LAW AND MOURNING

A VOLUME IN
The Amherst Series in Law,
Jurisprudence, and Social Thought

EDITED BY
Austin Sarat
Martha Merrill Umphrey
Lawrence Douglas

LAW AND MOURNING

Edited by
Austin Sarat
Lawrence Douglas
Martha Merrill Umphrey

University of Massachusetts Press
Amherst & Boston

Copyright © 2017 by University of Massachusetts Press
All rights reserved
Printed in the United States of America

ISBN 978-1-62534-279-9 (paper); 278-2 (hardcover)

Designed by Jack Harrison
Set in Scala
Printed and bound by Maple Press, Inc.

Cover design by Jack Harrison
Cover art: Jules-Eugéne Lenepveu (French, Angers 1819–1898 Paris), *Antigone Gives Token to the Body of Her Brother Polynices*, 1835–98. Ian Woodner Family Collection Fund, 1991, the Metropolitan Museum of Art, New York.

Library of Congress Cataloging-in-Publication Data

Names: Sarat, Austin, editor. | Douglas, Lawrence, editor. | Umphrey, Martha Merrill, editor.
Title: Law and mourning / edited by Austin Sarat, Lawrence Douglas, Martha Merrill Umphrey.
Description: Amherst : University of Massachusetts Press, 2017. | Series: Amherst series in law, jurisprudence, and social thought | Includes bibliographical references and index.
Identifiers: LCCN 2017012817| ISBN 9781625342836 (pbk. : alk. paper) | ISBN 9781625342829 (hardcover : alk. paper)
Subjects: LCSH: Mourning customs—United States. | Law—Social aspects—United States.
Classification: LCC GT3390 .L38 2017 | DDC 393/.9—dc23
LC record available at https://lccn.loc.gov/2017012817

British Library Cataloguing-in-Publication Data
A catalog record for this book is available from the British Library.

For our friend and colleague Nasser Hussain

Contents

Acknowledgments   ix

Law and Mourning: An Introduction   1
MARTHA MERRILL UMPHREY, AUSTIN SARAT, LAWRENCE DOUGLAS

1.
Mourning in America: What's Law Got to Do with It?   14
RAY D. MADOFF

2.
The Mourning After: Posthumous Sperm Retrieval and the
   New Laws of Mourning   36
SHAI J. LAVI

3.
To Weep Irish: Keening and the Law   59
ANDREA BRADY

4.
Listening within the "Grief of Distortions"   94
ANN PELLEGRINI

5.
Psychoanalysis, Mourning, and the Law: Schreber's Paranoia
   as Crisis of Judging   117
MARK SANDERS

6.
Does Mourning Become the Law? Commodity Fetishism
   and Political Contestation   148
CATHERINE KELLOGG

Contributors   167
Index   169

Acknowledgments

We are grateful to our Amherst College colleagues David Delaney and Adam Sitze for their intellectual companionship and our students in Amherst College's Department of Law, Jurisprudence, and Social Thought for their interest in the issues addressed in this book. We would like to express our appreciation for generous financial support provided by Amherst College's Corliss Lamont Fund. We dedicate this book to Nasser Hussain, whose untimely death deprived us, our students, and the world of a brilliant mind and a beautiful soul.

LAW AND MOURNING

Mourning and the Law
An Introduction

MARTHA MERRILL UMPHREY, AUSTIN SARAT,
AND LAWRENCE DOUGLAS

Yoking law and mourning together may seem counterintuitive. Mourning, Freud observes, "involves grave departures from the normal attitude toward life."[1] The painful experience of loss causes a mourner to lose interest in the outside world, temporarily pulling him or her into an altered temporality saturated by the past and devoid of an imaginable future. Death, it turns out, is no real end; rather, it is remarkably generative for those who live on, in ways both predictable and sometimes destabilizing. Those who mourn a loss seem immersed in another realm, detached from reality, indifferent or unresponsive to rule and reason, exempt from the usual rules and timetables of everyday life.

What does law have to do with such a deeply human, otherworldly state? As the chapters in this volume suggest, law is bound up with and responsive to mourning in many ways. Mourning is constituted in relation to social norms and institutions that, through rule and ritual, absorb, regulate, and contend with loss and its reverberations.

Law helps to give meaning to death and mourning, establishing rules that require a clear demarcation of the boundary between life and death, tell us what we can and cannot do with the remains of the dead, and create privileges and disabilities for survivors. These rules are found in criminal law, health law, and laws governing inheritance. Law seeks to channel the powerful emotions associated with it, and protect those vulnerable to them, in order to limit social confusion and conflict. Yet mourning can also generate critiques of existing legal and political orders that seem compelled by calls from the dead, unleashing an indifference to legal consequences in mourners that can undermine or destroy law.

To say one enters a "state" of mourning invokes a telling metaphor; to be "in mourning" is to be responsive to a different kind of authority. The dead make demands on the living: ritual acts must be performed, testimonials made, possessions rearranged, memories sifted, futures reimagined, and injustices redressed. Those demands can be weighty, and the grief attached to and derived from them can be powerful and unsettling. We give those in mourning space to dwell apart; indeed, in some times and places we require they dwell in such a space for a year or more,[2] or even die themselves.[3] To be both in mourning and in law's world, one is subject to different "sovereigns," sometimes aligned but sometimes at odds. The chapters that follow trace the borders arising from this state of mourning in law itself, between law and politics, and ultimately in acts of judgment and justice.

Governing the "State" of Mourning

We might characterize mourning as a psychic relation between the living and the lost, shaped in part by the surrounding social world. Mourning involves an internal process of detaching from someone or something that has passed away. In his classic essay "Mourning and Melancholia" (1917), Freud suggests that in mourning, "the existence of the lost object is psychically prolonged" internally, in opposition to the evident reality of loss. Mourners lack interest in the outside world, cannot adopt a new love object, and turn away from any activity not connected with thoughts of the lost object.[4] Building upon Freud's later work connecting this mourning dynamic with the constitution of the ego, Paul de Man argues that mourning "entails a movement in which an interiorizing idealization takes in itself or upon itself the body and voice of the other, the other's visage and person, ideally *and* quasi-literally devouring them. . . . [It] consists in recognizing that the dead are now only 'in us,' now only images 'for us.'"[5] Delineations of self and other collapse spatially as the image of the lost object emerges inside the subjectivity of mourners. Moreover, this incorporation of the lost object carries it forward temporally as memory, as part of the living, in ways that can generate action on behalf of the dead.

Those attachments play out in the social world as well. Anthropologists and sociologists identify the state of mourning in culturally defined acts—rites, rituals, and customs—that take place after a death and offer a means of transition for both the deceased and the bereaved.[6] Such transitions are a rite of passage involving, as Gorer describes it, a withdrawal from society, a period of seclusion, and ultimately social reentry.[7] They are the social expression of, or perhaps protective shell for, the painful psychic detachment mourning involves. While mourning may feel singular, individualized, and profoundly subjective, defined by an aloneness and apartness from the world, it simultaneously produces a powerful and continuing set of attachments among the living and with the dead.

Law plays an important role in organizing death and its reverberations. As Ray Madoff argues below, the law of the dead is everywhere, affecting not only what follows from an individual's death (e.g., the disposition of bodies and property) but the very definition of death itself.[8] We call on law first to define criteria for death, to name it performatively so as to transform a person into remains. These criteria can vary. Is death defined by the cessation of breath? Of brain activity or cellular deterioration? What can death mean when transplanted organs continue to support someone else's life? Law negotiates and fixes the otherwise confusing boundary between life and death.

Perhaps more familiarly, law regulates the material remainders of those who have died: their bodies, their money and property, their reputations. With the proliferation of new technologies (e.g., cryogenics) and legal instruments (in the form of, e.g., trust arrangements that constrain heirs in unusual or even unjust ways), this task has grown more and more complex. As Shai Lavi suggests below, perplexing questions arise with, the possibility of something like posthumous sperm retrieval. When is it ethical? Only under conditions in which it had prior authorization by the deceased, or when family or prospective family desires it? Addressing such questions, law mediates continuing relations between the living and the dead.

Law also recognizes and contains intense emotional responses to death. Most fundamentally, states impose laws, processes, and sanctions on wrongdoers as a means of quashing and delegitimizing acts of private vengeance.[9] In both civil and criminal contexts law produces metrics to calibrate the relation between bad acts and punishment or damages, imposing norms of proportionality on the unstable emotional landscape of mourning. We can see this struggle made manifest in debates around, for example, the role victim impact statements ought to play in the penalty phase of US criminal trials. Victim impact statements challenge courts to balance demands to acknowledge the depth of a mourner's loss with the need to maintain a fair process for those found guilty of killing.[10]

Outpourings of grief, contained and ritualized within the legal process,[11] can nevertheless threaten law's efforts to maintain itself as a site of reason and restraint as survivors themselves become victims, damaged beyond recognition by loss.

Mourning, Melancholia, and Injustice

Even as law seeks to guide and regulate mourners in their most vulnerable and volatile moments, mourning—as a state set apart from normality, responsive to the demands of the lost—generates calls for justice and provides ground for resistance to law. In the United States of the early twenty-first century we see widespread evidence of this dynamic. Our easy access to powerful weapons, driven by lax regulation, a thriving black market, vociferous ideological commitment to the Second Amendment, and a jurisprudence protective of police discretion, enables killing on an unprecedented peacetime scale. Out of the many deaths we see daily—police shooting young black men and women, mentally ill men killing targeted populations, young men killing bullies and rivals—political movements have taken shape. Such movements challenge laws and law enforcers, accusing them of doing injustice to the dead. Sometimes these movements make reformist demands for change; sometimes they generate civil disobedience, sometimes riot and destruction. Rage at the law becomes a way of displacing mourning.

Movements grounded in mourning arise not just from well-founded dissatisfaction but also from contact with traumatic loss to which law appears brazenly indifferent.[12] They derive their moral force from a close identification of mourner with mourned and from the incorporation of the dead into the living, blurring the boundary between living and dead, fueling hostility to law in reply to law's seeming indifference to loss.

We can see many manifestations of this theme in law and culture, and perhaps none more powerful than Sophocles' *Antigone*,[13] a play that famously illustrates the demands of mourning and their conflicts with positive law. As the play opens, a civil war pitting the sons of Oedipus against each other has ended. Creon, who has become king, declared that while Eteocles, defender of Thebes, is to have a ritual burial with full honor, the body of his rebellious brother Polyneices is to be left unburied, carrion for beastly consumption. Creon articulates a vision of sovereignty steeped in the language of positive law:

Polyneices, who broke his exile to come back with fire and sword against his native city and the shrines of his fathers' gods, whose one idea was to spill the blood of his blood and sell his own people into slavery—Polyneices, I say, is to have no burial: no man is to touch him or say the least prayer for him; he shall lie on the plain, unburied; and the birds and the scavenging dogs can do with him whatever they like.

This is my command, and you can see the wisdom behind it. As long as I am King, no traitor is going to be honored with the loyal man. But whoever shows by word and deed that he is on the side of the State—he may have my respect while he is living, and my reverence when he is dead.[14]

Antigone, Polyneices' sister, resists Creon's edicts, which would require her to abjure the rites of mourning required by kinship ties, by the laws of the gods, and by her love for her brother. In death, Polyneices makes demands on Antigone that put her own life at risk. Burying him defiantly, Antigone's mourning gives her legitimacy and standing to contest Creon's authority, a sacred threshold space in which the future seems to overlay the present, anchored by the bonds of kinship love. "I shall lie down / With him in death, and I shall/be as dear / To him as he is to me," she says.[15] In her mourning for Polyneices, Antigone conjures a scene of mimetic intimacy in the grave, a mirroring between brother and sister that suggests a near merging of identities—equally dead, equally near, equally dear. The scene is both a fantasy and a prediction, a not-unwelcome specter of the future that haunts the course of action she has chosen to take in the present. But Antigone's choice is also her duty: the dead Polyneices calls on her to assume the position of mourning kin and to respond to a demand that she can never escape.

Antigone is Creon's kin, but that relation is not in itself enough—particularly in the tangled world of Oedipus and his progeny—to overcome the chasm between them. Their clashes are the cold conflicts of competing sovereigns, not the hot arguments of family disputes.[16] Yet if Antigone seems unyielding with Creon, she nevertheless tells him that it is her "nature to join in love, not hate,"[17] and at the threshold of being buried alive she calls on the chorus:

> Be witness for me, denied all pity,
> Unjustly judged! and think a word of love
> For her whose path turns
> Under dark earth, where there are no more tears.[18]

Antigone enjoins the chorus to mourn her even as she remains alive, and in doing so issues a call for justice on the threshold of death. She asks the chorus to witness Creon's injustice; but her prayer for "a word of love" gives substance to the affective underlay of the duties mourning demands. For Antigone, justice comes not just from fulfilling a duty, but from a concatenation of law and love that propels critique of Creon's rule from beyond her grave, both spatially (the chorus remains outside to condemn the king) and temporally (the moment of her entombment generates a future beyond its time-bound eventness).

If Creon's attachment to positive law leads to hubris, a kind of madness that wrecks violence and injustice on those subject to it, Antigone's vision of law connects living and dead, present and future, through ties of affection. Such ties are, for her, both unavoidable and inviolable:

> Thebes, and you my fathers' gods
> And rulers of Thebes, you see me now, the last
> Unhappy daughter of a line of kings,
> Your kings, led away to death. You will remember
> What things I suffer, and at what men's hands,
> Because I would not transgress the laws of heaven.[19]

"You will remember..."—is it a prediction? An order? A simple statement of fact? However one reads them, Antigone's words connect witnessing, remembering, and attachment; and together lay upon Thebes a duty not only to mourn her loss but also to understand it as injustice. Memory itself appears to be an effect of death and constitutive of mourning; and the dead—Antigone, in particular—demand through memory a recognition of injustice. That recognition can produce a reversal; it can act as a call to do justice. For Antigone, the call is answered too late. Antigone's suffering at Creon's hands makes her a martyr. As Gillian Rose suggests, "Mourning draws on transcendent but representable justice, which makes the suffering of immediate experience visible and speakable."[20]

Returning to Freud, one might characterize Antigone not as a mourner but as a melancholic, suffering from a pathological state that involves a turning against one's own self, a "grand impoverishment of the ego" (246) and an overcoming of the instinct to cling to life.[21] Melancholia meets law's indifference to injustice with indifference not just to law but to life itself. By burying Polyneices, Antigone defies Creon's rule because she does not fear the consequences of her actions. She is, as Judith Butler suggests, already essentially dead at the beginning of the play. Her inevitable physical death—self-murder—generates a terrible mimetic strain of destruction: Haimon kills himself, and his mother and Creon's wife,

Eurydice, follows suit when she hears news of her son's death. Melancholic self-destruction spreads from body to body, ultimately destroying Creon's sovereignty as well.[22] Out of mourning, then, can emerge a politics enormously destructive to both mourner and law.

That kind of self-devouring catastrophe can occur outside the bounds of fiction, of course, but the dynamics of melancholia can also take on a politics more hopeful than destructive. As Jacques Derrida notes, "If we are to give the dead anything it can now be only in us, the living."[23] For Eng and Kazanjian, melancholia's open-endedness (distinct from a mourning process, which comes to closure) generates continuing and creative tensions between past and present. To them, "Loss is inseparable from what remains, for what is lost is known only by what remains of it, by how these remains are produced, read, and sustained."[24] They suggest that "psychic and material practices of loss and its remains are productive for history and for politics. . . . A world of remains [is] a world of new representations and alternative meanings."[25] Interiorizing those we have lost, we carry them forward. When we make demands on their behalf, we resignify their loss and turn it into the grounds of possibility for an alternative future.

Overview of the Book

The first two chapters explore law's regulation of mourning. Ray Madoff's "Mourning in America: What's Law Got to Do with It?" outlines the wide-ranging ways law shapes the mourning process. Madoff traces law's role as mourners negotiate three main steps in the bereavement process: acceptance, understanding, and the afterlife of the living. In the first step, acceptance, law (specifically US law) fixes the moment and definition of death via a standard of "irreversible cessation" of either circulation/respiration or brain, and regulates the disposition of bodies after death. Those regulations, Madoff claims, are arbitrary and often incomplete. Some mourners dispute law's definition of death (particularly "brain death") and fight to reinterpret it.

Madoff argues that American law's investment in testatorial freedom complicates bereavement's second step, reflection and understanding. In contrast to other countries, US law allows broad leeway for testators to disinherit family members and meddle in their lives posthumously, exacerbating the difficult emotional terrain of mourning. Finally, Madoff examines the ways in which law affects the fashioning of a person's afterlife. For example, even as the deceased's online archive is ephemeral and, by contract, made inaccessible to survivors, he/she loses the privacy protections of tort law following death, sometimes tarnishing memories and destroying reputations. On the other hand, laws governing charitable trusts allow a person's legacy to promote worthy goals in perpetuity. In regulating the after-effects of someone's death, Madoff argues, these laws create structures and set limits on the very experience and process of mourning.

Shai Lavi's chapter, "The Mourning After: Posthumous Sperm Retrieval and the New Laws of Mourning," explores the legal regulation of posthumous sperm retrieval (PMSR). Lavi begins with the Israeli army's practice of offering soldiers the chance to sign a "biological will" that orders sperm retrieval should they die. For Lavi, when new technologies open up distinctly modern ways of perpetuating life, we must rethink our familiar psychological framework for understanding mourning. Analyzing PMSR, Lavi suggests that mourning is not solely a psychological phenomenon bound up with grief, but also an expression of a social duty to continue the natural life cycle of death and birth.

Lavi surveys the varied terrain of PMSR regulation, noting the investment countries have in a liberal model that emphasizes the intent of the deceased even as some courts privilege the wishes of mourning relatives. But to Lavi, PMSR is better framed as a *calling* from the deceased that enjoins mourners to perpetuate life. Here Lavi turns to anthropological literature foregrounding social relationships among the corpse, the soul of the deceased, and the community of mourners that must help guide the soul to a place of rest. Until that duty is fulfilled the body, the soul, and the survivors dwell in a liminal space, outside the parameters of normal life.

Expanding the argument, Lavi considers the ancient biblical practice of levirate marriage, which requires that when a married man dies childless his brother must marry the widow, and that their first child be given the name of the deceased and become his legal heir. Such a practice expresses a desire for the continuation of the life cycle. Lavi argues that PMSR resembles levirate marriage insofar as it seems to articulate a similar desire, even as it enables the perpetuation of the deceased as an individual rather than as part of a family structure. Because of that technologically enabled shift, PMSR is a distinctly modern mode of mourning.

The next two chapters address the relationship between mourning and politics, and the ways in which mourners generate calls for justice and democratic practice. Andrea Brady's "To Weep Irish: Keening and the

Law" explores the ancient Irish tradition of keening, a cultural phenomenon and funerary practice that seventeenth-century British colonialists attempted to delegitimize and regulate legally. The failure of such regulations, Brady argues, indicates both law's difficulty in imposing social change and the limits of the colonizer's representations of the colonized.

Keening was an improvised poetic lamentation performed predominantly by women following the death of a family or community member. It expressed grief through a set of complex formal conventions. Yet to the ears of the English, mourners' wailing sounded like demonic, animalistic howling of pagans. Keening's unrestrained wailing expressed a form of mourning at once gendered and nationalized: for the English, women's excessive emotion and ritualized incivility fused with Irishness itself.

Brady describes the opinions of English protestant colonizers, emphasizing their view of the wildness of keening and the Irish language, evidence of Irish cultural and religious inferiority. Colonizers tried to subdue the Irish by eliminating their customs, imposing cultural conformity and secularized protestant values via legal and ecclesiastical decree. Such attempts were met with rebelliousness. Brady suggests that the uncontainability of keening in particular challenged English claims to sovereignty. Funerals, full of violent emotion, became demonstrations against the English church, disrupted civic life, and challenged colonial symbolic rule. While the English had some success in dismantling Irish legal structures, they were unable to eliminate keening, or to successfully reform the Irish people.

Ann Pellegrini's "Listening within the 'Grief of Distortions'" is a meditation on democratic politics, the psychic and social landscape of feelings in relation to existing social hierarchies in the United States, and larger psychic processes of disavowed vulnerability and blocked mourning. Taking a psychoanalytic approach to the deployment of anger, tolerance, civility, and the assertion of pain in political discourse, she explores the ways that defense mechanisms interfering with mourning can impede meaningful democratic practice.

Pellegrini begins by considering the place of anger in our politics as well as the claims of tolerance that she says are hollowed out in a larger context of social inequality. President Bush's post-9/11 call to move the nation quickly from grief to action, she argues, interrupted but could not fully end the mourning process that followed such loss. Moreover, assertions of tolerance, mixed with high-decibel moralism, provided a shield against the pain involved in mourning loss fully. Instead, the American majority engaged in fantasies of a politics of comfort, without anger.

Pellegrini also takes up the Supreme Court's decision in *Snyder v. Phelps*. In that case the Court held that the First Amendment protected Westboro Baptist Church's protest at a soldier's funeral. It consigned mourning to the private world of the family. It missed the arduous public dimensions of mourning essential to democratic practice. As Pellegrini argues, "Seeking to preserve life at all costs by cutting off mourning . . . all but guarantees carrying our grief to others in the form of the violent dealing out of death to 'our enemies.'" A better democratic politics would, she suggests, attend to the risks and vulnerabilities we all face rather than using law to comfort us against loss.

The final two chapters take up the nexus of mourning and legal theory. In "Psychoanalysis, Mourning, and the Law: Schreber's Paranoia as Crisis of Judging," Mark Sanders returns us to Freud to analyze the link between mourning, guilt, and legal culpability. Freud claims in "Mourning and Melancholia" and *Totem and Taboo*[26] that law originates in mourning, in the sense of guilt felt after the killing of the primal father. From that original guilt sprang a concept of crime, and from crime sprang law. In this sense, Sanders suggests, the mourner judges himself to be a murderer; hence mourning can be seen as law's ultimate source.

One can, of course, distinguish a generalized guilt felt by all from the actual legal culpability of an accused. Yet in criminal cases the psychic life of judges helps structure that culpability. If a judge—one like Schreber—is paranoid, then his guilt, via substitution, becomes the culpability of the accused in crossing "I am guilty" with "he is culpable." Sanders turns to Schreber's actual memoirs for evidence of this chiasmus. For Freud, paranoia has three attributes: love turns to hate; the hate is projected onto the one who was formerly loved; and this projection may occur, in transference, on a substitute. Guilt over feelings of hate for a loved object produces paranoia, which in turn generates a fantasmatic persecutor whom the paranoiac can judge and condemn.

Reading Schreber's memoirs through the work of Freud, Klein, and Lacan, Sanders argues that the judge's text exhibits precisely this dynamic. His memoirs display his lost capacity to judge, to gauge proportion; he exhibits symptoms of guilt for his ingratitude toward Flechsig, the doctor who once cured him. In his paranoid state he transposes his own guilt onto his doctor, accusing Flechsig of committing a crime against him. Indeed, for the paranoid judge, Sanders argues, there can be no judgment of another other than guilty. Schreber's memoirs display what Sanders sees as a crisis in judging. To the extent that mourning relations undergird that crisis, the very "condition of possibility for law itself must be thought as giving primacy to guilt."

Finally, Catherine Kellogg considers the relation between mourning and the very possibility of justice. She does so by offering a critique of the philosopher Gillian Rose's last works on love, law, and mourning. Rose's *Mourning Becomes the Law* argues that deconstructionists have left themselves in a state of interminable grief because the metaphysics they mourn (underlying concepts of justice, freedom, and the good) were, for postmodernists themselves, never really there. Hence for them mourning itself inescapably "becomes the law." And yet, Kellogg argues, Rose misses some of deconstruction's most critical dimensions. In deconstruction, mourning can never be completed precisely because metaphysics has at its heart an aporia: "the endless and unavoidable negotiation between the irreplaceability of the singular and the law of the concept."

Kellogg defends this deconstructive understanding of mourning and its relation to justice by taking up the concept of commodification. Derrida, Kellogg suggests, argues that there is no original thing prior to commodification, that "use-value" posits an original that never was. That identity as original is, on Derrida's terms, a retrospective fiction, and so a fetish replaces what was never lost to begin with. Rose, on the other hand, believes in metaphysics, in the reality of the original object; and to that extent, mourning its loss can restore the object to itself, prior to abstraction.

For Derrida, however, "justice" is "the remaking of the law in order to accommodate the singular infraction for which, in order to be law, it must have always-already been designed," or "the adequation between a thing and its ideal." In this line of thinking, mourning's work, Kellogg argues, is ultimately to "abolish the irreplaceability, the singularity of the singular." Psychoanalytically this process occurs once the libidinal energy attaching the mourner to a lost object is finally overcome by the reality principle, introjected back into the ego so that the ego can once again be free and uninhibited. If mourning—"letting go of the irreplaceability of singularity of the singular"—enhances and opens law on Rose's account, it is also a process that covers over what is lost in the transition from universal to particular. It cannot, Kellogg contends, guarantee justice; rather, it "makes law's reach to justice impossible." For Derrida, when law is applied to a specific case it must be remade, and therefore can never be fully authorized. And yet that very undecidability creates an opening that is always already present. That opening, for Kellogg, is itself justice. It is not, as Rose suggests, a metaphysical loss to be mourned.

Taken together, the work collected in this book maps law's mutual imbrication with mourning. On the one hand, loss is law's terrain to govern, building borders that can comfort and contain pain and grief. On the other hand, mourners inhabit a state apart from law, responding to the sometimes insurrectionary demands of the dead. In carrying the lost within them, mourners connect self and other, past and present. It is law that helps them to imagine a future.

NOTES

1. Sigmund Freud, "Mourning and Melancholia," in *The Standard Edition of the Complete Psychological Works of Sigmund Freud*, vol. 14, ed. and trans. James Strachey (London: Hogarth Press, 1981), 243–44. Even so, Freud continues, we do not regard such a state as pathological, and "we look upon any interference with it as useless or even harmful."

2. On funerary rites and mourning rituals, see Robert Hertz, *Death and the Right Hand*, trans. Rodney and Claudia Needham (London: Cohen and West, 1960), and Brandy Schillace, *Death's Summer Coat: What the History of Death and Dying Teaches Us about Life and Living* (New York: Pegasus Books, 2016).

3. On the Brahman practice of sati, see for example Mala Sen, *Death by Fire: Sati, Dowry Death, and Female Infanticide in Modern India* (New Brunswick, NJ: Rutgers University Press, 2002).

4. Freud, "Mourning," 244. In the normal course of events, over time a person in mourning experiences the painful process of detaching from a loved person or idea, a piece-by-piece withdrawal of the libido until "when the work of mourning is completed the ego, becomes free and uninhibited again." Freud, "Mourning," 245.

5. Jacques Derrida, *The Work of Mourning*, trans. Michael Naas and Pascale-Anne Brault (Chicago: University of Chicago Press, 2001), 34.

6. Paul C. Rosenblatt, R. Patricia Walsh, and Douglas A. Jackson, *Grief and Mourning in Cross-Cultural Perspective* (Minneapolis: HRAF Press, 1976), 2, 7.

7. Geoffrey Gorer, *Death, Grief, and Mourning* (Garden City, NY: Doubleday and Company, 1965), xxxiii.

8. See also Ray Madoff, *Immortality and the Law: The Rising Power of the American Dead* (New Haven, CT: Yale University Press, 2010).

9. See, for example, William Ian Miller, "Clint Eastwood and Equity: Popular Culture's Theory of Revenge," in *Law and the Domains of Culture*, ed. Austin Sarat and Thomas R. Kearns (Ann Arbor: University of Michigan Press, 1998).

10. The Supreme Court allowed victim impact statements into the penalty phase of criminal trials in *Payne v. Tennessee*, 501 U.S. 808 (1991). Elizabeth Joh, for example, worries that the effects of victim impact statements "legitimate popular notions of revenge, victimhood, and pain." Elizabeth E. Joh, "Narrating Pain: The Problem with Victim Impact Statements," 10 S. Cal. Interdisc. L.J. 17, 18 (Fall 2000).

11. See Paul Gewirtz, "Victims and Voyeurs: Two Narrative Problems at the Criminal Trial," in *Law's Stories*, ed. Peter Brooks and Paul Gewirtz (New Haven, CT: Yale University Press, 1998), 135–61. See also Martha Minow, "Surviving Victim Talk," 40 UCLA L. Rev. 1411 (1993); Susan A. Bandes and Jessica M. Salerno, "Emotion, Proof, and Prejudice: The Cognitive Science of Gruesome Photos and Victim Impact Statements," 46 Ariz. St. L.J. 1003 (Winter 2014).

12. In criminal law, "depraved indifference" is defined as conduct so wanton, so deficient in a moral sense of concern, so lacking in regard for the life or lives of others, and so blameworthy as to warrant the same criminal liability as that which the law imposes upon a person who intentionally causes a crime. See wwdefinistion.uslegal.com/d/depraved-indifference (accessed January 20, 2016).

13. Sophocles, *The Oedipus Cycle*, trans. Dudley Fitts and Robert Fitzgerald (San Diego, CA: Harcourt, 1977).

14. Ibid., 197.

15. Ibid.

16. As Judith Butler has observed, "Her words, understood as deeds, are chiasmically related to the vernacular of sovereign power, speaking in and against it, delivering and defying imperatives at the same time, inhabiting the language of sovereignty at the very moment in which she opposes sovereign power and is excluded from its terms." Butler, *Antigone's Claim*, 28.

17. Sophocles, *The Oedipus Cycle*, 211.

18. Ibid., 226.

19. Ibid., 228.

20. Gillian Rose, *Mourning Becomes the Law: Philosophy and Representation* (Cambridge: Cambridge University Press, 1996), 37.

21. Freud, "Mourning," 246.

22. As Butler suggests, "One might reapproach Antigone's 'fatality' with the question of whether the limit for which she stands, a limit for which no standing, no translatable representation is possible, is not precisely the trace of an alternate legality that haunts the conscious, public sphere as its scandalous future." Butler, *Antigone's Claim*, 40.

23. Derrida, *The Work of Mourning*, 9.

24. Ibid., 2.

25. David L. Eng and David Kazanjian, eds., *Loss: The Politics of Mourning* (Berkeley: University of California Press, 2003), 5.

26. Sigmund Freud, *Totem and Taboo: Some Points of Agreement between the Mental Lives of Savages and Neurotics*, in *The Standard Edition of the Complete Psychological Works of Sigmund Freud*, vol. 13, ed. and trans. James Strachey (London: Hogarth Press, 1981).

1
Mourning in America
What's Law Got to Do with It?

RAY D. MADOFF

Humans are intensely social creatures. We orient ourselves by our relationship to others. Whether it is our first relationships—to our mothers, fathers, siblings, and playmates—or our later relationships—to our lovers, spouses, children, friends, and other important people in our lives—other humans play a fundamental role in our understanding of ourselves and our sense of belonging in the world.

But what happens when a loved one dies? Given the primacy of our social connectedness, it is not surprising that the death of a loved one is one of the most disorienting and difficult experiences that humans must endure. The process of managing this loss—the mourning process—is a fundamental challenge of human existence.

The mourning process is the process through which an individual comes to understand and accept that a loved one has gone from a physical presence to a physical absence, and the process through which the survivor reconstitutes his or her life in the face of this absence. In the mourning process the bereaved gradually undoes the psychological bonds that bound her to the deceased, and incorporates the memory of the deceased in her on-going life.[1]

The mourning process is essentially an intellectual and emotional process whereby the bereaved becomes reoriented to a world that is missing something important. In this way, it appears to be fundamentally internal and private—far removed from anything as public and institutional as "the law." Yet closer examination shows how, contrary to this initial impression, the law in fact is intimately involved in all aspects of the mourning process. From the first moment of death—and even establishing that the moment of death has occurred—the law plays a fundamental role in shaping the mourning process. Whether the bereaved is coming to accept the loss, reaching an understanding of his relationship to the deceased, or finding a way to move forward with an image or place for the deceased in the mourner's ongoing life, the law (or the notable absence of law) is there, providing structure and support—and sometimes impediments—to the mourning process.

This chapter focuses on three steps of the bereavement process and the role of the law in each step: (1) "acceptance," whereby the mourner comes to accept the fact of death and the transition of the deceased from a living person to be cared for to a body to be disposed of, (2) "understanding," whereby the mourner comes to understand his or her former relationship with the now dead person, and (3) "the afterlife of the living," whereby the mourner finds a way to incorporate an image and a place for the decedent in the mourner's post-death life.

Acceptance

Mourning begins with recognition and acceptance of the death of a loved one. From the very beginning the law is there to determine (1) whether a death has occurred and (2) what is to be done with the body.

Has Death Occurred?

One of the most critical determinations that the law can make is that a person has passed from living to dead. Once a person has been declared dead, the many legal protections we have for the bodies of living people terminate, and the body becomes subject to possible autopsy, organ donation, and disposal.[2] Beyond determination of death and disposal of the body (and even in the absence of a body—for example, when a person has been missing and is presumed dead), the declaration of death produces many legal consequences, including the disposition of a person's property by will or intestacy, the ability to pay life insurance policies on a person's life, and the release of marital bonds as wives and husbands become widows and widowers free to marry others. Most importantly, from the survivors' point of view, law marks the division between being in relationship with another person—loving or otherwise—and being a mourner.

Mourning begins with the death of a loved one. But when is a person considered to be dead? While we might think of this as a factual question to be resolved by scientific inquiry, it turns out that the division between life and death is not so clear-cut and science can provide only limited assistance. The reason for this is that while we might think of death as occurring in a single moment—and the legal world requires this as well—in biological terms death is not a discrete event but a gradual process.[3] Even after a person's heart stops beating, other muscle, skin, and bone cells may live on for several days. Picking a moment in this process and calling that the moment of death is in some ways arbitrary and yet the job must be done, and the legal world is the one that is called on to do it.

The question of whether death has occurred has been, and continues to be, a surprisingly complicated question. For centuries, people knew (or at least thought they knew) what death was, but they didn't have adequate tools to determine whether death had occurred. A feather in front of a nose or a mirror in front of a mouth were not always up to the task of detecting flickering life and this resulted in many cases—and widespread fear—of premature burial.[4] In fact, one of the early scientists devoted to finding a definitive surgical test to determine whether death had occurred, Jean Jacques Winslow, came by his interest honestly. As a child he had twice been abandoned for dead, only to revive and discover that he had been placed in a coffin.[5]

With the advent of the stethoscope, the standard for determining death used throughout much of the twentieth century was "cessation of heart and lung function." This cardiopulmonary standard, combined with statutes requiring that death certificates be issued with the signature of a licensed physician who can attest to the fact of the person's death, made premature burial largely a thing of the past. However, no sooner had one practical problem been solved than other ones emerged.

The first of these was raised by the development of the mechanical ventilator, which made it possible to support a person's heart and lung function even after brain function had ceased. A person's heartbeat could now continue even when the patient had no discernible brain activity and respiration was mechanically sustained. This put hospitals in the difficult position of maintaining care for individuals who seemed to be more dead than alive. It also raised an additional problem that under a cardiopulmonary definition of death, the removal of a mechanical ventilator from a person with no brain activity technically constituted murder. This resulted in some peculiar legal cases, including one in which a defendant charged with murder argued that the doctors who removed the life support, and not him, caused the death of the victim.[6]

The possibility for organ transplants raised another practical problem for using the cardiopulmonary definition of death. That is, the cardiopulmonary definition of death impeded the availability of organs for transplant. The reason for this is that after the heart stops pumping, organs quickly begin to decay and soon are no longer suitable for transplant. To address this problem, proponents of organ transplant sought a way to be able to keep bodies on mechanical ventilators right up until the moment of harvesting organs for transplant. However, under the cardiopulmonary standard, this would result in transplant surgeons committing murder. In response to this problem, a highly influential report by an ad hoc committee at Harvard Medical School came to the rescue by proposing a new definition of death: cessation of brain function. This definition made a certain degree of sense in a society that associates personal identity with the brain. Happily, it also served the goals of organ transplants by providing that organs could be harvested from a body after the brain had ceased functioning, even if—due to mechanical ventilation—the person was still breathing and had a heart rate.

Today, the most widely adopted statute, the Uniform Determination of Death Act, provides that a person can be declared dead when he has sustained either (1) irreversible cessation of circulatory and respiratory functions or (2) irreversible cessation of all functions of the entire brain.[7] This statute has been adopted in thirty-eight states. States that have not adopted the Uniform Determination of Death Act have either adopted their own statutes or developed case law allowing the use of brain death as an alternative standard for determining death. Brain death has been adopted as a standard throughout much of the rest of the world as well.[8]

Despite this near-universal adoption of the brain death standard, complications remain. First, some religions have their own official views of when death occurs and these standards are sometimes at odds with the brain death standard. One version of this conflict played out in a 2007 case involving Cho Fook Cheng, a seventy-two-year-old grandfather who suffered a heart attack the day after Thanksgiving. He was brought to the hospital and placed on a ventilator. Soon thereafter, the doctors declared Cheng dead based on the brain death standard and sought to have him removed from life support. The family, however, practiced a Taiwanese form of Buddhism, in which a person is not considered dead until his heart stops beating. The case was heading for a court showdown but was rendered moot when Cheng's heart stopped on its own. Yet based on the plain meaning of the governing statutes, as well as case law from other jurisdictions, it seems likely that the hospital would have been within its legal rights to remove life support. Once a person is declared dead under the governing authority, the family is not entitled to demand life support measures.[9]

Even when religion is not an issue, the brain death standard can be problematic because a person who is brain dead does not necessarily appear dead to outsiders and loving family members can be reluctant to give up hope. Sometimes this can result in litigation between family members and hospitals over whether death has occurred.

In 2004 Jesse Koochin was a six-year-old boy suffering from inoperable and incurable brain cancer. He had been undergoing care in a hospital when the tumor grew so large that it broke through the base of his neck, cutting off blood to his brain and effectively killing him (at least according to doctors applying the brain death standard). Subsequently, two physicians independently determined that the child was "brain dead" and informed his parents that they would order life support removed within twenty four hours. Jesse's parents rejected the hospital's definition of death and sought instead to wait until cardiopulmonary death occurred. The parents won and took their child (or in the views of the hospital, their child's body) home, where he was maintained on a mechanical ventilator until his heart gave out the following month.[10]

According to the parents' attorney, the courts' decision provided a chance for a family to give medical care to a child in the way they thought was appropriate and, in the end, say goodbye in a manner that gave some closure and peace of mind.[11] However, the Koochin case raises complex issues of medical ethics. Professor Jacob Appel has outlined the competing positions as follows:

> From the Koochins's point of view, what is at stake is nothing less than their autonomous right to make medical decisions for their child. They do not wish to impose a cardiopulmonary death standard upon everyone. Rather, emphasizing that there is no universal societal consensus on brain death, they wish to carve out an exception to the general rule in accordance with their own values. The family fully acknowledges that their child's condition is dire. They would prefer, however, to continue to hope and pray until Jesse's heart stops beating. In other words, they want this to be an entirely private, family decision.
>
> Jesse's physicians, in contrast, insist this case (unlike the Quinlan or Schiavo cases) has nothing to do with decisions about how or when to die. Although the boy's heart may continue to beat for weeks or even months on "life support," Jesse—to the hospital's way of thinking—is already dead. His parents are seeking to take home and ventilate a corpse—a child as dead as Tony Perkins's mother in Psycho. If the couple believes otherwise, they

are in denial. Moreover, carving out an exception for the Koochins may do long term societal damage by undermining the perceived validity of brain death. Organ donation programmes, which rely on brain dead cadavers, will inevitably have a more difficult time obtaining familial consent. Cost is also a factor: in a society with limited healthcare resources, many question the expenditure necessary to maintain lifeless bodies.[12]

The mourning process can be particularly complicated when there is no body, such as when the loved one has gone missing. The question of whether and when a missing person will be declared dead is a legal one. Individual mourners will likely have differing responses to the declaration of death.

Consider the case of Natalee Holloway, an American student who vanished on a high school graduation trip to Aruba. Natalee was last seen in the early hours of May 30, 2005, leaving a nightclub with three men. In 2012, a judge declared Natalee dead at the request of her father, who said that the declaration of death would help him get closure. In contrast, Natalee's mother fought the declaration of death. According to news reports: "Beth's position is she has no proof or indication that Natalee is still alive, but absent any proof or indication that she is dead, she always wants to hang onto that slight glimmer of hope," said Beth Holloway's attorney, John Q. Kelly. "No mother likes to, without evidence, have her daughter declared dead. She wants to carry her around in her heart."[13]

What Can Be Done with the Body?

Once death has been declared, the law once again takes a primary role in setting the stage for the mourning process. As one judge elegantly described it:

> A corpse in some respects is the strangest thing on earth. A man who but yesterday breathed and thought and walked among us has passed away. Something has gone. The body is left still and cold, and is all that is visible to mortal eye of the man we knew. Around it cling love and memory. Beyond it may reach hope. It must be laid away. And the law—that rule of action which touches all human things—must touch also this thing of death.

Law sets limits on the way that mourners can deal with the disposition of the body. A mourner can't decide to keep the body of a loved one in their house, nor can they bury them in their backyard or dispose of them in a furnace.[14] State statutes generally require that a body must be disposed of in a prescribed manner and within a reasonable period of time. In Massachusetts, the relevant statute reads:

Except as otherwise provided by law, or in case of a dead body being rightfully carried through or removed from the commonwealth for the purpose of burial or disposition elsewhere, every dead body of a human being dying within the commonwealth, and the remains of any body after dissection therein, shall be decently buried, entombed in a mausoleum, vault or tomb or cremated within a reasonable time after death.[15]

Disposal of the body is a critical step in the mourning process. Religious practices and other customs for disposing of bodily remains have been designed to help mourners come to terms with their loved one's death. And yet, since there is only one body to be disposed of—and often many mourners—disagreements can arise about what to do with the body. Again, the law steps in to provide answers.[16]

Traditionally the law has responded to this problem of conflicting views of mourners by providing a hierarchy of decision makers.[17] Today the law has been revised in many states to allow individuals to leave their own burial instructions or choose a person to make the decision for them. But in the absence of advance planning, the hierarchy remains. This hierarchy can be deeply painful for the mourners who are lower down the hierarchy since that sends the societal message that their mourning is in some ways less legitimate than others. This is particularly likely to be problematic when the decedent had a nonmarital partner. The conflict between the partner and the family of birth is all too common and can be deeply painful for everyone involved.

In addition, the state-ordered autopsy can sometimes impede people mourning in the way that they would otherwise like. State laws generally give broad authority to conduct a full autopsy in the case of unnatural death or for any public health reason regardless of the wishes of the decedent or his or her family.[18] In addition, in many states when an autopsy is conducted, the coroner is also given the right to remove corneas, pituitary glands, and other organs for transplant without the consent of the decedent or his family.[19] Some mourners may have personal objections to the performance of an autopsy on their loved one's body. In addition, many religious and ethnic groups (such as Hmong, Orthodox Jews, Mexican Americans, Muslims, and Navaho) include adherents who believe that a person enters the afterlife with the body in its condition at the time of death, or that a body can continue to feel pain for as long as several days after bodily death, or that autopsies are proscribed as a mutilation of the human body. While some states allow people to register religious objections to autopsy, the vast majority do not. Moreover, even in those states that allow religious objections to be made, autopsies can nonetheless be allowed provided that the state has a strong enough need for the information an autopsy can provide.[20] These statutes have been widely accepted as constitutional.

Interestingly, while some aspects of disposal of the dead are highly regulated, American law leaves entirely unregulated some of the most important decisions regarding the use of the deceased person's body: (1) whether the body is cryonically frozen for possible future reanimation; and (2) whether genetic material is removed from the body for posthumous procreation.

Cryonics

Cryonics is a process in which people who are legally dead are cooled to extremely low temperatures in the hope that future technology will be able to revive and cure them of whatever illness was responsible for their death. Cryonics operates on the belief that there is a difference between clinical death and actual death. Thus, although the legal world speaks of cryonics as the process of freezing dead people and bringing them back to life, proponents of cryonics believe that they are suspending people who have been declared legally dead (because their heart has stopped beating) but who retain sufficient cell structure that they can be restored to biological life and then preserved in that state for future reanimation.

The technology for revival from cryonic suspension is currently not available, and its very feasibility is subject to serious doubt; as one skeptic said: "Believing cryonics could reanimate someone who has been frozen is like believing you can turn hamburger into a cow." However, others are more optimistic and believe that the successes of frozen reproductive technology and nanotechnology make cryonics a real possibility—even if not in the near future.

Who makes the decision of whether a body is buried or cryonically frozen for possible reanimation? Throughout most of the world, this is not an issue because cryonics has been explicitly prohibited.[21] However, while American law has been more responsive to the cryonics industry, it has left open many important issues, including whether a person can leave binding decisions about having his body cryonically preserved or not. (This is unlike the situation regarding the disposition of property, which is highly regulated.) Because of this, families can be torn apart by the decision of whether to freeze a loved one for possible future reanimation.

The most famous cryonics dispute involved baseball legend Ted Williams. In 1986 Williams wrote a will providing specific instructions for the disposition of his body at death: "I direct that my remains be cremated and my ashes sprinkled at sea off the coast of Florida where the water is very deep."

Nonetheless, when he died in 2002, his son and one of his two daughters had Williams's body sent to Arizona for cryonic preservation. In support of their actions, they submitted to the court a grease-stained scrap of paper dated 2000 that said the following: "JHW, Claudia and Dad all agree to be put into bio-stasis after we die. This is what we want, to be able to be together in the future, even if it is only a chance." The paper had the signatures of Williams and his two children.[22]

Did this paper reflect Williams's true wishes? It is impossible to say, and Williams's oldest daughter said that it didn't. On the one hand it seemed a clear statement of wishes written after his will; on the other hand it was written on a grease-stained scrap of paper (not the usual format for a document intending to have legal effect) and was signed "Ted Williams" the signature he used for autographs, not "Theodore S. Williams," the signature he used on all official documents intending to have legal effect. It was even suggested by some that Williams could have written his name as an autograph, and then the text could have been added around it. If this had been a dispute over property, there would have been legal requirements in place that set standards for when a document would be treated as having legal effect (including the requirement that there be at least two witnesses to the signing who are required to attest to the fact that the signature was the person's free act and deed). Instead, a court in this type of dispute is operating with far less guidance. As one local probate lawyer said, the judge is not bound to agree with the wishes expressed in a will or a note. "The judge is probably going to assess all the equities in the situation, and the wishes of the decedent if they can be determined." In the end, the case was settled without a court determination regarding Williams's true intent, and his body remains frozen at Alcor rather than in the deep waters off the coast of Florida.

Removing Genetic Material for Posthumous Procreation

Posthumous sperm retrieval (PSR) is a procedure in which spermatozoa are extracted from a man after he has been pronounced legally brain dead. The first report of PSR was in 1980, but since then it has been estimated that more than 1,000 requests are made each year.

The ability to exhume sperm from a dead man can have a profound effect on the mourning process. Consider the case of Nikolas Evans, a young college student who was assaulted outside a bar in Austin, Texas. He died ten days later, but before his death, his mother, Missy Evans, requested that the doctors exhume sperm from her son for posthumous conception. Twenty vials were eventually exhumed, and Missy Evans began to search for suitable women to act as egg donor and surrogate to create the child for her son that he was not able to do for himself.[23]

While PSR raises numerous ethical issues and is outlawed in many countries, it remains legal and unregulated in the United States.[24]

Reflection and Understanding

Death marks not just the end of a person's life, but also the end of that person's relationship with others. While people are alive, it is always possible to have more experiences and more conversations. Relationships can continue to grow and change for better and for worse. But once one of the individuals has died, the relationship is over. There are no more experiences to be shared, and no more conversations to be had. For the survivors, all that is left to do is reflect on the relationship and come to a final reckoning or understanding. Psychologist Anna Aragno has described this phase of the mourning process as "an all-consuming relationship review": "Every aspect, from the first meeting through myriad moments, scenarios and scenes, is summoned to recall, relived, remembered, again and again, and finally cast to memory."[25] This reflection and understanding is a critical part of the mourning process. Colin Murray Parkes and Holly Prigerson describe this aspect of the mourning process as a "gradual piecing together of the pieces of a jig-saw that eventually will enable us to find an image and a place in our lives for the people we have loved and lost."[26]

How does the mourner come to understand the relationship with the deceased? Internal reflection—sometimes with the assistance of therapists, family, and friends—is often the primary mechanism. However, this process can be complicated by the continuing legal expressions of the deceased that occur after death, as expressed in the last will and enforced under American law.

Consider the following all-too-typical case, and how the law acts to shape the parties' understanding of the situation:

> A widowed mother had two adult children with whom she generally had a good relationship. As the mother aged, she became frail and everyone began

to worry about her ability to live alone. The older child, a son, lived far away, with a busy career and a family of his own. The younger child, a daughter, did not have a career and was a single mother who struggled to make ends meet. It seemed like a good solution to everyone for the daughter to move in to the mother's house. The daughter would have free rent, and a good place to live with her child. The mother would have someone around to cook meals, take her to doctor's appointments and make sure that she was safe.

What could go wrong?

As time passed, the mother became frailer and more dependent on her daughter. While her son checked in regularly by phone and visited when he could, he was not able to do much in terms of providing day-to-day help. When the mother died, everyone was sad, but the son was also shocked to learn that shortly before her death the mother had changed her will to give almost her entire estate to her daughter and only a small share to her son.

If all goes well in life, children will have to mourn the loss of their parents. However, the legal rules that apply at this time can play a complex role in how this mourning process unfolds. The ability of a decedent to control his or her property at death (called freedom of testation) and the ability to impose conditions (which we will refer to as posthumous meddling) can both have profound effects on how children come to understand their relationship with their parents.

Freedom of Testation

The starting principle of American property law is that people have the ability to control their property at death. While there are some protections for surviving spouses, there are no obligations to provide for children (even if the children are minors, and even if, as a result of the disinheritance, the children would become wards of the state). It is freedom of testation that gives the mother the legal capacity to disinherit the son in the first place.

This Anglo-American approach differs from the laws of most of the world, which provide protection for children against disinheritance. For example, under French law, parents are obligated to give large portions of their estate outright to their children.[27] In this case, both son and daughter would, by law, be provided with one-third of the mother's estate. The mother would only have had the capacity to control the remaining one-third of her estate. If she chose to give that property to her daughter, it could easily be understood to reflect either (a) the mother's appreciation for the daughter's care or (b) the mother's understanding of the fact that the daughter, as a single mother, had more expenses and fewer resources than her brother. However, the fact that the brother also got a significant portion of the mother's estate would no doubt have made the brother feel that he too was a beloved member of the family.

Moreover, the law plays an important role in how the brother and sister come to understand what happened. Law is a powerful tool for shaping how people think about their dispute. As one scholar has described it: "Law provides a set of categories and frameworks through which the world is interpreted. Legal words and practices are cultural constructs which carry powerful meanings not just to those trained in the law or to those who routinely use it to manage their business transactions but to the ordinary person as well."[28] Legal rules frame a core story as to why the state is involved. This story reflects larger cultural values in that a legal claim recognizes that there has been a deviance from desired norms. The remedy reflects a view as to how to correct this deviance.

If the brother were to consult an attorney about this fact pattern, chances are that the attorney would tell him that he might have a claim that his caretaking sister exerted "undue influence" over their mother. The legal claim of undue influence is basically a claim that the daughter exerted so much control that the mother wrote a will in her favor that she otherwise would not have written. Undue influence, in conjunction with lack of mental capacity, is the most common ground for overturning wills. The remedy for the undue influence case would likely be the equal division of the property between the brother and the sister. The desire to share a portion of his mother's estate has now been changed—courtesy of the legal rules—into a different story. Now it is a story that the mother probably wanted her property to go to both children equally, but that the daughter did something wrong and overcame her mother's wishes, causing her to write a will that she otherwise would not have done.[29]

This conversion to a legal claim often has the effect of inflaming the dispute and polarizing the siblings. The daughter—who was previously considered "the good one" for taking care of mother—is now demonized for overcoming the will of the mother. The son—who may have had guilt feelings as a result of not living closer to Mom—can now claim victim status.[30] This reframing of the dispute is bound to play a significant role in the mourning process.

Posthumous Meddling

American law creates additional complexities for mourners due to the ability of the dead to exert control from beyond the grave. American law provides that not only can a person distribute her property as she chooses, but she can also impose conditions on that distribution of property. This "posthumous meddling" can significantly complicate the mourning process.[31]

Consider the case of Daniel Shapira, whose father, David Shapira, died when Daniel was still in college. Though we can't know for certain about their relationship during life, we can easily imagine that it was filled with the ups and downs, loving connectedness, and challenging disagreements that typically occur between parents and their children as the children grow up and seek their own identities, separate from the parents. As Daniel experienced the first freedoms of college, father and son might have had disagreements about Daniel's lifestyle or choice of girlfriends. No matter what the legal regime provided, after his father's death Daniel would no doubt have had much to process about the many phases of his relationship with his father.

However, American law adds an additional dimension to this process of reflection and understanding that can significantly affect the mourning process. Under American law, David Shapira was given the capacity to express his views and continue to impose his wishes from the grave—which, in fact, he did.

David Shapira had a strong religious identity and he cared deeply about the fate of the Jewish people. Reflecting this, his will included a provision that Daniel would receive a share of his father's estate only if, within seven years of his father's death, Daniel married "a Jewish girl whose both parents were Jewish" (this last stipulation was presumably intended to prevent Daniel from sidestepping the provision by having a non-Jewish girlfriend convert to Judaism and then marrying her).[32]

Imagine how this provision must have complicated Daniel's mourning process. One aspect of his father had become set in stone. It was no longer possible to have another conversation with his father, though Daniel might have believed he could have convinced his father that such a provision was unnecessary or wrong-headed. It is precisely because of the inability of the living to engage in renegotiation with the dead that Richard Posner has argued that these types of provisions should not be given effect:

> Consider, however, the possibilities for modification that would exist if the gift was inter vivos rather than testamentary. As the deadline approached, the son might come to his father and persuade him that a diligent search had revealed no marriageable Jewish girl who would accept him. The father might be persuaded to grant an extension or otherwise relax the condition.

But if he is dead, the kind of "recontracting" is impossible, and the presumption that the condition is a reasonable one fails. This argues for applying the cy pres approach in private as well as charitable trust cases unless the testator expressly rejects a power of judicial modification.[33]

Since David Shapira was no longer living, Daniel couldn't bring the arguments directly to his father and instead had to bring them against his father's legal representative (his executor) in a court of law. In the actual *Shapira* case, Daniel indeed argued that the marriage restriction provision should not be given effect, that seven years did not give him adequate time for making a good marital choice, and that the provision would encourage him to enter into a sham marriage (followed by a divorce) simply for the sake of getting his inheritance.[34]

While these arguments might have been successful if presented to his flesh-and-blood father, the court, in its role as applier of the law, was far more interested in the rights of Daniel's father to control his property after death—which are protected under American law—than it was in the right of Daniel to receive an inheritance free of restriction—which wasn't so protected.

If Daniel had been born in another country, his experiences after death would have been very different. Throughout most of the world, parents are not allowed to disinherit their children, and in many countries these types of restrictions are seen as against public policy. French law is explicitly adverse to the idea of parents exerting their control over their children.[35] As such, cases like *Shapira* could not happen there.

Daniel's experience might even have been different had it occurred at a different time. While American law has traditionally been extremely lenient toward posthumous meddling, in a recent case a lower court ruled that a provision in a will disinheriting grandchildren who married non-Jews was void as counter to public policy. While this decision was overturned on appeal, it is possible that later cases will adopt the reasoning of the lower court, particularly since this position was included in the latest version of the Restatement (Third) of Trusts: an intended trust or trust provision is invalid if it is contrary to public policy.[36] The Restatement generally includes in this category restraints on beneficiary behavior, including restraints on marriage or religious freedom, and those that disrupt family relationships and choice of careers, but it also calls for balancing of conflicting social values.

If the position of the Restatement were to be widely adopted, then lawyers would discourage their clients from including these types of provisions. This could have a significant ameliorative effect on the mourning process. Moreover, even if these provisions were included in a will, a court's refusal to enforce this type of posthumous meddling may have its own ameliorative effect on the mourning process.

The Afterlife of the Living—The Decedent as Memory

No matter how painful or disrupting the loss, mourners must live on. In this continuing afterlife of the living, the deceased person must be eventually transformed from a living, breathing person to an idea in the minds of the living. All of the processing about the relationship has been completed and the decedent becomes almost a cardboard cutout, an idealization.[37]

What are the forces that act to create memories of a loved one? Certainly many things that are not touched by law—memories of conversations and time spent with the loved one are no doubt primary. Nonetheless, even here, in the formation of memory, the law plays a critical role in several aspects of how a loved one is remembered; particularly in terms of (1) accessing memorial material, (2) protecting memories of the dead, and (3) creating ongoing legacies to the memory of the deceased.

Accessing Memorial Material

When a person dies, she leaves behind her personal effects, many of which provide the most powerful access to memories for mourners. In centuries past, the tangible manifestations of memory were limited to diaries, letters, and paintings of the deceased. In decades past, there would also be photographs of the deceased. As tangible personal property, all these objects would have passed as part of the deceased person's estate, along with her money and other property. It would be controlled by the executor or other personal representative of the decedent and passed along to family members or to other beneficiaries chosen by the decedent.

Today, however, many of the words and images most conducive to creating memories are captured in electronic—rather than tangible—form. Through email, Facebook pages, and Instagram, people can leave a rich array of material—including emails, videos, photos, and recordings of their thoughts in these electronic databases. However, under the current legal regime, survivors have little right to access this material. The reason is that these electronic images are not considered to be "property" of the deceased and therefore do not pass through the person's estate to the heirs. Instead, these accounts, and the images they contain, are governed by contract law. These contracts—written by the companies that provide the service—had previously provided that they terminate at death. There were numerous lawsuits brought against these companies by bereaved families seeking to preserve access to these documents. In most cases, however, the lawsuits were not successful, imposing extreme hardship on the mourners. Consider the following:

> Alison Atkins died on July 27 at age 16. Online, her family is losing its hold on her memory.
> Three days after the Toronto teen lost a long battle with a colon disease, her sister Jaclyn Atkins had a technician crack Alison's password-protected MacBook Pro. Her family wanted access to Alison's digital remains: Facebook, Twitter, Tumblr, Yahoo and Hotmail accounts that were her lifeline when illness isolated her at home.
> Since then, Ms. Atkins's attempts to recover Alison's online life have begun falling apart. The websites that previously logged in automatically on Alison's laptop began locking out Ms. Atkins as part of their standard security procedures. Her attempts to guess or reset her sister's passwords backfired. Some of the accounts have been shutting themselves down.
> On Nov. 21, Alison disappeared from Facebook, where her family used her account to communicate and share memories with more than 500 friends. "We have already lost Alison," says Ms. Atkins. Now the family says it fears losing another part of her.[38]

Despite this case law, the situation is changing. In the United States, the Uniform Law Commission has proposed a Fiduciary Access to Digital Assets Act, which has already been adopted in nineteen states and proposed in many more.[39] This statute allows an executor or other fiduciary to access or manage an individual's fiduciary assets, including electronic communications such as email, text messages, and social media accounts, but only if the original user consented in a will, trust, power of attorney, or other record.

Protecting Memories of the Dead

How are the dead remembered? While each person has his or her personal recollections and experiences, memories and reputations are also created in the words and images of others.

During life, there are numerous legal doctrines designed to afford protection for a person's reputation. The right of privacy protects against the disclosure of private information to the public. The tort of defamation protects an individual against intentional lies. However, under American law these protections are eliminated after death, and a person's secrets and reputations are up for grabs and sometimes destruction.

Consider the case of Sharon Riley, whose teenaged son Anthony committed suicide. While it is impossible to measure the pain of a mother following her son's suicide, it was no doubt deepened by the actions of local police officers who took photographs of the teen as he lay in his coffin and displayed the photographs at a public gathering. There, the officers made statements implying that the boy's involvement in gang-related activities had caused his death. The mother sued for invasion of privacy. The court, in rejecting her claim, ruled that there was no cause of action for invasion of privacy on behalf of the boy because he was dead and no cause of action on behalf of the mother, because any claim of right to privacy was personal to the son.[40]

Many other countries take a far more protective approach to the feelings of mourners and the privacy interests of the dead. This case stands in sharp contrast to a similar case from Italy involving a teen suicide. A newspaper had published pictures of the boy's house as well as the text of an essay that he had written on the day of his suicide. The boy's father asked that the newspaper stop publication of these things and also sought damages for past publication. The Italian agency charged with protecting privacy interests ruled that the privacy of minors after death is subject to special consideration. It ordered that damages be awarded and also that the newspaper had to stop publishing pictures of the house as well as excerpts from the boy's essay. The agency also ruled that there should be an investigation into how the reporter acquired the essay.[41]

Memories in Action—Creating Ongoing Legacies to Memories of the Dead

The search for meaning in life is an essential human activity. While alive, we each seek to develop this meaning for ourselves. Upon death, however, this possibility for continued human expression and impact comes to an end. One of the most difficult things for mourners is to manage this sense of annihilation of their loved one. In order to overcome this void, mourners often seek to channel their grief through carrying on the work of their loved one or creating some meaning out of their loved one's death.

This creation of legacy occurs outside of law in a variety of contexts. First, we often see the creation of legacy in funeral or memorial services in which mourners talk about the life the person lived and the impact of that life on others. We also see this in the tradition of making charitable gifts in a person's memory or in doing good deeds on the anniversary of a person's death.

Public law—as the embodiment of a society's values—is also often called on to serve as a legacy to a person's life. Consider some current examples from one day's newspaper:

- After the Newtown massacre of school children, many parents became involved in working toward legislation that would limit access to guns. As one parent said in his testimony before Congress: "I'm not here for the sympathy or the pat on the back," Heslin, a 50-year-old construction worker, told the senators, weeping openly during much of his hushed 11-minute testimony. "I'm here to speak up for my son."[42]
- After Aaron Swartz committed suicide in the wake of his prosecution, supporters began pushing lawmakers to revise the law under which Swartz was prosecuted. They have called this law "Aaron's Law."[43]

Many of the laws that we have today—Megan's Law, the Ryan White Care Act, the Lindbergh Law—were created as a legacy to the loss of an individual.[44]

Private law plays its own significant role in the creation of legacy. One of the most powerful devices for creating legacy is the creation of a perpetual charitable trust or charitable foundation devoted to the work and memory of a loved one, or a cause in which the decedent believed strongly. A charitable trust is an entity formed with donated funds that is committed to pursuing a goal that society recognizes as worthy through the granting of charitable status. Consider the following email appeal written by the widower of a woman who died suddenly at the age of fifty.

> *As you know, my beloved Alison died just three months ago. Her death shook the foundations of many lives and needless to say, overturned mine and that of Ben and Noah—our grief is a mountain.*
> *What you may not know is that the boys and I have decided to tackle that grief, while giving us a sense that we continue to live for Alison, by forming a foundation in her name and honour. The foundation will pay a lasting tribute to Alison's wonderful, purposeful life and carry on her amazing work as a leading employment lawyer, a strong supporter of victims of torture in her role as chairwoman of Freedom from Torture and as a brilliant and path-breaking advocate for women's rights. Alison fought tirelessly for people less fortunate than herself and would have given so much more to causes of fairness, equality and social mobility had she lived.*[45]

The charitable foundation is a particularly powerful device because (1) it affords official societal sanction of worthiness in the form of being granted tax-exempt status, and (2) charitable foundations can exist in perpetuity. In this way, charitable foundations have the capacity to provide the immortality that human life lacks.

Conclusion

We think of the mourning process—one of the most painful of human conditions—as a deeply private and personal affair. And yet this essay has argued that even in this most private affair, public law plays a central role in shaping the bereavement process. From creating the moment that death has occurred, to shaping the post-death relationship of the mourner to the deceased and, in some cases, providing a mechanism for the mourner to let their image of the dead "live on" though a charitable entity committed to good works, the law plays a central role all along the way.

What does this intermingling of the most private act of mourning and the most public entity of law tell us about the nature of mourning and the nature of law? Is this a product of some intentional effort of law to blend with and control the anarchy of mourning? I think not. Rather, I believe it is a sign of the all-consuming nature of both law and mourning. Each is so all-encompassing in their respective realms of the private and the public that it is not surprising that they overflow their boundaries and inevitably engage with each other in the interstices.

NOTES

1. For a discussion of the mourning process, see Colin Murray Parkes and Holly Prigerson, *Bereavement: Studies of Grief in Adult Life* (New York: Routledge, 2009).

2. In addition, depending on the cause of death, the declaration of death can result in someone being charged with actual murder instead of attempted murder.

3. Kenneth V. Iserson, *Death to Dust: What Happens to Dead Bodies* (Tucson, AZ: Galen Press, 2001), 17.

4. Norman L. Cantor, *After We Die: The Life and Times of the Human Cadaver* (Washington, DC: Georgetown University Press, 2010), 12.

5. Ray D. Madoff, *Immortality and the Law: The Rising Power of the American Dead* (New Haven, CT: Yale University Press, 2010), 35.

6. *State v. Schaffer*, 574 P. 2d 205 (1977); see also *People v. Eulo*, 472 N.E.2d 286 (N.Y. 1984).

7. Uniform Determination of Death Act, National Conference of Commissioners on Uniform State Laws (1980).

8. Madoff, *Immortality and the Law*, 37.

9. In response to such difficulties, some scholars have suggested that the moment of death be at least partially a function of individual choice. New Jersey has enacted a statute that does this by allowing a patient's religious belief to be taken into account in determining whether death has occurred. New Jersey's law is similar to the law of other

jurisdictions in providing for doctors to apply either the cardiopulmonary or brain death standard, but it goes on to provide that the brain death standard is not to be used if the physician authorized to declare death has reason to believe that the brain death would violate the person's religious beliefs. In such a case, only the cardiopulmonary standard is to be used. Health and Vital Statistics, N.J. Stat. Ann. § 26:6A.

10. Lois M. Collins and Linda Thomson, "Jesse Loses his Battle with Brain Tumor," *Deseret Morning News*, November 20, 2004, www.deseretnews.com/article/595106792/Jesse-loses-his-battle-with-brain-tumor.html?pg=all.

11. Ibid.

12. J. M. Appel, "Defining Death: When Physicians and Families Differ," *Journal of Medical Ethics* 31 (2005): 641.

13. See abcnews.go.com/News/judge-pronounces-natalee-holloway-dead/story?id=15346993.

14. *State v. Bradbury*, 9 A.2d 657 (Me. 1939); "Tells of Cremating Body of Sister, 76" *New York Times*, June 12, 1938, 37.

15. Permanent Disposition of Dead Body or Remains, Mass. Gen. Laws Ann. chap. 114, §43M.

16. When Anna Nicole Smith died, there was a lengthy trial over who was authorized to make the decision regarding the disposition of her body: the executor of her will, her mother, or one of the two potential fathers of her newborn daughter. The probate court judge ultimately ruled that the infant daughter was the appropriate decision maker. This case was a more public version of a controversy that has played out since this country's inception—fights among family members and others about controlling the disposition of a person's body after death. Frances H. Foster, "Individualized Justice in Disputes Over Dead Bodies," 61 Vand. L. Rev. 1351 (2008).

17. For example, Massachusetts law finds the order of decision makers as follows: (1) the surviving spouse of the deceased; (2) the surviving adult children of the deceased; (3) the surviving parent(s) of the deceased; (4) the surviving brother(s) or sister(s) of the deceased; (5) the guardian of the person of the deceased at the time of his or her death; (6) any other person authorized or obligated by law to dispose of the remains of the deceased. Persons Authorized to Make Gift, Mass. Gen. Laws chap. 113, § 8.

18. States have broad discretion to determine when a medical investigation into the death of an individual (including autopsy) should be held, as noted in *American Jurisprudence*, 2nd ed., Coroners § 7. In most states, a medical examiner may review any death that has occurred under violent or criminal circumstances. Likewise, most states provide that a coroner may investigate any deaths that occur "suddenly" when the decedent appeared to be in good health. For instance, see Florida and Virginia Laws: Unclaimed Dead Bodies or Human Remains, Fla. Stat. Ann. § 406.50; Investigations of Death, Va. Code Ann. § 32.1–283. Finally, states commonly provide for an autopsy in the event the death is considered to have occurred by accident or under any suspicious or unusual circumstances. See Examinations, Investigations and Autopsies, Fla. Stat. Ann. § 406.11.; Duty to Notify State Medical Examiner, Alaska Stat. § 12.65.005.

19. Madoff, *Immortality and the Law*, 31–32.

20. *Snyder v. Holy Cross Hosp.*, 352 A.2d 334 (Md. App. 1976) (a case in which the court allowed an autopsy to determine the cause of death, following the sudden and unexplained death of the father's eighteen-year-old son, who had been in apparent good health, over the religious objections of the father).

21. Though this, too, can raise issues for the mourning process. Consider the case from France where the child of believers of cryonics had to remove his parents from a refrigerated crypt in the basement of their chateau in the Loire Valley to bury or cremate them. Madoff, *Immortality and the Law*, 50.

22. Richard Sandomir, "Williams Children Agree to Keep Their Father Frozen," *New York Times*, December 21, 2002, www.nytimes.com/2002/12/21/sports/baseball-williams-children-agree-to-keep-their-father-frozen.html.

23. Dan P. Lee, "The Good Seed," *GQ*, June 2011, www.gq.com/news-politics /news makers/201112/nik-evans-sperm-paternity-fight-story-marissa-evans?printable=true; Susan Donaldson James, "Sperm Retrieval: Mother Creates Life after Death," *ABC News*, February 23, 2010, abcnews.go.com/Health/Wellness/mother-murdered-son -hopes-create-grandchild-post-mortem/story?id=9913939.

24. For a discussion of the ethical issues involved in PSR, see Carson Strong, Jeffrey R. Gingrich, and William H. Kutteh, "Ethics of Postmortem Sperm Retrieval," *Human Reproduction* 15 (2009): 739.

25. Anna Aragno, "Transforming Mourning: A New Psychoanalytic Perspective," in *On Deaths and Endings: Psychoanalysts' Reflections on Finality, Transformations and New Beginnings*, ed. Brent Willock et al. (New York: Routledge, 2007), 36.

26. Parkes and Prigerson, *Bereavement*, 81.

27. Ray D. Madoff, "A Tale of Two Countries: Comparing the Law of Inheritance in Two Seemingly Opposite Systems," 37 Boston Coll. Intl and Comp. L.J. 333 (2014).

28. Sally Engle Merry, *Getting Justice and Getting Even* (Chicago: University of Chicago Press, 1990).

29. Ray D. Madoff, "Lurking in the Shadow: The Unseen Hand of Doctrine in Dispute Resolution," 76 S. Cal. L.R. 180 (2002).

30. Note how different this is from divorce today: a party may go to a lawyer asserting claims of moral worth (e.g., I was a good person, my spouse was a bad person), and yet the lawyer in effect explains that this dispute is not about right and wrong but only about where to go from here.

31. The term "posthumous meddling" was coined by Jeffrey Sherman in his thoughtful 1999 article "Posthumous Meddling: An Instrumental Theory of Testamentary Restraints on Conjugal and Religious Choices," Univ. Illinois L.R. 1273 (1999).

32. *Shapira v. Union Nat. Bank*, 315 N.E.2d 825 (Ohio Ct. Com. Pl. 1974).

33. Richard A. Posner, "Economic Analysis of Law," §18.7 (7th ed. 2007), cited in Jesse Dukeminier and Stanley Johanson, *Wills, Trusts, and Estates* (New York: Aspen, 1999), 31.

34. While the court was not impressed with these arguments, see the case of the person who married several times in order to get a greater inheritance. Daniel Shapira also made more traditional legal arguments, notably that this type of provision violated his constitutional rights, but these too fell on deaf ears.

35. Ray D. Madoff and Pierre-Alain Conil, "Inheritance and Death: Legal Strategies in the United States, England and France," in *Routledge Handbook of Family Law and Policy*, ed. John Eekelaar and Rob George (New York: Routledge, 2014).

36. Restatement (Third) of Trusts § 29 (2003). Restatements are distillations of common law that are prepared by the American Law Institute (ALI), a prestigious organization comprising judges, professors, and lawyers. The ALI's aim is to distill the "black letter law" from cases to indicate trends in common law and occasionally to recommend what a rule of law should be.

37. While Freud spoke about the importance of exorcising the dead, modern psychologists have instead focused on the importance of incorporating the dead into the ongoing life of the living. Parkes and Prigerson, *Bereavement*, 71.

38. Geoffrey A. Fowler, "Lie and Death Online: Who Controls a Digital Legacy?," *Wall Street Journal*, January 5, 2013, http://www.wsj.com/articles/SB10001424127887324677 20457818822036423346.

39. The Uniform Law Commission (ULC), also known as the National Conference of Commissioners on Uniform State Laws (NCCUSL), provides draft legislation to the

states with the goal of bringing clarity, stability and uniformity to critical areas of state legislative law.

40. Riley v. St. Louis County of Missouri, 153 F.3d 627 (8th Cir. 1998). Even if the officer's statements about the boy were intentionally false, there would still be no cause of action because of the notion that the dead cannot be defamed.

41. Provvedimento del 11 ottobre 2006. Il Garante Per Law Protezione Dei Dati Personali; discussed in Madoff, *Immortality and the Law*, 127–29.

42. Alan Fram and Philip Elliot, "Newtown Victim's Father Urges Action in D.C.," *Boston Globe*, February 28, 2012, www.bostonglobe.com/news/nation/2013/02/28/father-newtown-victim-urges-ban-assault-weapons/6gYZYf6RRNpe72EMPIYYNO/story.html.

43. David Uberti, "Inquiry Widens into Swartz Prosecution," *Boston Globe*, February 28, 2013, www.bostonglobe.com/news/nation/2013/02/28/house-committee-broadens-inquiry-into-aaron-swartz-case/eGMQxBsUYidHp7fV6ROBXM/story.html.

44. Of course, one need not die to have a law named after him or her—the Brady Handgun Violence Prevention Act was named after James Brady, who was left permanently disabled after the 1981 assassination attempt on President Reagan.

45. Alison Wetherfield was a friend of the author and truly an extraordinary woman. Her obituary, published in the *London Times*, can be found here: http://www.thetimes.co.uk/tto/opinion/obituaries/article3526135.ece.

2

The Mourning After
Posthumous Sperm Retrieval and the New Laws of Mourning

SHAI J. LAVI

In November 2012, Israel was in the midst of a military operation in the Gaza Strip.[1] After a prolonged week of air raids, soldiers who had been recruited for military reserve duty under emergency orders were preparing themselves for a land invasion. Conscious of the dangers awaiting them, over thirty field soldiers asked to sign a "biological will." The document, drafted by New Family, an NGO promoting individuals' right to establish nonconventional families in Israel, is a legally binding testament, ordering the posthumous retrieval of the signee's sperm and allowing its future use in the case of death. Soldiers who fall in combat would be able to bring children into the world posthumously either upon the request of a spouse or, if single, with a yet-unknown woman who would volunteer to carry and raise their biological offspring. Postmortem sperm retrieval (PMSR) is not only a way for life to continue after death but also opens a new way to practice grief, bereavement, and mourning.

The procedure is neither new nor specific to Israel or to soldiers. The technology for sperm harvesting has been available since the late 1970s, and the first known case of birth from PMSR in the United States dates to 1999.[2] Gaby Vernoff, in her twenties, lost her husband in a car accident. His sperm was harvested thirty hours after his death at the wife's request. The couple was childless and Gaby, determined to bring a child into the world, turned to a reproduction clinic at a nearby hospital. Dr. Cappy Rothman, director of the Center for Reproductive Medicine at Century City Hospital in Los Angeles, agreed to perform the procedure. Justifying his decision, he remarked, "I just did it because the family was in so much stress and so much grief."[3]

Though no longer a novelty, PMSR remains highly controversial. Some countries have banned the procedure altogether, while others have introduced more lenient regulation.[4] In an obvious sense, the variety of regulatory regimes is an outcome of a clash of value systems and *weltanschauung*, which bioethicists and moral philosophers have sought to spell out.[5] But the controversy has a deeper and more important significance. The source and origin of the normative controversy lies in the anthropological ambivalence of the practice itself. PMSR both reaffirms and challenges modern society's approach to the cycle of life and death. It reflects deeply held convictions and equally deep anxieties that are widely shared. For many observers, PMSR is a violation of the laws of nature, but at the same time it is the fulfillment of very natural desires. It concerns the highly extraordinary wish of close kin to posthumously harvest the gametes of the young and childless dead, but it can only be understood within the very ordinary context of reproductive technologies, which have already transformed modern kinship relationships in a variety of much less controversial ways. Furthermore, the ambivalence toward PMSR stems from its liminal position between the unpredictable emergence of the new and the endurance of the old. Modern society is not the first to face the problem of the young and childless dead, and the novel solution that advance technologies offer to this problem simultaneously preserves yet utterly transforms traditional practices.

Most importantly, PMSR newly articulates the relationship between the living and the dead, and, in this sense, constitutes a distinctly modern relationship toward mourning. In PMSR, mourning is at stake not only and not simply because the spouse and parents of the dead must make the decision to harvest the sperm at the peak of their grief, within twenty-four to seventy-two hours after death.[6] PMSR raises anxieties because it threatens to prematurely alleviate and perhaps even substitute grief and mourning. Indeed, an oft-repeated justification for attempts to achieve a posthumous conception has been the amelioration of grief. Cappy Rothman, the surgeon who performed the first posthumous sperm extraction, suggested that collecting sperm in circumstances where there has been the sudden, usually violent, death of a young man, "gives people hope and lessens the pain of suddenly losing a loved one."[7]

As long as PMSR is understood merely as a reproductive technology, it is easy to see why it would be interpreted as a death-denying gesture that undermines the laws of nature. From this perspective, PMSR seeks to defy death by radicalizing the artificiality of the reproduction of life, and violates the taboo of death in the name of a dubious imperative to give life. But what if PMSR is not simply about overcoming death but also about the way in which the living bring to a peaceful resolution the passing away of the dead by regenerating the cycle of life and death? If this is the case, then could it be said that PMSR obeys the maxim that by the same token that life is followed by death, death, too, must be followed by life? If, nevertheless, PMSR stirs up anxieties, it is not so much because it denies death and privileges life, but rather because of the distinctly modern way in which it seeks to perpetuate the cycle of life and death. PMSR in this sense inscribes new laws of mourning, the mourning of the morning after. What are these laws?

In the final analysis, can the legal (Part 2), psychological (Part 3), and anthropological (Part 4) rules and laws that purport to govern our lives between birth and death capture life after death? Or does the case of posthumous birth understood as an extraordinary act of mourning offer us an opportunity to question these taken-for-granted frameworks and open for us new ways to contemplate our mortality (Part 5 and Conclusion)?

1. Introducing Life after Death

To understand PMSR we must first place it within the broader context of posthumous birth. Traditionally, and long before the development of artificial reproductive technologies, posthumous children were the unfortunate offspring of a father who had passed away during pregnancy. As a fiat of nature beyond human control, these cases raised few moral dilemmas. The one important legal question to address was whether the child should be considered a rightful heir of the deceased father. Most legal systems answered in the affirmative, as long as the child was born within a set time after the father's death.[8]

Posthumous fertilization as distinct from posthumous birth was made possible with the development of new biotechnologies and, specifically, of cryopreservation of sperm, which became available in the 1950s.[9] One of its first uses was to offer men in high-risk professions, such as astronauts and soldiers, an option for fathering children in the event of injury that would make them infertile. More recently, it has become a recommended procedure among patients who are undergoing cancer treatment.[10] Such patients are offered the opportunity to deposit their sperm prior to treatment for later use, preempting the common risk that chemotherapy will render them infertile. Another source of frozen sperm is gametes donated to sperm banks. Ethical and legal complications arise in the case of death. Should the sperm be destroyed or kept posthumously? If kept, who should have access to it and for what legitimate end?

Now-routine techniques that have been developed, such as oocyte preservation, in vitro fertilization (IVF), and cryopreserved embryo transfer, have expanded the possibilities of parenting after death. Furthermore, the development of cryopreservation of ova has extended the options for posthumous reproduction to the use of frozen ova, in similar ways to the use of sperm.[11]

Postmortem gamete retrieval, first reported in 1980, is a further development along similar lines.[12] Sperm has been extracted through a variety of means, including excision of the epididymis,[13] rectal probe electroejaculation, and testicular sperm extraction (TSE).[14] Extraction has a significantly high success rate within thirty-six hours of death, and in some reported cases has taken place seventy-hours hours after death. The retrieval is successful in nearly 100 percent of the cases, and in 80–90 percent of the cases the sperm is motile. Fertilization then takes place usually through in vitro fertilization, which is as successful as regular insemination.[15] More recently, in 2011, postmortem ova retrieval has been reported for the first time.[16]

A survey of fertility centers in the United States found that a total of forty centers reported eighty-two requests for postmortem sperm retrieval between 1980 and July 1995.[17] Pregnancy following postmortem sperm retrieval was reported for the first time in 1998,[18] and a subsequent birth was reported in March 1999.[19]

2. Regulating Postmortem Sperm Retrieval

PMSR is treated differently in different Western countries.[20] In several European countries PMSR is prohibited outright. These include Austria, Bulgaria, Denmark, Finland, France, Germany, Greece, Italy, Latvia, Portugal, Slovenia, and Sweden. In quite a few countries PMSR is permitted under restricted conditions, including in Belgium, the Czech Republic, Hungary, Netherlands, Spain, the United Kingdom, and Israel.[21] Yet in others, such as the United States, there are no specific national regulations, and the practice is governed by general norms concerning the treatment of the posthumous body.[22]

Though the details of regulation differ from one country to the next, the overarching concerns are similar. The regulation reflects a liberal sensitivity to the rights and welfare of the three main parties involved: the deceased, the gestational mother, and the expected child. The language of individual rights and interests is dominant in the legal discourse, but whether it fully captures the phenomenon is much less clear.

Countries which regulate PMSR require that the retrieval and subsequent use of the sperm will accord with the autonomy of the deceased. Consequently, the first and major hurdle to overcome is constructing posthumous intent.[23] There is significant latitude in the interpretation of this condition. Some jurisdictions require a written document. A clearly stated wish either in writing or orally will go a long way toward legitimizing PMSR, as the Ethics Committee of the American Society for Reproductive Medicine has suggested: "It would seem to be totally appropriate to honor this designation after their death in the absence of any adverse consequences to the living participants in the pregnancy or any expected children."[24] Naturally, this requirement can be fulfilled only in cases of foreseeable death, when dying patients store frozen gametes or embryos and designate them for posthumous use, or when individuals at risk sign a "biological will" instructing the posthumous retrieval of sperm. In most other cases, this condition is hardly ever attainable.

Even when the deceased did not explicitly discuss the issue, PMSR may still take place. In the absence of a written document, courts from different jurisdictions have relied on material evidence indicating the deceased's wish.[25] In quite a few cases, courts have based their approvals on the testimony of the spouse or parents of the deceased as well as on passing remarks and general impressions to establish the deceased's wish for progeny. In some cases, courts have relied on the legal presumption that a person in a long-term relationship who was already planning to have a child with his partner is likely to have granted his partner the permission to continue with the planned project without him.[26]

The Israeli directives go one step further and hold a broader presumption, namely, that all married men (or men in long-term relationships) would wish, if asked, to have a child after their death. There is little empirical evidence supporting this presumption, and if anything some preliminary studies have suggested that, if asked in advance, it is the female partner who is more likely to be interested in PMSR of her partner than the man himself.[27]

In many of these regulations, there seems to be some confusion between the will of the deceased to have children when he was still alive and his will to have a child after his death. These are obviously two very different questions, but they are constantly blurred by the courts and, occasionally, by the regulator as well. For example, the Israeli directive instructs: "With due caution, it can be said that when a person is married or when he ties his life with a female partner in a mutual life, it may reveal his presumed will to have children together with his partner."[28] Even if the assumption were correct, it would have little bearing on the more relevant question regarding desire to have posthumous children.

An internationally renowned UK case from the 1990s may help to highlight the tension between jurisdictions that hold to a strict interpretation of a "biological will" and those more flexible in their interpretation of the requirement. Four years after their marriage in 1995, Stephan Blood contracted meningitis and died. His wife, Diane, asked the doctors caring for her husband to remove sperm samples from him. The doctors complied and two samples were removed before her husband was pronounced clinically dead. Diane applied for permission to use the stored sperm to bear a child, but the UK Human Fertilisation and Embryology Authority (HFEA) refused. Diane turned to the court. In its ruling the Court pointed out that in the absence of the husband's consent, the sperm had been obtained illegally and thus could not be used in the UK. After a series of decisions and appeals, the Court granted Diane permission to use the sperm outside the UK, in EU countries where the regulation is not as strict. Diane became pregnant at a fertility clinic in Belgium and later gave birth to a son.[29]

More difficult are cases in which the deceased is unmarried, and the parents are asking for PMSR. Such was the recent US case of Daniel Thomas Christy, a twenty-three-year-old man, who was involved in a motorcycle accident, suffered severe head trauma, and was hospitalized. In the hospital, after seeing a small baby, Christy's fiancée, Amy Kruse, began contemplating the possibility of PMSR and discussed the matter with his parents. As his medical surrogate decision makers, the parents asked the hospital to retrieve his sperm. The ethics committee met to discuss the case but could not reach a decision, and consequently rejected the request. Daniel's parents filed an emergency order and the Iowa sixth district court decided in favor of Christy. Extending the Uniform Anatomical Gifts Act from 2006 to the case of PMSR, Judge Martha Beckelman ruled in favor of Ms. Kruse.[30]

An even more challenging scenario takes place when there is no woman involved in the life of the deceased, in which case the construction of the presumed will of the deceased is even sketchier. Such was the case of Idan Snir, a twenty-one-year-old Israeli man.[31] When Idan was diagnosed with cancer and before he began chemotherapy, he deposited a sperm sample at the Rambam Hospital in Haifa. As mentioned, sperm cryopreservation is a recommended procedure for cancer patients who are advised that the treatment is likely to make them infertile.[32] Depositing sperm in advance would allow Idan to procreate if and when he recovered. But he never did. Idan passed away at the age of twenty-two, single and childless. For Idan's parents this was not the end of the story. They decided to make use of the deposited sperm and find a woman who would bear Idan's posthumous child, their grandchild. Once they had located an appropriate candidate, a forty-year-old single woman, they requested the hospital to release their son's gamete. The sperm bank at the Rambam Hospital refused, claiming that Idan's parents had no legal claim over the sperm, and that in the absence of a legal document expressing the specific wish of the deceased, the existing directive limits the posthumous use of sperm to a long-term partner.

In an unprecedented decision, the court ruled in favor of the appellant and ordered the hospital to release the frozen sperm to the intended mother. The court reasoned that not only married men (or those living in a long-term relationship) may have the desire to bring children into the world postmortem. In a world of new family structures and advanced reproductive technologies, single women as much as married women may wish to have children, and single men may carry out their desire for a progeny with their assistance. The parents are best positioned to know and express the "true wish" of the deceased. Specifically, the court found a leading clue in a conversation Idan had had with his father. "Dad," Idan was reported to have said, "I promise you, life will not come to an end, it will be continued, it is impossible to bring life to a halt."[33] The court—well aware of the interpretive stretch—still insisted on reading into this statement a hint of the deceased's wish for posthumous procreation.[34]

The weight given to the will of the deceased is closely related to the legal status attributed to the sperm. Some jurisdictions have considered sperm as property and apply inheritance law to the frozen sperm and ova.[35] Others have rejected the equation of gametes with property and regulated the matter differently. Several states in the United States, for example, have applied the legal regulation of body transplants to posthumous sperm.[36] Others, such as Canada and Israel, have enacted special regulation to cover posthumous sperm retrieval and use.[37]

The diversity of legal regulations and variety of judicial interpretations undermine any attempt to generalize. Still, it is hard to ignore the ways in which certain jurisdictions have clearly deviated from the liberal model that bases PMSR on the presumed will of the deceased. Some scholars have concluded that in the final analysis the interests of the remaining relatives trump the autonomy and will (presumed or real) of the deceased.[38] While there is much truth to this observation, the question remains open as to whether the relatives themselves are making autonomous decisions.

Indeed, the will of the deceased is only one legal requirement for PMSR approval. An additional regulatory concern is with the interests of the widow, who under the influence of her personal tragedy might be unable to form a sound opinion as to carrying out a pregnancy. The concern is both with the internal psychological pressure of the widow's personal grief and with the potential undue influence coming from the parents of the deceased, who are themselves mourning and may pressure the spouse to give birth to a child in order to alleviate their own sense of loss. Aware of this danger, some legislators and policymakers have prohibited the use of the sperm during the mourning period, which is variably defined as a six-month to one-year period.[39] The European Society for Human Reproduction and Embryology (ESHRE) has called for a minimum one-year waiting period before the frozen eggs or sperm are actually used. The Israeli Directive stipulates a similar requirement, explaining that "the decision should not be made under the close and weighty influence of the entire feelings and emotions that accompany this event."[40] And, furthermore, it should be ensured that "the partner is not under any pressures or influences that may overpower her independent judgment and her personal approach to the problem of bearing a child from the sperm of her deceased partner."[41] In addition, some countries further require a social worker's report that confirms that the child will have a nourishing environment. "The wife," as one medical journal put it, "must consent to a 1-year period of specimen quarantine, so that additional counseling may be provided after the initial bereavement period has passed."[42]

A study on the practice of PMSR has shown that most of the widows or partners had wished to keep the spermatozoa initially (twenty-one widows, 52.5 percent), but subsequently retreated from their intention, with over half not following up with the treatment. Investigators concluded that the initial request reflects "the commonly perceived mourning period which is thought to last from 6 months up to 1 year," whereas the decision not to follow through "may in part reflect the counseling that is commonly conducted before any decision is taken."[43]

It is interesting to note, in this context, a certain tension in the regulation of the postmortem timeframe. Some jurisdictions, as we just saw, prohibit the postmortem use of the sperm within the first year after death, while others—quite to the contrary—require its use within the first year.[44] In both cases the assumption is that the deceased is more present during the first year of his departure and gradually fades thereafter, but each understands this presence differently—the first focuses on the gradually diminishing sense of loss, the second on the fading presence of the will.

The third and final consideration that guides regulation is the welfare of the child. In some countries, it is on this ground that PMSR is banned altogether. Scholars have written, in this context, of the dangers of "Planned Orphanage" and have emphasized the psychological damage that may be caused to a child, who will continue to search incessantly for his dead father.[45] Consequently, some regulators have insisted on including in the decision-making process a written review by a social worker who will report on the status of the designated mother and her living environment and lend support to judging whether the woman's decision to bring a child into the world under unusual circumstances will not harm the future child. The mourning process is seen in this context as yet another threat to the ability to make the right decision.

To summarize, under the liberal conceptualization the PMSR procedure is construed as fulfilling the verifiable choice of the deceased and reflects his autonomous decision. The sperm is thought of either as property or as a donation, but at any rate PMSR is an act of willful giving. Not only the deceased but also the gestating mother must conform to the model of deliberate choice-making. Thus, in order to safeguard the well-being of both mother and child, pregnancy should not be carried out within a period of six months to one year. Mourning is understood psychologically as grief and consequently as a potential impediment to the clear and rational judgment of spouse and parents. Proper management of grief through a mourning period and counseling may relieve these concerns and pave the way to a successful decision-making process.

This account, as commonsensical as it may sound, does not get to the heart of the matter. It eludes fundamental questions concerning postmortem sperm retrieval and the mourning of the dead. We may begin by asking: Is the wish to procreate truly the *living will* of the deceased?

Might it not be better understood as the will of the remaining spouse and parents masquerading as the will of the dead, as some critics have readily suggested? Or should we remain open to the possibility that it is not the will of the *living* at all and, for that matter, not at all a *willing*, but rather a calling from the dead? And consequently, we may ask, what role does mourning play in the tragedy of the childless dead? Is it merely an emotional breakdown awaiting catharsis? Or is mourning, in its originative sense, not a psychological modality, but rather a state of affairs that binds together the living and the dead and persists until the mourners fulfill their duty toward the deceased, helping to heal the broken cycle of life and death?

3. Mourning beyond Melancholy

Rachel Cohen's son, Keivan, was nineteen years old when he was hit by a bullet from a Palestinian sniper in 2002.[46] While the casualty notification unit was still in the family's living room, Rachel went into her son's room, took a large framed photo, and smashed it on the floor, crying out: "Keivan, where have you disappeared? Where is this pretty face? These eyes? Everything will be buried, nothing will remain. Where is the little Keivan you promised me?" Ten years later she recalls how the idea of PMSR occurred to her at that very moment: "And suddenly, it was as if I heard him. . . . Mom, he said to me, it's not too late. There's still something you can take from me. . . . What about the sperm? Don't you want it?"[47]

The army was helpful, and the sperm was harvested form the body within the thirty-six-hour time window. But in the absence of a spouse or a long-term relationship, the state was reluctant to allow its use. The family was in the possession of sixteen syringes that could allow nearly an infinite number of children to be reproduced, but they could use none. The parents, accompanied by a lawyer, turned to the attorney general, requesting his approval. After a prolonged period of negotiations, the parents discovered to their dismay that during the time they were waiting for his reply, the attorney general had prepared binding guidelines that allowed only partners of the deceased and not parents to use the sperm.[48] The family argued that the directives should not be applied retrospectively, and after two years of legal struggle their request was finally granted. But the story did not end there. There was still the problem of finding a suitable mother. Rachel began interviewing women to find the right match. The woman would not be offered money, and Rachel stipulated that she would need to accept the grandparents of Keivan's offspring as part of the extended family; most importantly, the woman would need to take upon herself the raising of a dead soldier's child along with the grandmother's expectations.

More than ten years after her son died, Rachel was still searching for the right woman. In the course of the years, three women, each in turn, tried to conceive but, even after extensive hormone therapy and numerous trials, failed. When asked how much longer she would pursue this mission, Rachel responded: "A friend of mine had a dream. He [Keivan] came to her and asked, 'Tell my mother she should not give up and should continue.' So my friend asked him, 'Why won't you tell her that yourself?' and he replied, 'My mother is in a difficult psychological state, and I cannot go to her. You go.' This was five years ago," she continues. "He too wants his child and I hope I will carry out the task. Sometimes I wonder to myself whether this task is not too big, and I ask, 'Keivan, why isn't it working? How much strength do I have? I can't.' But I don't have an alternative. I will keep going until the last drop of sperm."

Time has not been a cure to Mrs. Cohen. The specters of the dead continue to haunt her. She seemed fixated on the idea and could not give up. She felt that giving up would be a betrayal of her son. Rachel placed a shrine in the memory of her son at the entrance to the apartment and tested the women she brought home for their reaction—how moved were they by the photos of the dead soldier? How authentic was their reaction? She was unable to move on in life and by her own account could not find joy in her other children and grandchildren. In 2013, however, eleven years after Keivan's death, the endeavor finally materialized. Rachel found a mother for her grandchild and a baby girl was born named Osher, Hebrew for "felicity."

Rachel's story lends itself, perhaps too readily, to a Freudian framework. Freud famously draws a distinction between mourning and melancholia.[49] While mourning, he explains, is the common reaction to the loss of a loved person, in some people the same loss produces the pathological disposition of melancholia. Freud emphasizes that mourning, too, involves a grave departure from the normal attitude to life, but is not regarded as a pathological condition. We believe time is the best cure and that any interference with it is useless or even harmful. Freud captures succinctly the distinction between the normal and the pathological response to loss: "The melancholic displays something else besides which is lacking in mourning—an extraordinary diminution in his self-regard, an impoverishment of his ego on a grand scale. In mourning it is the world which has become poor and empty; in melancholia it is the ego itself."[50]

The psychological soundness of PMSR is a challenge that proponents of the practice have had to face. During the Parliament Committee discussion in Israel, Dr. Zelina Ben-Gershon, from the Israeli Chief Scientist's Office, warned: "Parents try to bring time to a halt from the moment their child dies to prevent anything from changing. Sometimes they leave the room as it was for years, wear the clothes, listen to the same songs, try to do everything to keep the world from turning, so as not to bid farewell, so that death will be as naught. . . . The commemoration of a lost son [via PMSR] is an almost obsessive act for parents. It does not resemble anything logical, rational that a person would do. I cannot imagine even one family of mourning parents that will be able to afford not to use this option." Ben-Gershon is worried that, once available, the technology will tempt mourning parents to make use of it.[51]

While post-Freudian psychological theory offers an important perspective on mourning, it is nonetheless a limited one. A familiar objection comes from the ranks of liberals. During the same Parliament discussion, Asa Kasher, one of Israel's leading bioethicists, offered the liberal response to these concerns: "There's an attempt to tell the widow how to live. They say to her 'Pull out, depart, disengage.' They tell her Freudian tales from the beginning of the previous century, even though Freud himself behaved differently when his daughter passed away. They tell us things that are obsolete."[52]

But the liberal response is merely one response, and not the one that Rachel Cohen adopted. Rachel's wish to use her son's sperm was not part of his "living will." His desire to bring children became concrete and pressing only posthumously. Rachel speaks of the duty she owes to her son ("Tell my mother she should not give up") as well as the duty he owes her ("Where is the little Keivan you promised me?"). It is not a will that Keivan expressed during his lifetime and which endured after his death, nor is it a posthumous approximation of his living wish. Quite to the contrary, it is only after his death that the idea was born. What lay at stake was not Keivan's wish for progeny, nor simply Rachel's desire for a grandchild. It was first and foremost the fact that Keivan died young and childless and that his mother had the possibility of doing something about it.

But for the very same reason, one must object to any attempt to pathologize her response and reduce it to its psychological dimensions. The psychological account focuses on the individual survivors and their perception of loss, not on the loss itself. Rather than address the loss, psychology sees only the imprints that it leaves on the individual psyche. Death is treated as an emotional loss, to which the mourners must face up and gradually adjust. Furthermore, psychology can only treat Rachel Cohen's loss as an individual experience, which of course it was. But it would be a mistake to ignore the fact that her son's death was not only her personal loss and that she was responding to something which melancholia simply cannot capture, namely, the tragic circumstances that threatened to interrupt the intergenerational cycle of life followed by death followed by new life. It was now her role as a mother to make sure the chain would not be broken. Rachel's wish, overstated, obsessive, and disturbing as it may appear, was not idiosyncratic and surely not reducible to a personal pathology. It was grounded in the human condition that anthropologists have long documented. One available key to understanding Rachel's quest is by examining its anthropological underpinnings.

Indeed, we should not limit our understanding of mourning to the psychological study of emotions, as both the liberal and the psychological accounts, each in its own way, suggest.[53] Though mourning is often confused with grief and bereavement, the former is not identical with the latter two. While grief and bereavement are emotional responses to death, mourning reaches beyond the individual psyche. Mourning is a multilayered phenomenon that requires a multilayered analysis. We may begin with the anthropological insight that mourning unsettles the cosmological order and not merely the psychological one.

4. The Anthropological Condition of Mourning

In his important contribution to the study of mourning, the French anthropologist Robert Hertz sought to understand the laws of mourning beyond individual sentiment.[54] As his teacher and mentor, Emile Durkheim, had treated the study of suicide, Hertz saw the potential of approaching sociologically what ordinarily seemed like a highly personal experience, and appropriately named his study "The Collective Representation of Death." The essay studies the mortuary practices among the Dayak tribes of Borneo. Hertz was struck by the fact that the burial of the dead took place in two separate stages. Among the peoples of the Malay, Hertz notes, the custom is not to take the body at once to its final burial ground. During this provisional stage, the body is placed in shelter and gradually decomposes and the soul of the dead remains in the vicinity and is seen simultaneously as a source of danger and of protection. The liminal status of the body and the soul is further reflected in the liminal status of the mourning kin. They, too, are placed at the margins of society and have unique obligations toward the dead. Only after a certain time—which may be short or long—is the body brought to its final burial ground. Only then does the soul join the society of the dead, and only then do the living kin reintegrate into society. The death of the person brings about the disintegration of society, the body, and the soul and is followed by a reinstallation from which the collectivity emerges "triumphant" after death.

For Hertz, mourning is not limited to emotions and, furthermore, it is not only about the surviving relatives. Mourning is about the triangular relationship of the corpse, the soul, and the community of mourners. In the process of mourning all three inhabit a liminal position. The corpse is placed between the living and the dead. It no longer walks among the living, but neither does it share the eternal life of the dead. The soul, which has left the body, continues to hover close to the dead body, not yet fulfilling its journey to the afterworld. And finally, there are the mourners, who, like the soul and the corpse, are placed on the outskirts of society. As Hertz put it, "Indeed, the close relatives, because they are as it were one with the deceased, share his condition, are included with him in the feelings which he inspires in the community, and are subject, like him, to a taboo during the whole interval between the death and the second funeral."[55]

Once mourning is understood anthropologically rather than psychologically, we may begin to understand how PMSR constitutes a modern practice of mourning. Here, too, the body of the dead is not immediately put to rest. Following Hertz, Eric Venbroux distinguishes between "flesh-type" and "bone-type" kinds of objects.[56] While the former disintegrate shortly after death, the latter remain intact throughout the period of mourning and await the second burial. The sperm of the deceased is a bone-type object par excellence. It is what is left of the body and continues to bind together the deceased and his relatives in their liminal condition. Eventually, the bone-type object, too, is brought to rest and the mourning period comes to an end. This happens once the sperm is either used or discarded. During the interval, the mourners are attached to the dead and cannot continue with their ordinary lives. From this perspective, the law, which sets a mourning period of six months to a year, is not simply guarding the widow and the parents from making hasty decisions. It also commits them to a period during which the sperm as a bone-type object cannot rest in peace and during which the soul of the deceased continues to hover over the body. The mourning period set by the law can be prolonged for years, as the case of Rachel Cohen demonstrates. During this period the soul of the dead is closely tied to his body. If, in this case, the sperm stands in for the body, it is the name of the deceased that stands for his soul. The soul of the deceased may carry on, either in memory or in the offspring that will spring from the sperm.

PMSR, in this sense, neatly maps onto well-known anthropological categories, perhaps too neatly. Indeed, these anthropological insights allow us to push our inquiry one step further and ask: Is PMSR a modern reincarnation of ancient practices of mourning? Is there nothing new about the new technologies? Are life and death, body and soul, the living and the dead, constant universal categories that take different shapes and forms but ultimately represent unchanging anthropological structures? To examine the purview of the structuralist analysis and its limitations, we may wish to compare and contrast PMSR with a telling historical analogy, the biblical practice of levirate marriage.

5. The Levirate Duty

The new technology of posthumous birth brings to mind the much older biblical practice of levirate marriage. According to the book of Deuteronomy (25:5–6), when a married man dies childless, his brother comes under an obligation to marry the new widow. The first child to be born of the wedlock will carry the name of the deceased and will be his legal heir. Etymologically, levirate comes from the Latin *levir*, the husband's brother, and the practice seems to have been common in the Near East.[57] What is distinct about the Israelite practice is its justification. As opposed to other Mesopotamian cultures that tied the practice to inheritance laws, the additional explanation the Bible gives for the ancient practice concerns the continuity of the man who dies childless, so "that his name may not be blotted out of Israel."[58]

The levirate marriage is an important duty, and one biblical story (Genesis 38) tells of the consequences of defying the obligation. It is the story of Onan the son of Judah, the founder of one of the Israelite tribes. When Onan's brother Er died childless, leaving his wife Tamar a widow, Judah ordered his second son to carry out the levirate obligation and bear a child from his sister-in-law. "And Judah said unto Onan, 'Go in unto thy brother's wife, and marry her, and raise a seed to thy brother.'"[59] Onan, knowing that the child would be named after his brother, and thus would not be his own, refused to carry out the obligation and spilled his semen on the ground (hence the word onanism). God was displeased and punished Onan by death.

It lies beyond the scope of this paper to trace the origins and purpose of the levirate marriage.[60] Scholars have offered different explanations for the practice, including provision of an heir so that property can remain within the family, care for the widow and her reabsorption into the family, and the continuation of the name of the deceased in the life of his brother's son. As mentioned, scholars consider inheritance as less central to the Jewish tradition and, accordingly, this is why the Bible emphasizes the notion of a "name."[61] Jewish mysticism has also emphasized the importance of having an heir to perform the ritual duties in memory of the dead that children perform toward their father.

The fear of dying without leaving a descendant seems to have been a concern among the ancient Israelites. Thus, for example, Absalom the son of King David realizes that he will leave the world without an offspring: "Now Absalom in his lifetime had taken and reared up for himself a pillar, which is in the King's Valley. For he said, 'I have no son to keep my name in remembrance.' And he called the pillar after his own name. And it is called unto this day, Absalom's pillar."[62]

The affinities between levirate marriage and PMSR are striking—so much so that the comparison is not a scholarly imposition, but has been raised during legislative processes. In a discussion of PMSR in the British House of Lords, Lord Winston, a medical doctor and a practicing Orthodox Jew, made the following observation:

> I am reminded that there is of course biblical precedent. Your Lordships will be aware, for example, of Levirate marriage, clearly stated in Deuteronomy. There is a notion that if a man dies prematurely and his wife is without issue, then she is allowed to marry her late husband's brother because that promotes the generation and preserves her lost husband's name in society. Indeed, in biblical law that child is named after the lost father and not after the brother whom she marries.[63]

Similarly, the directive issued by the Israeli attorney general itself makes the connection between the historic levirate marriage and contemporary posthumous reproduction:

> The desire for continuity and for existence [kiyum] after death by means of remaining offspring is a basic desire of most individuals in society. A concrete expression of this will can be found in Jewish heritage and in Jewish

law [halacha]. The stories of the forefathers in the book of Genesis, generation after generation—Abraham and Sara, Isaac and Rebecca, Jacob and Rachel—revolve around their longing for a seed [zera] and for a fruit of the womb. In another sense, the raising up of offspring to the dead lies at the foundation of the laws of the levirate marriage. It should also be recalled that the commandment to be fruitful and multiply is the first of the Torah commandments.[64]

With the death of a childless person, the cycle of life and death is tragically interrupted. It is almost as if the dead cannot rest in peace without having progeny. It is the duty of the living toward the dead to complete the cycle. This means more than expressing grief. There is an unfinished matter that must be attended to, and it is the responsibility of the kin to accommodate it. From this perspective, PMSR is not new, but a repetition with little variation of old practices.

PMSR, like levirate marriage, is about repairing the broken cycle of life and death. It provides concrete content to the community's obligation toward their dead before the latter are brought to eternal rest. The process of mourning is understood precisely as a closing of this gap and the rejuvenation of society in the face of death. Mourning rebuilds the interrupted cycle of life and death. Edmond Leach has made a similar point, suggesting that "our inherently ambiguous concept of time facilitates the assertion that birth comes after death as day comes after night. The category 'time' covers two quite different kinds of experience: time as repetitive and time as irreversible duration. By merging both kinds of experience within the same category we manage . . . to muddle them up and to avoid recognizing irreversibility by assimilating it to repetition."[65]

The affinities between levirate marriage and PMSR seem to suggest that both are equally anchored in the human condition. Indeed, Don Seeman has argued against the tendency to exaggerate the novelty and transformative power of new reproductive technologies and in favor of facing the commonalities between old and new reproductive strategies.[66] Seeman calls for a shift from "a discourse of ethical, religious, and reproductive *norms* in the language of academic bioethics, to a discourse of cultural, religious, and reproductive *strategies*." From this perspective, he argues, "Technologies available to accomplish this goal [of procreation] vary, as do the social institutions that make it possible, but modern technological surrogacy and the servant-surrogacy of the Hebrew Bible are at least comparable, as are the Levirate and today's controversial postmortem collection and delivery of sperm cells."[67]

Seeman is surely right in noting the similarities between the levirate and PMSR, but the comparison he insists on may also highlight fundamental differences. Furthermore, his recommendation to shift the analysis from norms to strategies is itself telling. While it may be true that thinking of levirate marriage as a "strategy" may help us see the affinities it shares with PMSR, its construction as a strategy may be incongruent with the understanding of the practice as part of a nomos. PMSR is not merely a new technological means for achieving a preexisting, universally recognized, human end. The technology itself belongs to a new moral world that gives rise to novel objectives along with state-of-the-art means for pursuing them.

Conclusion: PMSR and the New Laws of Mourning

The affinities between levirate practice and PMSR are quite striking and must be seriously considered. The two share in common a concern with the problem of the childless dead and the wish to afford him posthumous progeny. From this perspective, PMSR is a modern variation and a closer approximation to the biblical desire to "raise a seed" to the dead. And yet, PMSR is not only a revival of the ancient levirate practice by advanced technological means. While the affinity between the two is striking, the variations are at least of equal importance. The comparison of PMSR with levirate marriage may highlight the shifts in our understandings and practices of "raising a seed" to the dead.

Returning to Hertz's tripartite analytic framework, which breaks down mourning into its three leading protagonists—the relatives, the corpse, and the soul—we can see how each of these has taken a radically new form in PMSR. First, the relatives of the deceased take on very different roles. In the levirate, the brother of the deceased has the legal duty to marry the widow and she is not allowed to marry anyone else. Only if the two perform a special ritual, known as *haliza,* are they released from this mutual obligation. The levirate marriage aims at continuing the individual as a member of an extended family, not his individuality per se. It would be tempting to argue that PMSR, in contradistinction, is about the deceased as an atomized individual. Indeed, there are good reasons to believe this is the case. The primacy of the individual in PMSR is highlighted by the fact that PMSR is grounded in fulfilling the will of the deceased and his right over his sperm, which carries on after death, while the levirate is about the family's obligation and the wishes of the deceased are entirely irrelevant.

The aim of PMSR, it would seem, is to continue the "seed" of the deceased in an individualized fashion. Furthermore, in PMSR the deceased need not be married, and in many of the Israeli cases the future mother is not even known to the deceased.

And yet, it would be a mistake to conclude with Marilyn Strathern that while the contemporary reproductive practices concerns the *individual*, older customs, including the levirate marriage, are about the *dividual*. Dividuals in her account "contain a generalized sociality within. Indeed, persons are frequently constructed as the plural and composite site of the relationships that produce them."[68] Rather, and as we have seen, PMSR is not concerned with the isolated individual. It is concerned with the individual imbedded in new family ties, and new biosocial relations. In the absence of a spouse or girlfriend, the future grandparents will step into the shoes of the deceased and court strangers for the role of potential mothers. Posthumously, the deceased becomes a member of a newly formed family, one he did not necessarily know nor could have imagined. It is a posthumous family, a family of the future, not of the past.

The second difference concerns the soul of the deceased. Admittedly, neither the biblical text nor PMSR make explicit reference to the soul. In fact, the biblical text does not know of the Christian (and rabbinic) dualism of body and soul. But the "soul" in Hertz's account should not be limited to the Christian "soul" as an ephemeral entity. The soul, as opposed to the corpse, is that which remains of the dead and passes on. In the Bible, which knew nothing of an afterlife, it is the "name" of the deceased. But what precisely is this "name"? In the levirate practice, the name of the deceased is the continuation of the deceased patriarchic name through the matrimony of his brother and the widowed wife. In PMSR, the "name" of the deceased that carries on after death is not a familial legacy but a genetic heritage. In the age of reproductive technologies, personhood is understood biologically, and individual continuity is interpreted as hereditary material. The modern soul, striking as it may sound to the uninitiated, lies in a long polymer of deoxyribonucleic acid, which is made of repeating units of nucleotides.

The third and final element in this transformation is the corpse. PMSR sees in the corpse a source of biological material. It extracts from the dead the remaining, albeit fleeting, powers of life. The corpse becomes a resource, a potentiality of life that may be harvested. PMSR turns on its head the traditional distinction between soul and body—the soul is biological, whereas the physical corpse is spiritualized, in the distinctly modern sense in which the material world is seen as a source of energy that can be exploited for human ends. The biblical treatment of the corpse is not part of the levirate code. It is excluded from use and some rabbis have objected to PMSR precisely on those grounds.

Taken together, the body, the soul, and the relatives constitute the three elements of mourning. It is tempting to think, as some scholars have suggested, that PMSR is a death-denying practice both psychologically and sociologically: psychologically, in a failure to come to terms with the death of a beloved person, and sociologically, with the general attempt of modern humanity to overcome death. What we have seen is something quite different. On the one hand, PMSR manifests the wish to perpetuate the cycle of life and death. On the other hand, PMSR gives a totally new sense to the biblical commandment of "raising a seed" for the dead. We may conclude that while both the levirate and PMSR may emerge from the same human condition, the latter radically transforms this condition.

NOTES

The chapter greatly benefitted from its discussion at the Law, Jurisprudence, and Social Thought Program at Amherst College and at Cornell Law School Faculty Seminar. The author would also like to thank Joel Fox and Nir Gonen for their excellent research assistance.

1. The following is based on Ronny Linder-Ganz and Dan Even, "Reservists Ask for Their Sperm to Be Frozen If They Die," *Haaretz*, November 20, 2012, http://www.haaretz.com/new/diplomacy-defense/reservists-ask-for-their-sprem-to-be-frozen-if-they-die.premium-1.479114.

2. There were several earlier cases of PMSR, but this is the first publicly known case in which a baby was born. There was a case two years earlier in France. "Woman Has Baby Conceived from Dead Spouse's Sperm," *Deseret News*, March 27, 1999, http://news.google.com/newspapers?nid=336&dat=19990327&id=8uwjAAAAIBAJ&sjid=zOwDAAAAIBAJ&pg=6519,5408737.

3. Ibid.

4. See discussion below.

5. See, for example, Ravi V. Desai, Mahesh Krishnamurthy, Harish Patel, and David N. Hoffman, "Postmortem Sperm Retrieval: An Ethical Dilemma," *American Journal of Medicine* 116 (2004): 858; Ruth Landau, "Posthumous Sperm Retrieval for the Purpose of Later Insemination or IVF in Israel: An Ethical and Psychosocial Critique," *Human Reproduction* 19 (2004): 1952–56.

6. Joshua M. Hurwitz and Frances R. Batzer, "Posthumous Sperm Procurement: Demand and Concerns," *Obstetrics and Gynecology Survey* 59 (2004): 806–8.

7. Philip Cohen, "Life after Death: New York State Moves to Keep Dead Men's Sperm in the Family," *New Scientist* 2126 (1998); Bob Simpson, "Making 'Bad' Deaths

'Good': The Kinship Consequences of Posthumous Conception," *Journal of the Royal Anthropological Institute* 7, no. 1 (2001): 1–18.

8. For an alternative approach, see discussion of the "sleeping baby" doctrine in Morocco in Satyel Larson, "Bearing Knowledge: Law, Reproduction and the Female Body in Modern Morocco, 1912–Present" (PhD diss., University of California, Berkeley, 2012).

9. Y. Shufaro and J. G. Schenker, "Cryopreservation of Human Genetic Material," Ann. N.Y. Acad Sci. 1205 (September 2010): 220–24; S. Gilbert, "Fatherhood from the Grave: An Analysis of Postmortem Insemination," Hofstra L. R. 22, no. 2 (1993): 521–65.

10. Though the guidelines of the American Society of Clinical Oncology (ASCO) recommend that all patients of childbearing age be given information about fertility preservation, a study from 2009 suggests that in practice only 47 percent of relevant cancer patients are routinely referred to a reproductive endocrinologist or infertility specialist. Egg freezing is a more invasive procedure and considered experimental. See Caprice Knapp, Gwendolyn Quinn, Bethanne Bower, and Laurie Zoloth, "Posthumous Reproduction and Palliative Care," *Journal of Palliative Medicine* 14, no. 8 (2011): 895–98.

11. James J. Finnerty, Ted S. Thomas, Robert J. Boyle, Stuart S. Howards, and Logan B. Karns, "Gamete Retrieval in Terminal Conditions," *American Journal of Obstetrics and Gynecology* 185, no. 2 (2001): 300–307.

12. Cappy Rothman, "A Method for Obtaining Viable Sperm in the Postmortem State," *Fertility and Sterility* 34, no. 5 (1980): 512.

13. Ibid.

14. Murphy F. Towsend III, Joseph R. Richard, and Michael A. Witt, "Artificially Stimulated Ejaculation in the Brain-dead Patient: A Case Report," *Urology* 47 (2009): 760–62.

15. See Carson Strong, Jeffrey R. Gingrich, and Will H. Kutteh, "Ethics of Postmortem Sperm Retrieval," *Human Reproduction* 15, no. 4 (2000): 739–45.

16. The new procedure was applied in an Israeli case involving the death of a seventeen-year-old woman. Chen Ayash was hit by a car and diagnosed as brain-dead. Her family decided to donate her organs and retrieve her ova. The initial intention of the family was to immediately fertilize the eggs with donated sperm and freeze them as embryos, since frozen embryos have a greater chance of ultimately producing a child than eggs frozen before fertilization. But the hospital refused to fertilize the ova and the courts limited their approval to the harvesting and freezing of the dead child's eggs. See Dan Even, "Dead Woman's Ova Harvested after Court Okays Family Request," *Haaretz*, August 8, 2011, http://www.haaretz.com/print-edition/news/dead-woman-s-ova-harvested-after-court-okays-family-request-1.377495. Since this procedure is novel, most of the remaining discussion focuses on sperm retrieval, though much of what is said applies equally to the case of ova.

17. Susan M. Kerr, Arthur Caplan, Glenn Polin, Steve Smugar, Kathryn O'Neill, and Sara Urowitz, "Postmortem Sperm Procurement," *Journal of Urology* 157, no. 6 (1997): 2154–58.

18. John A. Allan and Amanda S. Cotman, "A New Method for Freezing Testicular Biopsy Sperm: Three Pregnancies with Sperm Extracted from Cryopreserved Sections of Seminiferous Tubule," *Fertility and Sterility* 68 (1997): 741–44.

19. Lotta L., "Baby Born from Dead Father's Sperm," Associated Press, March 26, 1999.

20. For lack of space, I do not discuss here the legal situation in non-Western liberal traditions. For Islam, see, for example, Reza Omani Samani et al., "Posthumous Assisted Reproduction from Islamic Perspective," *International Journal of Fertility and Sterility* 2 (2008): 96–100; for Japan, see Noriyuki Ueda et al., "Study of Views on Posthumous

Reproduction, Focusing on Its Relation with Views on Family and Religion in Modern Japan," *Acta Medica Okayama* 62, no. 5 (2008): 286–96.

21. J. Dostal et al., "Post-mortem Sperm Retrieval in New European Union Countries: Case Report," *Human Reproduction* 20, no. 8 (2006): 2359–61; Strong et al., "Ethics of Postmortem Sperm Retrieval," 740.

22. Steven E. Kahan, Allen D. Seftel, and Martini I. Resnick, "Postmortem Sperm Procurement: A Legal Perspective," *Journal of Urology* 161 (1999): 1840–43.

23.vSorin Hostiuc and Cristian G. Curca, "Informed Consent in Posthumous Sperm Procurement," *Archives of Gynecology and Obstetrics* 282, no. 4 (2010): 433–38.

24. Ethics Committee of the American Society for Reproductive Medicine, "Posthumous Collection and Use of Reproductive Tissue: A Committee Opinion," *Fertility and Sterility* 82 (2004): 261.

25. Carson Strong, "Gamete Retrieval after Death or Irreversible Unconsciousness: What Counts as Informed Consent?," *Cambridge Quarterly of Healthcare Ethics* 15, no. 2 (2006): 161–71.

26. Family Case 11870/03, Kfar Saba Family Court, September 29, 2003, Nevo Legal Database (by subscription, in Hebrew) (Israel).

27.v Yael Hashiloni-Dolev, "Posthumous Reproduction (PHR) in Israel: Policy Rationales Versus Lay People's Concerns, a Preliminary Study," *Culture, Medicine, and Psychiatry* 39 (2015): 634–50.

28. Elyakim Rubinstein, "Postmortem Sperm Retrieval and Its Use," *Israel Attorney General Guidelines* 1.2202 (2003): 5.

29. "Widow Allowed Dead Husband's Baby," *BBC News*, February 6, 1997, http://news.bbc.co.uk/onthisday/hi/dates/stories/february/6/newsid_2536000/2536119.stm.

30. Bethany Spielman, "Pushing the Dead into the Next Reproductive Frontier: Post Mortem Gamete Retrieval under the Uniform Anatomical Gift Act," *Journal of Law, Medicine and Ethics* 37, no. 2 (2009): 331–43.

31. Tomer Zarchin, "Parents Ask Court to Allow Use of Dead Son's Sperm," *Haaretz*, February 7, 2011, http://www.haaretz.com/parents-ask-court-to-allow-use-of-dead-son-s-sperm-1.341689.

32. Marie A. Achille et al., "Facilitators and Obstacles to Sperm Banking in Young Men Receiving Gonadotoxic Chemotherapy for Cancer: The Perspective of Survivors and Health Care Professionals," *Human Reproduction* 21, no. 12 (2006): 3206–16; Joanne Freankel Kelvin and Joyce Reinecke, "Institutional Approaches to Implementing Fertility Preservation for Cancer Patients," *Advances in Experimental Medicine and Biology* 732 (2011): 165–73.

33. Family Case 13583/08, Krayot Family Court, November 13, 2008, Nevo Legal Database (by subscription, in Hebrew) (Israel).

34. Ibid.

35. Spielman, "Pushing the Dead into the Next Reproductive Frontier."

36. Jason D. Hans, "Attitudes toward Posthumous Harvesting and Reproduction," *Death Studies Journal* 32 (2008): 840–41.

37. Bryce Weber, Ron Kodama, and Keith Jarvi, "Postmortem Sperm Retrieval: The Canadian Perspective," *Journal of Andrology* 30, no. 4 (2009): 409; Ruth Landau, "Posthumous Sperm Retrieval for the purpose of Later Insemination or IVF in Israel: An Ethical and Psychosocial Critique," *Human Reproduction* 19, no. 9 (2004): 1952–56.

38. Yael Hashiloni-Dolev, Dafna Hacker, and Hagai Boas, "The Will of the Deceased: Three Israeli Case Studies," *Israeli Sociology* 16 (2014): 31–53.

39. Usha Ahluwalia and Mala Arora, "Postmortem Reproduction and Its Legal Perspective," *International Journal of Infertility and Fetal Medicine* 2, no. 1 (2011): 9–14

("Prior to embarking on ART procedures, adequate mourning time of at least one year should have elapsed for the surviving partner").

40. "Postmortem Sperm Retrieval and Its Use," *Israel Attorney General Guidelines* 10.
41. Ibid., 9–10.
42. Jennifer A. Tash et al., "Postmortem Sperm Retrieval: The Effect of Instituting Guidelines," *Journal of Urology* 170, no. 5 (2003): 1922–25.
43. G. Bahadur, "Death and Conception," *Human Reproduction* 17 (2002): 2773.
44. Kristine S. Knaplund, "Assisted Reproductive Technology," *Real Property, Probate and Trust Law Journal* 28, no. 2 (2014).
45. Ruth Landau, "Planned Orphanhood," *Social Science and Medicine* 49, no. 2 (1999): 185–96.
46. "Living Memory," *Yediot Aharonot*, October 17, 2014.
47. Ibid.
48. Vardit Ravitsky, "Posthumous Reproduction Guidelines in Israel," *Hastings Center Report* 34, no. 2 (2004): 6–7.
49. Sigmund Freud, James Strachey, and Anna Freud, *The Standard Edition of the Complete Psychological Works of Sigmund Freud* (London: Hogarth Press, 1953).
50. Ibid., 245.
51. "Postmortem Sperm Retrieval," *Knesset Science and Technology Committee* 97, September 30, 2002, 9.
52. Ibid., 7.
53. Cf. Clive Seale, *Constructing Death: The Sociology of Dying and Bereavement* (New York: Cambridge University Press, 1998).
54. Robert Hertz, *Death & the Right Hand* (Glencoe, IL: Free Press, 1960).
55. Ibid., 200.
56. Eric Venbrux, "Robert Hertz's Seminal Essay and Mortuary Rites in the Pacific Region," *Le Journal de la Société des Océanistes* 124 (2007): 5–10.
57. See, for example, Millar Burrows, "The Ancient Oriental Background of Hebrew Levirate Marriage," *Bulletin of the American Schools of Oriental Research* 77 (1940): 2–15.
58. Ibid.
59. Genesis 38:8.
60. See, for example, Philip Cohen, "Life after Death: New York State Moves to Keep Dead Men's Sperm in the Family," *New Scientist* 2126 (1998); Bob Simpson, "Making 'Bad' Deaths 'Good': The Kinship Consequences of Posthumous Conception," *Journal of the Royal Anthropological Institute* 7, no. 1 (2001): 1–18.
61. Millar Burrows, "Levirate Marriage in Israel," *Journal of Biblical Literature* 59, no. 1 (1940): 23–33.
62. 2 Samuel 18:18.
63. Robert Winston, *Lords Hansard*, December 5, 1996: col. 806.
64. "Postmortem Sperm Retrieval and Its Use," *Israel Attorney General Guidelines*, 2.
65. Maurice Bloch and Jonathan Parry, *Death and the Regeneration of Life* (New York: Cambridge University Press, 1982), 9–10.
66. Don Seeman, in Daphna Birenbaum-Carmeli and Yoram S. Carmeli, *Kin, Gene, Community: Reproductive Technologies among Jewish Israelis, Fertility, Reproduction, and Sexuality* (New York: Berghahn Books, 2010).
67. Ibid., 345.
68. Marilyn Strathern, *The Gender of the Gift: Problems with Women and Problems with Society in Melanesia*, Studies in Melanesian Anthropology (Berkeley: University of California Press, 1988), 13.

3
To Weep Irish
Keening and the Law

ANDREA BRADY

Introduction

The *caoineadh* or keen was a tradition of poetic lamentation and ritual mourning that was performed in Ireland from at least the seventh century until the early twentieth century.[1] These improvised verse compositions occupy a liminal position between poem and song, or between highly organized thematic compositions and musical wailing. They were mainly performed by women, either bereaved family members or hired professional mourners. Incorporating ritual mourning gestures and vocalizations, keening took place at the time of death and following the wake, usually during the funeral procession. The custom seems to have filled important social functions in allowing individuals and communities to negotiate the crises that are often provoked by death. During the sixteenth and seventeenth centuries keening was widely disparaged by New English commentators (colonial administrators, soldiers, and servitors who arrived from the 1530s onward), who described the practice as mercenary and insincere. This essay examines keening as a site of colonial conflict that resisted legal and ecclesiastical reformation, and was important to community formation and to the articulation of resistance and dissent. Focusing in particular on New English accounts of the practice, it demonstrates how this phenomenon was used to characterize the Irish as barbaric or pagan, in opposition to English civility and reformed religion.[2] But it also examines the formal qualities and performance conditions of keening in order to show how much of the complexity of Irish subjectivity was repressed in order to produce the stereotype of the "wild Irish," figures who were both feared and derided, and subsequently subjected to intense colonial violence.

New English writers firmly associated keening with the Gaelic Irish (also identified disparagingly as the "native," "wild," or "mere" Irish), and in fact adopted it as a proverb for insincerity. Edmund Campion (1540–1581), who traveled to Dublin in 1571 and later became a Jesuit (he was executed in England), describes how the Irish "follow the dead corpes to the grave with howlings and barbarous out-cryes, pittyfull in apparance, whereof grew (as I suppose) the Proverbe, to weepe Irish."[3] Campion's description of keening as animalistic and barbaric was written during the 1570s, a period of intense colonial violence. In this period the Lord Deputy Sir Henry Sidney (1529–1586) attempted to demonstrate the "civilising" powers of English colonial rule, and "New English officials articulated the view that the Gaelic Irish were an unreasonable people and that normal ethical restraints were unnecessary when dealing with them."[4] Language of the kind used by Campion was applied in legal attempts to reform Irish customs and behaviors, as well as in arguments (most notably by Edmund Spenser) which supposed that the Irish "have never yet beene . . . made to learn obedience unto lawes, scarcely to know the name of law, but instead thereof have always preserved and kept their owne law, which is the Brehon law."[5] Such language can also be found in commentary on the "degeneration" of the Old English (settlers who had lived among the Gaelic Irish since the Norman conquest, and had adopted their customs, faith, and language) through contact with the Irish. The notion of degeneration was particularly powerful for New English settlers anxious to preserve their cultural distinction in a hostile environment.

Keening epitomizes the profound religious, cultural, political, and legal conflict between the Gaelic Irish and New English in early modern Ireland. The two groups understood ritual mourning in opposite ways. Clodagh Tait has argued that for English colonizers, the keen was "profoundly disrespectful to the deceased, to his or her family, and especially to God, since excessive gestures of mourning indicated a criminal lack of acceptance of his ways," but for Irish mourners it expressed "the grief and sense of loss (and sometimes anger or bewilderment) experienced by the community at the death of one of its members," as well as a show of respect that could strengthen community bonds.[6] Modern anthropology tends to side with the latter reading and affirms that ritual mourning can reinforce social cohesion by creating a space in which anger, sorrow, and resentments can be expressed and diffused.⁷ Historians of early modern Ireland have also argued that keening, however destructive, could permit mourners to articulate forms of social and emotional dissonance, including anger at the powerful, criticism of their own kin, or complaints of mistreatment by the dead.⁸

Keening is a significant example of what Pierre Bourdieu terms "bodily hexis," a relation to the social world inscribed on the body's bearing, movements, gestures, and space that "is a practical way of experiencing and expressing one's own sense of social value, . . . one's relationship to the social world and to one's proper place in it."⁹ The passionately embodied actions and utterances of keening women were read by other mourners specifically as affirmations of the social value of the deceased, but they also represented a commitment to indigenous religion and culture and resistance to colonial repression. For Bourdieu, bodily hexis as an embodied repertoire of social value acts "like a theatrical costume, to awaken, by the evocative power of bodily mimesis, a universe of ready-made feelings and experiences" (474). The theatricality of keening was also used an indictment of its inauthenticity, as we will see. But Bourdieu's terms also draw attention to what Judith Butler would term the performativity of the gendered and raced body of the Irish woman, as it is produced through this ritual action which is both autonomous and under multiple forms of duress: from ancient traditions, clashing Catholic and Protestant ideology, familial obligations, Brehon and common law regulations, and family, local, and national pressures.¹⁰

This essay examines the rhetorical and political function of keening as part of the discourses of sixteenth- and seventeenth-century English colonial administration. First, it shows that ritual mourning was a well-known phenomenon from numerous classical and contemporary societies. It then examines the specificity of the Irish *caoineadh,* and engages with the New English critiques of keening on aesthetic, gendered, and doctrinal grounds. The latter leads to a consideration of the use of keening and ritual mourning behaviors as resistance to Reformed religion, and to English rule more generally. Finally I show how the ecclesiastical and civil laws enacted to prevent keening and other funerary rituals such as wake games and feasting were part of a campaign to enforce English civility and customs in Ireland. Many early modern colonial commentators cited keening as evidence of the ungovernability of the Irish, and a sign that their conversion from paganism and Catholicism and their subjection to the English sovereign was incomplete. The persistence of the practice was blamed on the corruption and inefficiency of the Reformed Church in Ireland and its inability to convert the Gaelic Irish away from their "pagan" and Catholic customs, and on the irresolution and inadequacy of the English crown. Keening consequently became an emblem of the failure of English sovereignty in Ireland, but it was fundamentally a complex poetic form whose content was too readily erased in New English critiques.

Ritual Mourning across Cultures

Keening was an ancient practice that can be found in many cultures, and would have been familiar to English commentators from classical texts, where it was mainly the work of female mourners. Homer alludes to two kinds of professional mourners: those who led the melody in a dirge, and those who chanted a song of sorrow, with female mourners wailing in refrain—a division of the work of mourning that is also characteristic of Irish keening.[11] In the sixth century BCE, Solon attempted to restrain women's mourning as an attempt to diminish the power of aristocratic clans. He forbade women "at the buriall of the dead, to teare and spoyle them selues with blowes, to make lamentations in verses, to weepe at the funeralles of a straunger not being their kinsemen" and so forth.[12] Officers were engaged "to controll and reforme the abuses of women, as womanish persones and faynte harted, which suffer them selues to be ouercome with such passions and fondnes in their mourning" (99), drawing a connection between ritual mourning, effeminacy, and fear that was also significant in the accounts of Irish mortuary customs. Herodotus also describes the women of Sparta lamenting and beating their heads with their hands, and Egyptian women exposing their breasts and striking themselves for seventy days while singing a dirge.[13] Ancient Hebraic ritual mourning also involved keening.[14] Allusions to keening can also be found in Virgil's *Aeneid,* Cicero, and Propertius.[15] Lucian critiques funeral customs including "the howlings of women, teares of acquaintance, percussion of brests, tearing of haire, cheekes bloudyed, garments rent, and heads sprinkled with dust . . . they many times roll themselves on the floore, and dash their heads against the ground."[16] Lucian also satirizes the hiring of professional mourners: "these senselesse people do both howle themselves, and hire some Sophister, whose trade is lamentation; who mustering up many old calamities, is imploy'd as the leader, and captaine of the franticke solemnitie; and where he begins, they follow, and make up the ridiculous consort" (212). These customs benefit neither the dead nor the living; they are merely intended to induce the pity of bystanders. The bereaved father who expostulates with his dead son "acts this distemper for the spectators sakes" (212)—a standard criticism of keening's theatricality.

John Aubrey draws a connection between antique practices cited in Plautus and "Irish Howlings at Funeralls, also in Yorkshire within these 70 yeares (1688). *Ducit supremos Nœnia nulla toros.*—(sc. after their banishment) Præficæ, mulieres ad lamentandum conductæ."[17] The Praeficae in Roman antiquity were women hired to precede the corpse, beating themselves until they were bloody, baring their breasts and singing and lamenting, but it is notable that Aubrey draws the comparison also between Irish keening and Yorkshire folk traditions, showing that the Reformation was also incomplete in England. This grounding of contemporary ritual mourning in ancient practices was rarely adopted by New English commentators in Ireland. One exception would be Spenser's comparison of Irish customs to the Scythians, symbols of barbarism since Herodotus and Colossians 3:11.[18] (I return to the theme of Irish barbarism below.)

There are similarities between ancient British practices described by antiquarians and the physical displays associated with Irish keening. Drawing on Tacitus, William Camden (1551–1623) records that when Suetonius Paulinus attempted to invade the Isle of Anglesey, he found arrayed against him "the enemies armies on the shore thicke set in aray, well appointed with men and weapons, and women also running in, too and fro among them, like furies of hell, in mourning attyre, their haire about their eares, and with firebrands in their hands." These women joined with the Druids in cursing the invaders, who were "not able to stire their joints" until their captain encouraged them "not to feare a flocke of franticke women, and fantasticall persons."[19] Though Camden is not specifically referring to keening, his description presents the conjunction of "mourning" and disheveled women, furious resistance to foreign invaders, and occult Celtic powers that often feature in New English commentary on keening.

Susan Leigh Fry also draws attention to the similarity between Irish keening and the account in the ancient Welsh *Mabinogion* of "the Lady of the Fountain," "a yellow-haired lady with her hair over her shoulders, and many a gout of blood on her tresses, and a torn garment of yellow brocaded silk about her" who beat her hands so hard in sorrow that "it was a marvel that the ends of her fingers were not maimed. . . . And louder was her shrieking than what there was of man and horn in the host."[20]

In anthropological terms, the unbound hair, unrestrained grief, and self-mutilation of this bereaved woman mark her out as a ritual participant in a stage of liminality, whose charismatic power allows her temporarily to overcome the sound of "man and horn." Heather Larson has also argued that the keening woman resembled the wild man of Irish folklore, an association that protected her from the consequences of her outspoken behavior.[21] Like all the examples discussed above, ritual mourning seems to be practiced by women and has the potential to have a powerful effect on men who encounter it.

Aubrey's conflation of ancient and modern customs also features in the description by the antiquarian John Weever (1575/6–1632) of ritual mourning in Rome, where "suborned counterfeit hired mourners" are employed, being "women of the loudest voices, who betimes in the morning did meete at appointed places, and then cried out mainly, beating of their breasts, tearing their haire, their faces, and garments, joyning therewith the prayers of the defunct, . . . keeping time with the melancholicke musicke."[22] For Weever, lamentation is "a custome observed at this day in some parts of Ireland, but above all Nations the Jewes are best skilled in these lamentations" (15). This comparison of Irish and Jewish mourning gestures toward its heterodoxy. But the use of Irish keening as a point of reference for English readers when introducing a new culture shows how well known the phenomenon had become.

In travelers' tales, keening is also revealed to be a common practice among non-European peoples, and in some instances Ireland is again used as a way of familiarizing this alien custom. Cristóbal Acuña (b. 1597) describes the Amazonian Cacique, who "celebrate their Funerals for many Days together, with continual Mourning and Weeping, which they only interrupt with Drinking."[23] (This combination of excessive mourning with revelry and drunkenness was also frequently cited in indictments of Irish funeral customs.) The seventeenth-century cleric Lancelot Addison (1632–1703) described Jewish mourning in Tangiers: "They often every Week repair to his Grave, where they make great Lamentation and bitter Weeping over him," returning frequently to cemeteries as spaces for "contemplation of their own Mortality" and for lamentation.[24] A traveler to Russia, Samuel Collins (1619?–1670), described the "strange" burials practiced there:

> The Wife of the deceased is obliged to howl most pitifully, and hire others to do the like, but little reason have they to do it, considering their severe usage; but custom, not love, may possibly incite them to do it. . . . The Russians count that the greatest Funeral where are most Women-mourners; such

were the *Praeficae* among the old Romans. These therefore in a doleful tone cry out (as the wild Irish do, *O hone*) *Timminny Dooshinca;* Alas my Dear, why hast thou left me . . . ?²⁵

Collins uses the familiar keening refrain "O hone," the English translation of the *caoineadh* refrain *ochon*. He compares Russian and Irish customs: keening, expostulation, the correlation between mourning and social prestige, and the supposed lack of real grief among the bereaved. As in many of these examples, the Irish keen serves simultaneously as a token of cultural difference and a touchstone of familiarity for readers encountering strange customs and cultures through the medium of print.

Aesthetics: The Music of the Keen

The ritual mourning described in these sources shares general features: beating of breasts, self-mutilation, loud outcries, disheveled appearances, passionate or even violent exclamations, and expostulations with the dead. Some of these features, as we will see, were apparent in Irish keening, but it incorporated a more specific poetic form known as the *caoineadh* (I use the Gaelic spelling to denote the specific, formalized verse compositions, and the Anglicized "keening" to refer to the more diffuse range of ritual mourning behaviors). Archival records of early modern keening are difficult to obtain:²⁶ the *caoineadh* is not normally recorded in the *duanairí* (family manuscript anthologies), though keening behaviors are depicted in bardic poems.²⁷ These primarily oral compositions came to the attention of historians with the development of folklore studies in the nineteenth century, but even then there were strong taboos on performing the keen outside the context of a funeral, and only a handful of early recordings exist.

Nonetheless, references to keening can be found in an eighth-century poem by Blathmac mac Con Brettan, as well as saints' lives and an Old Irish Penitential from c. 800.²⁸ Keening is also regularly described in topographical and historical surveys, chronicles, travelogues, poems, and prose satires. Many of these sources simply reframe the twelfth-century account of Irish customs by the monk Gerald of Wales (Giraldus Cambrensis, born c.1146; died c. 1220–1223). Comparing Irish and Spanish lamentations in a topographical study from the late 1180s, Gerald described how dirges can intensify or tranquilize intense feeling:

> Unde et gens Hibernica et Hispanica, aliaeque nationes nonnullae, inter lugubres funerum planctus musicas efferunt lamentationes: quatinus vel dolorem instantem augeant et recentem, vel forte ut minuant jam remissum.²⁹

(Thus the Irish and Spanish, as well as some other nations, mix sorrowful music with their funeral lamentations, augmenting their present grief as well as diminishing it when the worst is past.)

Gerald, like some of the authors discussed above, recognizes keening as a transcultural practice that could both intensify and assuage feelings of sorrow.

The *caoineadh* is distinct from another ancient Irish poetic form, the bardic *Marbhnai* or elegies, which were composed by the *fileadha*, a hereditary class of professional, highly educated poets retained in great households.[30] The *caoineadh* was an improvised oral composition, usually performed by women. Surviving examples show that it was a highly stylized and rhetorical performance of verse memorial and lament, interspersed with a refrain of nonverbal wailing. John Kerrigan has argued that "keening, though a complex art, can sound like grief's own idiom. To wail and sob is to approach language through melopoeia."[31] Many early modern English commentators heard keening as simple noise, devoid of sense, but the wailing was typically mixed with Gaelic-language verses of sustained metrical and semantic complexity. Led by the *bean caointe*, usually a close relative, women would gather around the body and lament the deceased in song. The leader would use a phrase such as "*och, ochón*" as a cue to begin the wail. The meter was generally additive, with each stanza making use of a single assonance, maintained in the same position in each phrase-line; these phrases were joined paratactically, their grammatical independence facilitating improvisation.[32] The lines were short, with two or three stresses in each and no fixed syllable count. Several literary keens are composed in the ancient *Rosc* meter.[33] The song's short, tense lines were performed in passionate and exclamatory style.[34] The content often included direct address to the corpse, usually delivered in its presence. Each stanza might begin with a simple term of endearment, or call on other mourners, as in the formula "*Druidigí thaart, a mhná*" (gather round me, women!).[35] Topoi included apostrophes to the dead, terms of endearment, ecphonetic calls, and references to dreams and premonitions of death.[36] It was not uncommon for keening women to curse the dead person's enemies, criticize each other, or engage in verbal sparring, as in the famous eighteenth-century keen for Art O'Leary (*Airt Ui Laoghaire*), in which Art's sister accuses his wife, Eileen, of having slept, which Eileen denies; or the *Keen for Diarmait MacCarthy*, in which the mother curses the son-in-law who beats her daughter.[37]

Despite these complex conventions, most early-modern English accounts of keening describe it as wild, unmusical "howling." Barnabe Rich

(1542–1617) was a "strenuous Protestant" and career soldier whose opinions of Ireland were developed in the violent nexus of the 1570s and 1580s: he first went to Ireland with the forces of the first earl of Essex in Ulster in 1573, fought in the second Desmond rebellion (1575–83), and served under the second Earl in 1599.[38] In his published work he is often critical of what he describes as Irish Catholic superstition and moral depravity. He described the "houling and barbarous outcries" of keening women as so intense that "he that should but heare them, and did not know the ceremony, would rather thinke they did sing then weepe."[39] However, Rich insists that the keen is not song: it is not organized or musical. Like many New English commentators, Rich denies that it has any meaningful content, and does not attempt to translate or even acknowledge the content of the verse lament. Presumably he could not understand it. Instead he derides it as a "brutish kinde of lamentation," which should put the listener in mind of some "prodigious presagement prognosticating some vnlucky or ill successe, as they vse to attribute to the houling of dogges, to the croaking of Rauens, and to the shrieking of Owles, fitter for Infidels and Barbarians, then to be in vse and custome among Christians" (4). Like many of his contemporaries, Rich uses keening to demonstrate the obduracy of Irish paganism: though "a people so many yeares professing Christianitie," they are yet "more Heathen like, then those, that neuer heard of God."[40] Rich's references to croaking ravens and shrieking owls also exemplifies the tendency to associate keening with occult practices or witchcraft, as well as pagan mortuary practices including expostulating with the dead at the crossroads.[41]

Rich's reduction of Irish language and song to mere animal howling recalls a famous scene from Shakespeare's *Henry IV, Part I*, written in the late 1590s. While a guest in the castle of the Welsh hero Owen Glendower, Hotspur and his wife watch her brother Mortimer, who speaks no Welsh, and his wife, the daughter of Glendower who speaks no English, struggle to communicate. Lady Percy asks the irritable Hotspur to "Lye still ye Theefe, and heare the Lady sing in Welsh." Hotspur answers: "I had rather heare (Lady) my Brach howle in Irish."[42] Having already satirized Glendower's Celtic superstition, Hotspur casually equates the Welsh song of the daughter with the Irish language, dismissing it as a feminine form (the brach is a bitch-hound) no better than howling. His joke reflects the early modern English perception of the Irish, Welsh, and Scots as effeminate, barbaric, and given to lamentation. It also partakes of a colonial discourse in which, Patricia Palmer has argued, "Irish was consistently equated with bestial utterance—and, more specifically, with the metaphorically beastly dialect of the ungodly: of heathens, witches, papists."[43]

These two representations of Irish (or Celtic) mourning song are consistent with New English characterizations of Irish language and music as mournful, false, and discordant. Sir Richard Cox (1650–1733), a Tory from Cork who later served as lord chancellor of Ireland, complains about the use of the "Bagpipe" (probably the *uilleann* or elbow-pipes) in Irish funerals. Though it is but a "a squealing Engine, fit only for a Bear-Garden," the bagpipe is used at burials

> to encrease the Noyse, and encourage the Women to Cry, and follow the Corps, for there is nothing coveted more by the Friends of the deceased, than to have abundance of Company at the Burial, and a great Cry for the Defunct; which they think argues, That he was a Person of Figure and Merit, and was well-beloved in his Country; therefore they bury their Dead with great Ululations or *Allelews*, after the Egyptian manner, and hire Women to encrease the Cry.[44]

Cox recognizes that the number and loudness of the keening women is supposed to reflect the status of the deceased. But their music, which Cox associates with the Bear Garden (and perhaps by extension with the theater), does not encourage self-restraint but intemperance. This form of mourning is corrupt, with families seeking to convey their social status by hiring mourning women to cry on cue. The comparison to ancient transcultural practices of ritual mourning did not elevate it; rather, for Cox the conspicuous management of the ceremony by women is a sign of its depravity.

Gender: Keening and the Work of Mourning

In traditional Irish mortuary ritual the deceased were mourned by their kin, sometimes through the night, with women and bards taking a central role.[45] The princess Nualaith Ní Dhomhnaill, whose brothers were buried in Rome, was promised that "beside the pillars there would be no leave for repose or for psalm-chanting; there would be no gap without a crowd of women, no palm by noon that did not glisten."[46] The palms may be glistening with blood after being beaten for hours by these keening women. Katherine Simms has shown that bards mourned dead chieftains as if for a lover, often lying on the grave all night, weeping, beating their hands, singing, and howling: as one poem from c. 1430 puts it, "We are lying with you now, as we were with you before; o king, your white frost-covered gravestone is colder for me than for you."⁴⁷ In these contexts, keening was a poetic and embodied ritual dominated by women that demonstrated loyalty and kinship, and asserted an affective and social continuity between the dead and the living mediated through the poet as mourner.

Like many New English commentators, Richard Stanihurst calls attention to the gendered distribution of keening as part of his critique. Stanihurst (1547–1618) was an Old English Catholic born in the Pale who studied in Oxford with Edmund Campion. Although his remarks on Gaelic culture were often condescending, Stanihurst's attitude toward Ireland's ancient heritage was ambivalent, occasionally even admiring.⁴⁸ Nonetheless, he disparaged the "loud and effeminate weeping" and "wolf-ish and shrieking cries" of keening women: "They shout dolefully through swollen cheeks, they cast off their necklaces, they bare their heads, they tear their hair, they beat their brows, they excite emotion on all sides, they spread their palms, they raise their hands to the heavens, they shake the coffin, tear open the shroud, embrace and kiss the corpse and scarcely allow the funeral to take place."⁴⁹ Women disrupt the funeral, stalling the community in a liminal temporality where normal codes of behavior are suspended. While he does not object to moderate mourning, Stanihurst rejects this "perverse" custom "in the fashion of old women," and insists that it must be "completely uprooted from among the women by concentrated preaching and thundering threats."

Women's ritual mourning behavior—bare breasts, loose hair—often calls attention to their gender.⁵⁰ In some ways, it confirms the humoral model of gender and the passions. Women, reputedly colder and wetter than men, were physiologically predisposed to weep: "Why, there are women so prone to weeping that tears distill on their eyes if their brain contracts the slightest bit."⁵¹ Tears were considered an effeminate discharge, and though tears of grief were in some cases acceptable, immoderate public grief was not; civility "identified rigorous self-control as an essential masculine attribute."⁵² The French theologian Pierre Charron (1541–1603) argues that the "strange and effeminate" habit of sorrow "taketh away whatsoever is manly and generous in us, and puts upon us the countenances and infirmities of women," and "makes men eunuches." It is for this reason that the martial Romans "forbad these effeminate lamentations."⁵³ These beliefs also affected the representation of Irish women, whose effusions of milk, blood, and tears were criticized in many of the same texts discussed in this essay. Irish women were often depicted (as

Jean Feerick has shown) as violating "the New English insistence on a well-bounded, temperate body," and "the site of dangerous contaminations and mixtures."⁵⁴ The closed, masculine body of the New English colonist should enclose its tears, as an outward sign of the Christian and Stoic commitment to encounter grief rigorously; succumbing to immoderate sorrow was evidence not only of a lack faith in the resurrection, but of a dangerous effeminacy.

Through history, legal constraints on ritual mourning have acknowledged its costliness, potential for civil unrest, and doctrinal problems, but the centrality of women in these rituals, from the Roman *Praeficiae* to the Irish *bean caointe*, also led to demands for its regulation. The rituals of death were sites of considerable power, and leaving them in the control of women—who, as Gail Horst-Warhaft notes, "as child-bearers and midwives already have a certain control over birth"⁵⁵—displaced men from the social and spiritual authority that could be derived from these important rites of passage. Attempts by civic authorities to impose their authority on predominantly feminine, and potentially effeminizing, ritual mourning can be found throughout the classical and early modern periods. Petrarch (1304–1374) urged the rulers of Padua to restrain women from public outbursts of grief, and to limit female participation in the funerary rites.⁵⁶ In early modern Florence, city fathers banned women from funeral processions in order to prevent them from provoking vendettas by wild displays of grief, a legislative action that Sharon Strocchia argues coincided with the quattrocento move from a corporatist to a paternalistic social order "that bound issues of gender and family to the consolidation of political power."⁵⁷ This consolidation of authority over public behavior also had the effect, Juliana Schiesari has argued, of defeminizing the public sphere.⁵⁸ Moreover, keening was characterized by many of the stereotypes of women—excessive emotionality, impairment of reason, a tendency toward uncivil behavior—which English commentators attributed to the Irish in general.

Doctrine: The Heterodoxy of Ritual Mourning

Keening was characterized by many of the stereotypes of women—excessive emotionality, impairment of reason, a tendency toward uncivil behavior—which English commentators attributed to the Irish in general. In *The Irish Hubbub, or, The English Hue and Crie* (1617), Rich characterizes the Irish as people of excess, who are given to immoderate laughter and immoderate weeping, and uses these excesses in the service of his satire on English vices.[59] He was not alone in using Irish customs to define English standards of civility and moderation. For example, in an anonymous 1648 elegy for Abigail Sherard, identified as the daughter of Philip, second son of William the first Baron of Leitrim, the poet avers that

> I cannot (as the wilder Irish use)
> Or screeke or houle, and so their dead abuse;
> I can scarce weep, but I can sigh my part,
> And keepe a solemne Funerall in my heart....[60]

This *recusatio* allows the author to represent himself as a good mourner, not howling wild abuse, but constrained by the conventions of English moderation and poetic form. Invoking the keening woman for hire also allows him to assert, in characteristic elegiac fashion, that his own poetic lament is not mercenary but sincere. Such distinctions were particularly important to hold onto in Ireland, where the Old English are regularly cited as a model of the dangers of "degeneration" that arise from intimate and prolonged contact with the Irish.[61]

Irish keening was critiqued not only for its aesthetic qualities and effeminacy, but also its doctrinal implications. Ritual mourning had been condemned for centuries as a violation of the counsel of Paul, in 1 Thessalonians 4:13: "I would not have you to be ignorant, brethren, concerning them which are asleep, that ye sorrow not, even as others which have no hope." Citing this passage, John Chrysostom disapproved of "hiring women, pagans, as mourners to make the mourning more intense, to fan the fires of grief, ignoring the words of St Paul."[62] Although Calvin cautioned in his commentary on Thessalonians that "they who misuse this testimony to establish Stoic apatheia, that is, an iron sensibility, among Christians, find nothing of the kind in Paul's words,"[63] they were frequently used to counsel the bereaved against immoderate (or sometimes any) expressions of grief. In his famous *ars moriendi* of 1658, Jeremy Taylor (1613–1667) approved of "solemn and appointed mournings" as "good expressions of our dearnesse to the departed soul, and of his worth, and our value of him," but cautioned that demonstrative mourning soon excites other, more violent emotions, especially in crowds.[64] For this reason, keening was both a theological and a civic problem.

In Ireland, Christian exhortations to moderate the passions competed with traditional mortuary rituals in which keening and displays of despondency played an important part. There are some Irish examples of what

G. W. Pigman has called "rigorism," meaning an attempt to constrain grief, as well as Irish consolatory discourses that stressed the need for moderation.[65] An elegy by the seventeenth-century Munster poet Cúchonnacht Ó Dálaigh counseled the bereaved Uná to restrain her grief, not waste her appearance with unnecessary lamentation.[66] Nonetheless, conventions around constraining grief had not yet taken root in Ireland; indeed, they were hardly established in England either.[67] Attitudes toward grief were also affected by the upheavals of doctrine and observance during the Reformation and Counter-Reformation. In England, the progress of the Reformation had involved a destruction of the Catholic cult of the dead, through the abolition of Purgatory, reforms to the order of service for burial, and the seizure of endowments of guilds established to endow masses for the poor and chantries. These reforms had the effect of eliminating the dead as an ancestral age-group with which the living were in constant contact. They also marked an epochal historical break. Andy Wood has described the Reformation as "an assault upon local memory": "sweeping away the signifiers of an earlier culture of remembrance," the Reformation caused the people of late Tudor and Stuart England to feel "that they were separated from their pre-Reformation ancestors by a yawning chasm, a breakage within the remembrance culture that hitherto had bound their communities together."[68] For English observers, consequently, Irish mortuary customs resembled the unreformed and even pagan customs of their own history.

New English commentators described those customs as demonstrating a lack of faith in the resurrection. Camden observed that "such as visit and sit by one that lieth sicke in bed, never speake word of God, nor of the salvation of his soule, ne yet of making his will, but all to put him in hope of his recovering," neglecting their duty of care for the spiritual and temporal needs of the dying.[69] Instead, keening women would expostulate with the dying or dead, contrasting the attractions of earthly life with the horror of death.[70] According to Camden, when someone is dying

> certaine women hired of purpose to lament, standing in the meeting of crosse high-waies, and holding their hands all abroad, call unto him, with certayne out-cries fitted for the nonce, and goe about to stay his soule as it laboureth to get forth of the bodie, by reckoning up the commodities that hee enjoyeth of worldly goods, of wives, of beauty, fame, kinsfolke, friends, and horses; and demanding of him, why hee will depart, and whither? and to whom? yea they expostulate with his soule, objecting that she is unthankfull.[71]

They then lament that the soul is ready to leave the body and be surrendered to "these kinde of haggish women that appear by night and in darknesse." The women "keepe a mourning and wailing for it, with loud howling and clapping of their hands together," following the corpse to its burial with a devastating "peale of out cries."[72] Preserving the ancient Christian custom of *conclamatio*, the Irish mourners harangue the dying and the dead from the occult space of the crossroads. Their attempt to persuade the dying to cling on to life violated the Reformed *ars moriendi*, which required mourners to assist the dying in their crucial encounter with the terrors of death.[73]

The custom of expostulation endured far beyond the moment of death. In a visit to Kildare in 1682, Thomas Monk observed bereaved women expostulating with the deceased in the graveyard "perhaps, five, ten, or twenty yeares after their husband friend or relacon has been buried":

> they kneele over them—knocking and beatinge upon the grave and praiseing the partie, repeatinge the former kindnesse passed between them, intreatinge that they would attend and give ear to them, then in an odd tone sorrowing and lamentinge their losse, complain and tell them how they are misused, and by whom injured, and theron pray their help . . . soe they return well satisfied as haveing given an account to one that in time may redresse their injuries, revenge or relieve them.[74]

Monk believed that expostulation allowed the bereaved to articulate their grievances against other members of the community and arrive at some "satisfaction." This suggests that keening served as an outlet for conflicts and tensions, while also retaining the deceased as a member of the community.

In his "Character of Ireland" of 1699, written after a brief visit to the country in 1698, the English bookseller John Dunton (1659–1732) also describes the custom of expostulation, but in more satirical terms:

> Instead of a *Funeral Oration*, they bawl out these or the like querulous Lamentations, *O hone! O hone! Dear Joy, why didst thou dye and leave us? Hadst thou not Pigs and a Potato Garden? Hadst thou not some Sheep and a Cow, Oatcake, and good Usquebaugh [whisky] to comfort thy Heart, and put Mirth upon thy Friends? Then, wherefore wouldst thou leave this good World, and thy poor Wife and Children? O hone! O hone!* with much more such stuff.[75]

Here, the real grievances of the bereaved are belittled, but it is notable perhaps that Dunton makes use of comedy rather than anger and occult imagery to criticize keening women at the end of the seventeenth century, a period when keening had gone into decline among all but the lower classes (as signaled here by the pigs and potato garden).⁷⁶ Dunton attacks these customs both on aesthetic and doctrinal grounds:

> however careless they be of the *Living*, they are mightily concerned for the *Dead*, having a Custom, of *howling* when they carry any one to Burial; and *screaming* over their *Graves*, not like other *Christians*, but like People without *Hope:* and sooner than this shall be omitted, they do hire a whole Herd of these *Crocodils* to accompany the *Corps;* who with their counterfeit *Tears* and *Sighs*, and confused *Clamour* and *Noise*, do seem heartily to bemoan the departed Friend; though all this is with no more concern and reality, than an Actor on the Theatre for the feigned Death of his *Dearest* in a *Tragedy*. (402)

As Dunton points out, Irish keening women were often paid for their work of mourning. Rich also represents Irish mourning as duplicitous for this reason: "they wil hyre a number of women to bring the corps to the place of buriall, that for some small recompence giuen them, will furnish the cry, with greater shriking and howling, then those that are grieued indeede."⁷⁷ Both Rich and Dunton agree that Irish mourning customs display a lack of faith in the resurrection; they are mercenary, false, and theatrical, with women producing tears for hire like actors on the profane stage. Not only are the mourners "hired," but their concern is also fake: if it were real, they would provide faithful counsel or consolation instead of noisy expostulations. But there is also something more sinister in the allegation that keening women cried crocodile tears. In this period it was believed that human beings were the only animals capable of shedding tears of sorrow; crocodiles were famous for weeping hypocritically before they devoured their prey.⁷⁸ It is worth noting that Dunton's libel is as immoderate as the practices it critiques, and perhaps as bestial too: after all, satirists in this period were frequently represented as snarling dogs.⁷⁹

Keening, Resistance, and Disorder

The anger and violence that Dunton and others recognize in the customs of keening and expostulation demonstrate the function of mortuary ritual in giving expression to social and emotional dissonance, including anger at the powerful, criticism of their own kin, or complaints of mistreatment by the dead.⁸⁰ The *caoineadh*'s antiphonal structure, tropes of verbal sparring and complaint, and association with the custom of expostulating with the dead all make it well suited to the articulation of such dissonance. It could also endorse, poetically at least, transgressive behavior such as drinking the spilled blood of the dead. Such behavior is attested in the famous eighteenth-century keen for Art O'Leary, but other Irish elegiac poems also include references to blood-drinking.[81] Edmund Spenser (1552?–1599) also mentions blood-drinking in his description of the execution of Murrough O'Brien in Limerick in 1577. According to Spenser, the man's foster-mother was seen to "take up his head, whilst he was quartered, and sucked up all the blood that runne thereout" as she keened: she "steeped her face and breast, and tore her hair, crying out and shrieking most terribly."[82] Symbolic reincorporation of the dead into the living through ingestion is not unusual in funerary ritual, and has obvious resonances with the ritual of the Eucharist, though for Spenser the practice brings to light the inherent barbarism of the Irish.

As this example shows, the funeral, keening, and the often raucous revelry of the wake provided ritual authorization for extremities of action and utterance. Thomas Monk depicts a wake in Kildare in 1682 as resembling the "revellinge as if one of the feasts of Bacus." The following day, "so soone as the bearers have taken up the body they begin their shrill cries and hidious hooleings, and if there be not enough to make out a good cry, they hyre the best and deepest mouthed in all the countrie."[83] Sir Henry Piers (1628–1691), who compiled information on Westmeath for the Molyneux survey, described in 1682 how wakes are celebrated in a manner "more befitting heathens than christians." In the presence of the corpse,

> they spend most of the night in obscene stories, and bawdy songs, until the hour comes for the exercise of their devotions; then the priest calls on them to fall to their prayers for the soul of the dead. . . . When the time of burial comes, all the women run out like mad, and now the scene is altered, nothing heard but wretched exclamations, howling and clapping of hands, enough to destroy their own and others sense of hearing.[84]

The radical switching between modes of merriness and lamentation in which Barnabe Rich delighted renders the authenticity of the latter suspect for Piers. Dunton also describes a wake toward the end of the seventeenth century as a perverse display of contrasts. The corpse is carried during the night, "without any shouting or noise," into a barn, where it is watched by mourners in a state of "constrained silence." This reverence ended at midnight, when feasting was followed by outrageous games, "in such a place where such an object of mortality lay; to which not one that I saw showed the least regard." The next day, following a requiem mass and more feasting, "the corpse was brought forth (but first let me tell you that I saw about 20 women guzzling Usquebagh or aqua vitae: I inquired who they were, and was told that they were the *Mna Keenta* or howling women who had this given them to support their spirits in that laborious work)."[85] For Dunton keening is a performance by women whose drunkenness, and that of the other mourners, shows a lack of reverence for the dead.

The wake was a carnivalesque occasion of inversions, ribald play, and carnality, where games were played that included the staging of mock funerals (including keening by hooded women), mock marriages, erotic play, and burlesques of the clergy. Such games assert social vitality, often in the presence of the corpse that was sometimes stored under or at the end of the table on which Mass was celebrated, or even used as a prop and included in the feasting.[86] They also constituted symbolic attacks on the authority of church and state, and provided an outlet for social tensions that could overspill the ritual occasion. One of those tensions centered on attempts to impose Anglican forms of worship on Catholic communities.

The Elizabethan settlement in 1560 had attempted to reform Irish devotional practices through the application of Reformation statutes by both civil and ecclesiastical authorities. However, these reforms could not be nationally enacted due to significant structural weaknesses in the colonial administration, as well as loyalty to Catholic beliefs and practices among the Gaelic Irish and some Old English, and both commoners and gentry.[87] Indeed, the success of the Irish Counter-Reformation during the seventeenth century was facilitated by the systematic failure of the Tudor reformation.[88] By the late 1570s, "outright recusancy was apparently beginning to replace reluctant conformity as the typical response to the Elizabethan settlement."[89] From the 1590s onward, the Irish Catholic church consolidated its bureaucracy and embarked on a program of Tridentine reforms. At the same time, Irish Catholic mourners adopted various strategies to bypass civil and ecclesiastical controls (both Catholic and Protestant) on traditional burial rites. In the late sixteenth and early seventeenth centuries, it was commonly presumed that public funerals which followed the form of the Book of Common Prayer were merely a cover for secret rites committed elsewhere. The virulently anti-Catholic bishop of Waterford, Marmaduke Middleton (d. 1593), complained in 1580 that there was "no burial of the dead according to the Book of Common Prayer, but burial in their own houses with dirges and after cast into the ground like dogs."[90] Middleton notes that pre-Reformation customs persisted, such as the "ringing of bells and praying for the dead, and dressing their graves divers times in the year with flower pots and wax candles." These practices had not been totally extinguished in "reformed" England either.[91] Other strategies included double funerals and secret night burials (which had also become popular in England as a way of avoiding the controls and costs of a heraldic funeral, and of asserting affective bonds between mourners and the dead).[92] A case in Star Chamber in 1606 referred to the practice of filling the coffin with clay so that the body could be buried elsewhere using Catholic rites; it was also alleged that "it is a secret practice of the Papists to wrap their dead bodies in two sheets, and in one of them they strew earth that they themselves have hallowed and so bury them they care not where, for they say they are thus buried in consecrated earth."[93] Patrick Corish notes that in the early seventeenth century, cemeteries were the legal property of the established church, but that Catholics continued to be buried in them with Catholic rites.[94] From the 1630s, Catholics were able to pay a fee to the Protestant minister if they wished for a Catholic priest to preside over a funeral (Corish 106).

The resistance of Catholic mourners to interference by Protestant ministers in their burial rituals, and their boldness in proclaiming their confessional allegiance, made the funeral an occasion for widely publicized demonstrations against the English church. These demonstrations made use of violent mourning, weeping, shouting, self-harm, and destruction, transgressive behaviors that were central to keening rituals. In 1612 Rich described how at a funeral on the outskirts of Dublin,

> a dead corps beynge brought to be buryed, the mynyster of the parysh presentynge hym self to do hys duty acordyng to the prescryptyon of hys majesties lawes was not onely wythstode but was lykwyse so beaten & brused that it had lyke to haue cost hym hys lyfe, and a popysh pryst brought in that buryed the corps acordyng to the popysh manner. The very lyke was offered in the towne of Waxforde wher the mynyster was beaten that he kept hys bed many monethes after.[95]

On another occasion in Dublin, "a dead corps was caryed to the buryall wyth a crosse borne openly through the streates before it," notwithstanding "the late proclamatyon set forth by hys majesty for the avoydance of prystes, they are styll reteyned & the proclamatyon scoffed at" (140). Like many commentators, Rich draws attention to the failure of the law to curb these behaviors.

Attacks on ministers at funerals were not uncommon either.[96] In 1608, the prerogative Court of Castle Chamber (Corish characterizes the court as "a fearsome instrument in that it was not bound by the procedures of common law or the penalties of statute law"),[97] heard testimony by Thomas Meredythe, vicar of Balrotherie, about troubles at a funeral held by the influential Pale family the Barnewalls.[98] When he "attended at his church both to say divine service and also to bury the corpse of James Barnewall's mother," the defendants,

> having resolved "to bury the said corpse after a superstitious and idolatrous fasion, and not according to the King's Majesty's injunctions and ordinances," riotously entered the church, assaulted and wounded him—pulling away a great part of his beard and causing his nose to gush forth with blood—struck the book of Common Prayer from his hand and trod it disdainfully under foot, and that James Barnewell did moreover beat his [the plaintiff's] wife and threw her to the ground, she being great with child.[99]

In the context of the funeral, this transgressive behavior is reminiscent of the violent forms of mourning associated with keening, though in the latter mourners tend to harm themselves rather than others. The defendants were ordered to pay fines between £20 and £100, and Barnewell was imprisoned in Dublin Castle. This steep fine should be viewed as part of the campaign by the Lord Deputy Sir Arthur Chichester (1563–1625) against recusancy, in which he harassed leading Papists through the court of the Castle Chamber, although his use of the court as a "spiritual consistory" was met with resistance even by Protestant loyalists in the Pale, and the Privy Council urged Chichester to "take a temperate course between both extremes, neither yielding any hope of toleration of their superstition, nor startling the multitude by any general or rigorous compulsion."[100] This order shows that there was some sensitivity among the English authorities to the difficulty in forcing Gaelic Irish and Old English to adopt reformed practices.

These "riotous" attacks assert the primal right of the community to ownership of and control over the corpse and its manner of interment. They can be read as a transfer of the violence of ritual mourning that was expressed in the keen from the mourner's own body to the body of the authority figure (the minister). This reading is supported by evidence that it was often women who drove the protests. A letter of September 10, 1623, from the Archbishop of Canterbury to Sir Edward Conway described another disturbance in 1623 at the Protestant funeral of Susanna, Lady Killeen.[101] She was the Protestant wife of the Catholic Lucas Plunket, the first earl of Fingall,[102] and daughter of Lord Brabazon who had "lyved and dyed in good religion" (Protestantism). Her funeral was attended by "the Lord Moore and Sir Roger Jones two Counsellers of that State and the Sheriffe and diverse other gentlemen of quality," but these august presences did not deter "fowre weomen being the Captainesses and of these two being sisters to the Lord Killeene with about foure score other weomen" who assaulted the minister,

> rent his surplis, toare out a leafe of the Communion booke, and with blowes did offer him such violence that the better disposed people were inforced to reskue him. The body being brought into the churche, and the minister in the pulpitt ready to preache, the weomen with shoutes and outcries interrupted him and made him to desist and when by advise of the better sorte hee came downe and would onely have read the prayers for the buryall of the dead, they made such a hubbub and outcrye that hee was forced to leave that also.[103]

These Catholic women use keening behaviors to interrupt the Protestant order of service, exposing a religious fault line within this family. The Archbishop warned Conway to keep the king informed about the case and warned him "that the Lord Deputy instantly did take care to see it severely punished." Accordingly, the Lord Deputy remanded the four women in custody against "their appearance this next Terme in the Castle Chamber, where they are like to bee made examples of iustice and severity," though Lady Susanna's husband was not judged to have set them on: "The Lord Killeene is founde cleere in this businesse, permitting his wife in her life time to inioy the full exercise of her religion, and suffering the minister at her death to dispose her soule religiously and Christianly to God."[104]

Keening and the Law

Edward Muir has argued that over time, early modern authorities became "less tolerant of popular rites that led to disorder," regulating those carnivalesque spaces and times such as the wake that had provided an outlet for disruptive social energies.[105] This is certainly true of Ireland, where there were many attempts to impose civil and ecclesiastical controls on mortuary ritual. The difficulty of imposing such controls can be measured by the frequency with which legislation was passed by ecclesiastical and civil authorities. These attempts were not only mounted by the New English colonizers but also by the Irish Catholic hierarchy, whose efforts to prevent keening and funeral disorder date back to medieval times. Susan Leigh Fry notes that an Irish penitential from c. 800 ordained that keening of a "layman or laywoman" carried a punishment of "50 days on bread and water," while keening of an "anchorite or a bishop or a scribe or a great prince or a righteous king" was punishable by fifteen days on bread and water. However, she also traces multiple examples of keening in subsequent centuries: in a mid-eighth-century poem by Blathmac mac Con Brettan; in the "Book of Fenagh"; at the funeral of Sheeda Mac Conmara in 1310; in the Latin life of saints Ethnea et Fedelmia (late twelfth or early thirteenth century); in the fourteenth-century Book of Magauran; and so on.[106]

As the seventeenth century progressed, the Catholic hierarchy attempted to assert its control over keening and other mortuary practices. Samantha Meigs notes that the first Counter-Reformation synods in Ireland in 1614 did not legislate against funerary customs, though the Synod of Armagh in 1624 was explicit in its condemnation of the wake as an occasion of excessive expenditure, feasting, obscenity, and keening.[107] In 1660 the synods of Armagh and Tuam attempted to prohibit the hiring of female keeners, while the Dublin synod in 1670 ordered that "all the parish priests to use every endeavour to prevent the clamour and vociferation of the women who accompany the funerals of the deceased."[108] A similar resolution was adopted in Armagh in 1670, announcing that no priest could attend a wake or funeral at which keening was practiced, under threat of the removal of his parish.[109] In 1748, the bishop of Kildare was still trying to stamp out the "heathenish customs of loud cries and howlings at wakes and burials" as "contrary to the express commandment" of Paul. He deplored the "vanity" of those who "glory in the number of cries" and "do even send far and near to hire men and women to cry and compose vain fulsome rhymes in praise of their deceased friends." While the composition of epideictic "rhymes" on the dead was a respectable and well-established part of funeral ritual in England, the bishop commands priests and "religious laymen"

> to use all possible means to banish from Christian burials such anti-christian practies, by imposing arbitrary punishment of prayers, fasting, alms and such like wholseome injunctions on as many men and women as will loudly cry or howl at burials. But as to such men and women as will or do make it their trade to cry or make rhyme at burials, we decree . . . that for the first crime of this kind they shall not be absolved by any but the Ordinary or his representatives, and in case of a relapse, the aforesaid cries or rhymers are to be excluded from Mass and the Sacraments, and in case of perseverance in this detestable practice, they are to be excommunicated and denounced.[110]

When "wholesome injunctions" and "arbitrary punishment" failed, keening was to be punished with exclusion from the community of worship. The persistence of decrees against keening into the late nineteenth century shows that these ecclesiastical inhibitions were largely ineffective in restraining it.[111]

Alongside religious law, there were many failed attempts to use common law to reform native Irish cultural practices during the sixteenth and seventeenth centuries.¹¹² Kilkenny corporation decreed in 1609 that "no outcries to be made in the streets at funerals, on pain of 6d."¹¹³ The same council ruled in 1638 that "if any howling or crying be at any such burial, the Mayor and company to withdraw till they leave off howling."¹¹⁴ Legislation proposed by the Irish Privy Council in 1611 included "An Act for abolishing of barbarous and rude customs; as howling and crying at the burial of the dead, drawing their plough-cattle only fastened by the tails, and blowing their milch cattle to make them give milk, & c., and pulling of sheep."¹¹⁵ In 1626, the town of Galway decreed that "noe outcrye, houling or shooting [shouting] be made in or out of the streetes of this towne upon the buriall or at the buriall of any deceased person or persones whatsoever within this towne."¹¹⁶ Responsibility for enforcing this ban lay with the mayor and the sheriffs, who were charged with ensuring that "all and every corpse be caried to his grave here in a sivill orderly fashione, according to the forme in all good places observed."

These measures should be seen in the context of other legal attempts to reform native Irish cultural practices during the sixteenth and seventeenth centuries.¹¹⁷ Tudor legislation attempted to force the Irish to assimilate to English manners, asserting that differences of habit and dress corroded the unity of the kingdoms. The 1537 "Act for the English Order, Habit, and Language," 28 Hen. VIII. c. 15, ordained that the Irish should have "a conformity, concordance, and familiarity in language, tongue, in manners, order and apparel, with them that be civil people, and do profess and acknowledge Christ's religion, and civil and politic orders, laws and directions," citing the manners of the New English planters living in the Pale.¹¹⁸ The Act stipulates

> that there is again nothing which doth more contain and keep many of his subjects of this his said land, in a certain savage and wild kind and manner of living, than the diversity that is betwixt them in tongue, language, order and habit, which by the eye deceiveth the multitude, and persuadeth unto them, that they should be as it were of sundry sorts, or rather of sundry countries, where indeed they be wholly together one body, whereof his Highness is the only head under God.

Because cultural differences reinforce Irish identity as separate from the "civil" manners and body politic of the English, the act seeks to produce unity through conformity. This policy asserts that "divergence from English cultural standards is regarded not only as barbarism but even as a subversion of legal authority" that precludes them from enjoying civil rights under English law.¹¹⁹ While the act focuses on promoting harmony and the subjugation of the Irish to their English king, this characterization of the Irish as savage, wild, and barbaric continued to be used to justify their violent repression throughout the seventeenth century.

Sir William Herbert (c.1553–1593), an English associate of Sidney who landed in Cork in 1586 as undertaker for Munster, served as a Justice of the Peace and sheriff in Kerry. Soon after leaving Ireland in 1590 he composed an essay on its reformation, in which he uses terms familiar from the 1537 legislation to urge that "conformity in laws, dress and habits together with similarity in customs would all induce harmony, unity of spirit and friendship. As a result that alienation which springs from different and discrepant dress, laws and customs would be abolished and disappear."¹²⁰ His own efforts to establish an effectively Anglicized and Protestant society in Munster were rather less savage than those advocated by others including Spenser. Nonetheless, Herbert insisted that "the barbarous laws and habits of the inhabitants ought to have been destroyed and stamped out together with their religious usages, their pomps and their wicked and rude customs."¹²¹ This is the language not of legal reform but of tyrannical violence, and reflects the view that the Irish were too barbaric to be managed merely by the rule of law. As Irenius puts it in Spenser's *View*, "sithence wee cannot now apply lawes fit to the people, as in the first institutions of comon-wealths it ought to bee, wee will apply the people, and fit them unto the lawes, as it most conveniently may bee": the "sworde" of royal power must clear the way for the "halter" of legal reform.¹²²

Sir John Temple (1600–1677) exemplifies the hardening of this ideological tendency over the following century of conflict. Temple was a gentleman pensioner, judge, and MP who was born in Ireland, and whose hyperbolic account of the 1641 rebellion inflamed English opinion and demanded the waging of a bloody *lex talionis* against the Irish.¹²³ He looks back to the Irish in the time of Henry as "generally devoid of all manner of civility, governed by no setled lawes, living like beasts, biting and devouring one another, without all rules, customes, or reasonable constitutions either for regulation of Property, or against open force and violence."¹²⁴ Temple argues that reformations of the kind Herbert recommended had been pursued under Elizabeth's "prudent and religious Governours," who enacted "many wholesome Laws . . . against the barbarous customs of the Irish" (8). "But all was in vain" (9): the "perverse" Irish resisted reformation, because "the malignant impressions of irreligion and barbarisme, transmitted down, whether by infusion from their ancestors, or naturall generation, had irrefragably stiffned their necks, and hardned their hearts against all the most powerfull endeavours of Reformation" (10). In this propagandistic text, Temple asserts that the failure to subject the Irish to "wholesom Laws" in such apparently trivial matters as their mourning customs, haircuts, and apparel encourages their general rebelliousness and brought the whole premise of English sovereignty into question.

Temple's judgement is repeated across historical writings of the period, most of which are highly critical of failures to impose the rule of English law. Stanihurst insisted that conquest signified "three things, to witte, law, apparayle, and language. For where the countrey is subdued, there the inhabitants ought to be ruled by the same law that the conquerour is gouerned, to weare the same fashion of attyre, wherewith the victour is vested, and speake the same language, that the vanquisher parleth. And if anye of these three lacke, doubtlesse the conquest limpeth."[125] The persistence of native Irish customs such as keening, and their adoption by the Old English, suggested that the conquest did indeed limp. Throughout the seventeenth century, New English writers continued to cite keening among other Irish cultural practices such as mantles and glibs, fosterage, tanistry and gavelkind, coinage, livery, Brehon law, and the bards, as signs of the limits of English sovereignty. In 1689, Sir Richard Cox blamed the failure of Irish cultural conformity for the economic and political suffering of the country: "I do impute the Ignorance and Barbarity of the Irish meerly to their evil Customs, which are so exceeding bad, that as Sir *John Davys* says, *Whoever use them must needs be Rebels to all good Government, and destroy the Commonwealth wherein they live, and bring Barbarism and Desolation upon the Richest and most fruitful Land in the World.*"[126] As Thomas Hobbes (1588–1679) put it, "'tis not therefore the word of the Law, but the Power of a Man that has the strength of a nation, that makes the Laws effectual."[127] Ineffectual laws, by inversion, show up the sovereign as powerless. Keening not only disrupted public order directly, through the release of affective energies into protests against specific church or civil authorities; its persistence in spite of legal and ecclesiastical attempts to suppress it also presented a symbolic challenge to English sovereignty.

Conclusion

Keening represents a confrontation between conflicting cultures: on the one side, the New English, Protestant planters who endorsed the authority of common law as well as emotional self-restraint as vital for the maintenance of public order; on the other, the indigenous "wild" Irish, whose funeral customs included many elements with pagan origins that had only recently begun to be eliminated in English folk culture and whose allegiances to kinship groups, indigenous customs, and Brehon law represented a challenge to that authority. The keen's generic form, history, and performance conditions all made it particularly suited to evoking that conflict. However, the accounts of Irish mourning by New English writers refused to acknowledge the form, function, or history of the *caoineadh*, scorning Irish ritual mourning as mere animal howling. But the frequency and vehemence with which it is derided in English colonial discourse suggests that it had a powerful effect on outside observers.

New English depictions of Irish mourning mix scorn with fear and anger. Encircled by rebellious figures whose language they could not understand, insufficiently supported by their own sovereign, these writers suppress the content of Irish complaint and project responsibility for the failures of the plantation onto the Irish themselves. But the satirical elements in these texts cannot disguise the fear which keening could also provoke. Listening to the sound, anyone would think "that a company of Hags or hellish Fiendes, were carrying a dead body to some infernall Mansion; for what with the vnseemlinesse of their shewes, and the ilfaring noyse they doe make, with their howling and crying, an ignorant man would sooner beleeue they were Deuils of Hell, then Christian people."[128] Rich's description is framed as satire, but it also suggests that keening could invoke real terror. The most famous literary discussion of the terrifying power of Irish sound can be found in Edmund Spenser's *Colin Clout's Come Home Again*. Contrasting bucolic England with a haunted and devastated Ireland, Spenser describes a land where the keen has become universal:

> No wayling there nor wretchednesse is heard,
> No bloodie issues nor no leprosies,
> No griesly famine, nor no raging sweard,
> No nightly bodrags [*búaidred*, disturbance] nor no hue and cries.[129]

Ireland is a place of blood, disease, famine, and violence, in which the "hue and cry" of approaching war merges with the "wailing" of a suffering people. Many critics have argued that such moments reflect Spenser's own perception of the Irish, whose language he demotes to confusion and senselessness, stripped of its capacity for semantic signification and producing nothing but fear and estrangement in the English listener—just as the content of the keen, where historic and personal grievances are expressed in a virtuosic verse composition, is obliterated and replaced with an impression of the howling of wounded animals.[130] Indeed, when the Blatant Beast is first introduced at the end of V.xii, in a section of the poem that explicitly depicts the failure of the Elizabethan court to manage Irish rebellion, he is produced by Envy and Detraction, two hideous old hags who attack Artegall with sound, and "loudly cryde, / As it had bene two shepheards curres." Envy then "towards him runs, and with rude flaring lockes / About her eares, does beat her brest, and forhead knockes," an image that resonates with the depictions of keening women discussed throughout this essay.[131]

The violence of New English repudiations of keening reveals how intensely these commentators were affected by these sounds, despite their own supposedly superior rationality, faith, and self-control. Andy Wood has argued that the "governing elite of Tudor England . . . conceived of popular politics in auditory terms: as a 'commotion,' a 'mumur,' as 'complaining and murmuring,' as a great hurlie burlie among the multitude.'"[132] For Tudor and early Stuart rulers, he adds, "popular politics was about noise," and particularly about collective threatening speech. The murmuring, exclamations, cries, and noise of the populace were intimidating violations of decorum and class and gender hierarchies, and could be both the cause and consequence of riot and rebellion. Keening was perceived as a particularly Irish phenomenon, consistent with the "whining" tones of Gaelic language and music, and with the immoderate temperaments of Irish people. It could even be used as a touchstone for depictions of non-European savages. At the same time, these noises formed part of the political soundscape of England and invoked memories of rebellious underclasses. As I have argued elsewhere, the hubbub or Irish war cry—another sound stripped of semantic content, derided but feared—migrated to depictions of religious and political disorder in mid-seventeenth-century England. It seemed impossible to force the Irish to conform to English manners, or even to preserve distinctions between the two groups. When New English writers used the keen to complain that the Gaelic Irish had not been fully subjected to English power, the violence of their rhetoric and their repeated references to the "degeneration" of the Old English display an anxiety that it was the New English themselves who were in danger of being assimilated.

Keening also recalled English traditions of mourning that had not yet been fully extinguished by the Reformation. The history of the many attempts to manage this liminal site of mourning reveals how the process of colonization entails not just legal limits, but also the imposition of cultural and affective norms. Catherine Lutz has argued that emotion is "an important metaphor for perceived threats to established authority; the emotionality of repressed groups becomes a symbol of their antistructural tendencies."[133] Irish keening, and the funerary rituals of which it was a part, posed a direct threat to the authority of church and state through the violent disorder it sometimes released. But it also represented a threat to norms of emotional self-government that were notoriously difficult for English subjects to impose on themselves, particularly in times of grief. As a defense against such threats, the poetry of the *caoineadh* was dismissed as mere howling. This sought to turn Irish poetic traditions into a *terra nullius*, a space empty of signification that could be colonized by meanings imposed onto it, rather than an embodied poetic performance of community crisis and cohesion, political protest, or sorrow.

NOTES

I am grateful to Deirdre Ní Chonghaile, Marie-Louise Coolahan, Dorothy Cross, John Kerrigan, Patricia Palmer, and Katherine Simms for their advice and critiques of this essay.

1. Susan Leigh Fry, *Burial in Medieval Ireland, 900–1500* (Dublin: Four Courts, 1999), 85.

2. Discussions of the relationship between characterizations of the Irish as "barbarians," the imposition of English "civility," and colonial atrocities can be found in Nicholas Canny, *The Elizabethan Conquest of Ireland: A Pattern Established, 1565–76* (Sussex: Harvester, 1976), 125–36; Patricia Palmer, *Language and Conquest in Early Modern Ireland* (Cambridge: Cambridge University Press, 2001), 15–28; Andrew Hadfield, *Edmund Spenser's Irish Experience: Wilde Fruit and Salvage Soyl* (Oxford: Clarendon, 1997), 32, 40; and Joseph Th. Leerssen, *Mere Irish and Fíor-Ghael: Studies in the Idea of Irish Nationality* (Amsterdam: John Benjamins, 1986), 33–66.

3. Edmund Campion, *Two Histories of Ireland* (Dublin: Society of Stationers, 1633), 13–14.

4. Vincent Carey, "John Derricke's Image of Ireland, Sir Henry Sidney, and the Massacre at Mullaghmast, 1578," *Irish Historical Studies* 31, no. 123 (May 1999): 305–27 (308).

5. Edmund Spenser, *A View of the State of Ireland*, ed. Andrew Hadfield and Willy Maley (Oxford: Blackwell, 1997), 14. A discussion of Brehon law can be found in Colm Lennon, *Sixteenth-Century Ireland: The Incomplete Conquest* (Dublin: Gill and Macmillan, 1994), 57–60.

6. Clodagh Tait, *Death, Burial and Commemoration in Ireland, 1550–1650* (Basingstoke: Palgrave Macmillan, 2002), 37.

7. There are numerous cross-cultural examples of such practices, but a representative selection of essays on female ritual mourning might include Karen J. Brison, "You Will Never Forget: Narrative, Bereavement and Worldview among Kwanga Women," *Ethos* 23, no. 4 (December 1995): 474–88; Elizabeth Tolbert, "Women Cry with Words: Symbolization of Affect in the Karelian Lament," *Yearbook for Traditional Music* 22 (1990): 80–105; Margaret Alexiou, *The Ritual Lament in Greek Tradition* (Cambridge: Cambridge University Press, 1974); Ile-Ife Badwe Ajuwon, "Lament for the Dead as a Universal Folk Tradition," *Fabula* 22 (1981): 272–80; Nigel Barley, *Dancing on the Grave: Encounters with Death* (London: Abacus, 1997); Lauri Honko, "Balto-Finnic Lament Poetry," *Studia Fennica* 17 (1974): 9–61; Anne-Margrethe Hustad, "The North Russian Lament in the Light of the Religious Songs of the Old Believers," *Scando-Slavica* 27 (1981): 47–67; Ildiko Kriza, "The Rural Form of Death Dirges in Hungary," *Jahrbuch für Volksliedforschung* 39 (1994): 110–16; and Gail Holst-Warhaft, *The Cue for Passion: Grief and Its Political Uses* (Cambridge, MA: Harvard University Press, 2000), which includes a brief discussion of Irish keening.

8. Angela Bourke, "More in Anger Than in Sorrow: Irish Women's Lament Poetry," *Feminist Messages: Coding Strategies in Women's Folklore*, ed. J. N. Radner (Chicago: University of Chicago Press, 1992), 160–82 (160).

9. Pierre Bourdieu, *Distinction: A Social Critique of the Judgement of Taste*, trans. Richard Nice (Cambridge, MA: Harvard University Press, 1984), 474.

10. Judith Butler, "Performative Acts and Gender Constitution: An Essay in Phenomenology and Feminist Theory," *Theatre Journal* 40, no. 4 (December 1988): 519–31; see also her *Gender Trouble: Feminism and the Subversion of Identity* (New York: Routledge, 1990).

11. Donovan J. Ochs, *Consolatory Rhetoric: Grief, Symbol, and Ritual in the Greco-Roman Era* (Columbia: University of South Carolina Press, 1993), 43.

12. Plutarch, *Lives of the Noble Grecians and Romanes*, trans. Thomas North (London: Thomas Vautroullier and John Wight, 1579), 99.

13. "The Lacedaemonians have likewise a custom at the demise of their kings which is common to them with the barbarians of Asia—indeed with the greater number of the barbarians everywhere—namely, that when one of their kings dies, not only the Spartans, but a certain number of the country people from every part of Laconia are forced, whether they will or no, to attend the funeral. So these persons and the helots, and likewise the Spartans themselves, flock together to the number of several thousands, men and women intermingled; and all of them smite their foreheads violently, and weep and wail without stint, saying always that their last king was the best." Herodotus, *History of the Persian Wars*, trans. George Rawlinson (New York: Modern Library, 1947), Book VI, §58.

14. See for example Jeremiah 9:17–20 and Ezekiel 27:29–32.

15. Cicero, *De Legibus* II.23; Propertius, *Elegiae* II, 13, 27. Cited in Seán O'Súilleabháin, *Irish Wake Amusements* (Cork: Mercier, 1967), 134.

16. Jasper Mayne, *Part of Lucian made English* (Oxford: H. Hall for R. Davis, 1663), 211–12. Cf. *De luctu* [Of Mourning], in *The Works of Lucian of Samosata*, trans. H. W. Fowler (Oxford: Clarendon, 1905), §12–20.

17. John Aubrey, *Remaines of Gentilisme and Judaisme*, in *Three Prose Works*, ed. John Buchanan-Brown (Carbondale: Southern Illinois University Press, 1972), 176. Aubrey is citing Ovid, *Fasti* VI.668 ("The hollow flute was missed in the theatre, missed at the altars; no dirge accompanied the bier on the last march"), and Festus's epitome of Verrius Flaccus, *De verborum significatu*.

18. On Spenser's Scythians, see Palmer, *Language and Conquest*, 105; Nicholas Canny, *Making Ireland British* (Oxford: Oxford University Press, 2001), 48; Andrew Murphy, *But the Irish Sea Betwixt Us: Ireland, Colonialism, and Renaissance Literature* (Lexington: University Press of Kentucky, 1999), 67–68; Anne Rosalind Jones and Peter Stallybrass, "Dismantling Irena: The Sexualizing of Ireland in Early Modern England," in *Nationalisms and Sexualities*, ed. Andrew Parker, Mary Russo, Doris Summer, and Patricia Yaeger (New York: Routledge, 1992), 157–71 (159).

19. William Camden, *Britain, or A Chorographicall Description*, trans. Philemon Holland (London: George Bishop and John Norton, 1610), 671.

20. *The Mabinogion*, trans. Gwyn Jones and Thomas Jones (New York: Dutton, 1949), 166.

21. Heather J. Larson, "Keening, Crooning, and Casting Spells," *Proceedings of the Harvard Celtic Colloquium* 18/19 (1998–99): 134–49. For further parallels see Angela Partridge [Bourke], "Wild Men and Wailing Women," *Éigse* 18 (1980–81): 25–37 (25).

22. John Weever, *Ancient Funerall Monuments . . . of Great Britain, Ireland, and the Islands Adjacent* (London: Thomas Harper, 1631), 15.

23. Christopher D'Acugna [Cristóbal Acuña], *Voyages and Discoveries in South-America* (London: S. Buckley, 1698), 99.

24. Lancelot Addison, *The Present State of the Jews* (London: J.C. for William Crooke and John Courtney, 1675), 219–20.

25. Samuel Collins, *The Present State of Russia* (London: John Winter for Dorman Newman, 1671), 20–21.

26. Tait, *Death, Burial and Commemoration*, 2, explains some of the archival difficulties.

27. Keening is referred to in at least thirty-seven poems catalogued in Katharine Simms's important database of Irish bardic poetry, http://bardic.celtdias.ei/.

28. Ludwig Bieler, ed., *The Irish Penitentials* (Dublin: Dublin Institute for Advanced Studies, 1963), 231, 163.

29. James F. Dimock, ed., *Giraldi Cambrensis Opera*, vol. 5: *Topographia Hibernica* (London: Longman, Green, Reader, and Dyer, 1867), chap. 12, 157.

30. Rachel Bromwich, "The Keen for Art O'Leary, Its Background and Its Place in the Tradition of Gaelic Keening," *Éigse* 5 (1945–47): 236–52 (241). There are some interesting exceptions, however, in which it is women who produce bardic elegies. See Marie-Louise Coolahan, "Caitlin Dubh's Keens: Literary Negotiations in Early Modern Ireland," in *Early Modern Women's Manuscript Writing*, ed. Victoria Burke and Jonathan Gibson (Aldershot: Ashgate, 2004), 91–110.

31. John Kerrigan, *Motives of Woe: Shakespeare and Female Complaint* (Oxford: Clarendon, 1991), 17.

32. Seán Ó Coileáin, "The Irish Lament: An Oral Genre," *Studia Hibernica* 24 (1988): 97–117 (101).

33. Patricia Lysaght, "*Caoineadh os Cionn Coirp*: The Lament for the Dead in Ireland," *Folklore* 108 (1997): 65–82 (71).

34. Bromwich, "The Keen for Art O'Leary," 242.

35. Bourke, "More in Anger," 168.

36. Bromwich, "The Keen for Art O'Leary," 242.

37. Larson, "Keening, Crooning, and Casting Spells," 144; see also Lysaght, "*Caoineadh os Cionn Coirp*," 71–73; Bromwich, "The Keen for Art O'Leary," 243; and Bourke, "More in Anger," 160, 170.

38. Leerssen, *Mere Irish and Fíor-Ghael*, 57; Thomas M. Cranfill and Dorothy Hart Bruce, *Barnaby Rich: A Short Biography* (Austin: University of Texas Press, 1953); Richard Helgerson, "Lyly, Greene, Sidney, and Barnaby Rich's 'Brusanus,'" *Huntington Library*

Quarterly 36, no. 2 (1973): 105–18; and Willy Maley, "Rich, Barnaby (1542–1617), Soldier and Author," *Oxford Dictionary of National Biography*.

39. Barnabe Rich, *The Irish Hubbub or, The English Hue and Crie* (London: John Marriot, 1617), 3.

40. Barnabe Rich, *A New Description of Ireland* (London: William Jaggard for Thomas Adams, 1610), 12.

41. Tait, *Death, Burial and Commemoration* (36) and others also connect the *bean caointe* to the *bean sí* or banshee. See also Patricia Lysaght, *The Banshee: The Irish Supernatural Death Messenger* (Dublin: Glendale, 1986); Patricia Lysaght, "An Bhean Chaointe: The Supernatural Woman in Irish Folklore," *Eire-Ireland* 14, no. 4 (1979): 7–29; B. N. Kimpton, "Blow the House Down: Coding, the Banshee, and Woman's Place," *Proceedings of the Harvard Celtic Colloquium* 13 (1993): 39–47; and Coolahan, "Caitlin Dubh's Keens," 98, 102.

42. William Shakespeare, *Henry IV, Part I*, in *Comedies, Histories and Tragedies: The First Folio* (1623), III.i.38–39, facs. ed. Doug Moston (New York: Routledge, 1998), 382.

43. Palmer, *Language and Conquest*, 92.

44. Sir Richard Cox, "An Apparatus: Or Introductory Discourse," *Hibernia Anglicana: or, The History of Ireland* (London: H. Clark for Joseph Watts, 1689), [n.p.] sigs. liv and l2r.

45. Katherine Simms, "The Poet as Chieftain's Widow: Bardic Elegies," in *Sages, Saints and Storytellers*, ed. Liam Breathnach, Kim McCone, and Donnchadh Ó Corráin (Maynouth: An Sagart, 1989), 400–411 (401).

46. Eleanor Knott, "Mac an Bhaird's Elegy on the Ulster Lords," *Celtica* 5 (1960): 161–71 (163, 165).

47. Cú Chonnacht Mac Rithbheartaigh to Tomás Mór Mag Uidhir, 1430. Cited in Simms, "The Poet as Chieftain's Widow," 403.

48. Brendan Bradshaw, *The Irish Constitutional Revolution of the Sixteenth Century* (Cambridge: Cambridge University Press, 1979), 282–84; see also Leerssen, *Mere Irish and Fíor-Ghael*, 43–47.

49. Richard Stanihurst, "On Ireland's Past: De Rebus in Hibernia Gestis," in Colm Lennon, *Richard Stanihurst the Dubliner* (Dublin: Irish Academic Press, 1981), 156.

50. Bourke, "More in Anger," 166.

51. Laurent Joubert, *Treatise of Laughter* (1579), trans. Gregory David de Roucher (Tuscaloosa: University of Alabama Press, 1980).

52. Bernard Capp, "'Jesus Wept' but Did the Englishman? Masculinity and Emotion in Early Modern England," *Past & Present* 224 (2014): 75–108 (79).

53. Peter Charron, *Of Wisdome*, trans. Samson Lennard (London: Edward Blount, [1608]), 97.

54. Jean E. Feerick, *Strangers in Blood: Relocating Race in the Renaissance* (Toronto: University of Toronto Press, 2010), 63–64.

55. Gail Holst-Warhaft, *Dangerous Voices: Women's Laments and Greek Literature* (London: Routledge, 1995), 99.

56. Petrarch, *Rerum senilium liber XIV: Ad magnificum Franciscum de Carraria Padue dominum, Epistola I*, ed. Vincenzo Ussani (Padua, 1922); cited in Allison Levy, "Augustine's Concessions and Other Failures: Mourning and Masculinity in Fifteenth-Century Tuscany," in *Grief and Gender, 700–1700*, ed. Jennifer C. Vaught and Lynne Dickson Bruckner (Basingstoke: Palgrave Macmillan, 2003), 81–93 (87).

57. Edward Muir, *Ritual in Early Modern Europe* (Cambridge: Cambridge University Press, 1997), 49; Sharon T. Strocchia, "Funerals and the Politics of Gender in Early Renaissance Florence," in *Refiguring Women: Perspectives on Gender and the Italian*

Renaissance, ed. Marilyn Migiel and Juliana Schiesari (Ithaca, NY: Cornell University Press, 1991), 155–168 (161).

58. Juliana Schiesari, *The Gendering of Melancholia: Feminism, Psychoanalysis, and the Symbolics of Loss in Renaissance Literature* (Ithaca, NY: Cornell University Press, 1992), 162.

59. See also my discussion of Rich's satirical pamphlet in "Hubbub and Satire," *Renaissance Studies* 30, no. 1 (2016): 120–36.

60. *An Elegie, and Epitaph for Mistris Abigail Sherard, Daughter of the Right Honourable Philip Baron of Lentrimm* (1648), n.p.

61. Hadfield, *Edmund Spenser's Irish Experience*, 23.

62. Cited in Phillipe Ariès, *The Hour of Our Death* (New York: Knopf, 1981), 144.

63. John Calvin, *Ioannis Calvini in Omnes D. Pauli Epostolas* (Geneva, 1551), 481–82; cited in G. W. Pigman III, *Grief and English Renaissance Elegy* (Cambridge: Cambridge University Press, 1985), 137.

64. Jeremy Taylor, *Holy Living and Holy Dying* (1658), two vols., ed. P. G. Stanwood (Oxford: Clarendon, 1989), vol. 2, 225, 229.

65. Pigman, *Grief and English Renaissance Elegy*.

66. Simms, "Bardic Poems," 227.

67. For a fuller discussion of conflicting attitudes toward the Stoic or Christian rigorist conventions of restrained grief, see my *English Funerary Elegy in the Seventeenth Century: Laws in Mourning* (Basingstoke: Palgrave Macmillan, 2006), chap. 2.

68. Andy Wood, *The Memory of the People: Custom and Popular Senses of the Past in Early Modern England* (Cambridge: Cambridge University Press, 2013), 92.

69. Camden, *Britain*, "Ireland and the Smaller Ilands," 147.

70. Fynes Moryson also describes the custom of expostulating with the dead, "An Itinerary or Ten Years' Travel" (1600, 1617, c. 1626), in *Illustrations of Irish History and Topography, Mainly of the Seventeenth Century*, ed. Litton Falkiner (London: Longmans, 1904), 320.

71. Ibid.

72. Ibid.

73. Nancy Lee Beaty, *The Craft of Dying: A Study in the Literary Tradition of the Ars Moriendi in England* (New Haven, CT: Yale University Press, 1970), gives a comprehensive overview of the tradition.

74. Thomas Monk, "A Descriptive Account of the County of Kildare in 1682," *Journal of the Kildare Archaeological Society* 6, no. 4 (1910): 339–46 (346).

75. John Dunton, *The Dublin Scuffle* (London: A. Baldwin and Booksellers in Dublin, 1699), 402.

76. Samantha Meigs argues that there was a "growing disparity between the funeral observances of the 'richer and poorer sort' in the seventeenth century: she demonstrates that keening could be heard in the house of a Dublin merchant in 1635, but that by 1681 a priest in Wexford noted approvingly that after a death "the parishioners meete, consolating the afflicted, and interring the defunct without any rude Euilations or Clamours, but counterfeit Presentment of seeming sorrow." *The Reformations in Ireland: Tradition and Confessionalism, 1400–1690* (Basingstoke: Palgrave Macmillan, 1997), 117–18.

77. Rich, *A New Description*, 13.

78. On early sources for this myth, see Ad Vingerhoets, *Why Only Humans Weep: Unravelling the Mysteries of Tears* (Oxford: Oxford University Press, 2013), 16–18.

79. See for example *Micro-Cynicon, Sixe Snarling Satyres* (London: Thomas Creede for Thomas Bushell, 1599), or William Goddard's *A Mastif Whelp with Other Ruff-Island-lik Currs fetcht from amongst the Antipedes* (1599), which includes a title-page woodcut of a snarling dog; or John Marston, *The Scourge of Villanie* (London: J[ames] R[oberts] for John Buzbie, 1598), 'Satyre IX,' sig. G7r.

80. Bourke, "More in Anger," 160.

81. On blood-drinking, Bourke cites "The Romance of Mis and Dubh Ruis" ("More in Anger," 166); Bromwich cites Deirdre's fifteenth-century *Lament for the Sons of Uisneach* and Emer's keen for Cú Chulainn ("The Keen for Art O'Leary," 249).

82. Spenser, *A View*, 66.

83. Thomas Monk, "A Descriptive Account of the County of Kildare in 1682," *Journal of the Kildare Archaeological Society* 6, no. 4 (1910): 339–46 (346).

84. Sir Henry Piers, "A Chorographical Description of the County of West-Meath, Written AD 1682," *Collectanea de Rebus Hibernicis*, vol. 1, ed. Major Charles Vallancey (Dublin: Luke White, 1770), 124. Cited in Patricia Lysaght, "Hospitality at Wakes and Funerals in Ireland from the Seventeenth to the Nineteenth Century: Some Evidence from the Written Record," *Folklore* 114, no. 3 (December 2003): 403–26 (406–7).

85. Edward MacLysaght, *Irish Life in the Seventeenth Century after Cromwell*, 2nd ed. (Dublin and Cork: Talbot, 1950), 360–61.

86. Lysaght, "Hospitality," 420.

87. Lennon, *Sixteenth-Century Ireland*, 304–24.

88. Patrick Corish discusses this failure in detail in *The Irish Catholic Experience* (Dublin: Michael Glazier, 1985), 67–95. See also Meigs, *The Reformations in Ireland*, 75–76, 94.

89. Steven G. Ellis, *Ireland in the Age of the Tudors 1447–1603* (New York: Longman, 1998), 239.

90. Marmaduke Middleton, Bishop of Waterford and Lismore, letter to Walsingham, June 29, 1580; *State Papers of the Irish Church in the Time of Queen Elizabeth*, ed. W. Maziere Brady (London: Longmans, 1868), 39; cited in John Brady, "Funeral Customs of the Past," *Irish Ecclesiastical Record* 78 (1952): 330–39 (330).

91. See for example Peter Marshall, *Beliefs and the Dead in Reformation England* (Oxford: Oxford University Press, 2002); Eamon Duffy, *The Stripping of the Altars: Traditional Religion in England c. 1400–1580* (New Haven, CT: Yale University Press, 1992); Keith Thomas, *Religion and the Decline of Magic* (London: Penguin, 2003); and Stephen Greenblatt, *Hamlet in Purgatory* (Princeton, NJ: Princeton University Press, 2002).

92. Canny, *Making Ireland British*, 448. On night burials in England, John Weever complained that noblemen and gentlemen "are either silently buried in the night time, with a Torch, a two-penie Linke, and a Lanterne" (*Ancient Funerall Monuments*, xviii). See also Claire Gittings, *Death, Burial and the Individual in Early Modern England* (Kent: Croom Helm, 1984), 168, 34; Ralph Houlbrooke, "Death, Church, and Family in England between the Late Fifteenth and the Early Eighteenth Centuries," in *Death, Ritual, and Bereavement*, ed. Ralph Houlbrooke (New York: Routledge, 1989), 34.

93. George Harrison, *Elizabethan and Jacobean Journals 1591–1610*, vol. 4, *A Jacobean Journal 1603–1606* (London: Butler and Tanner, 1941), 311, cited in John Brady, "Funeral Customs of the Past," 332.

94. Corish, *The Irish Catholic Experience*, 103.

95. Cæsar Litton Falkiner, "Barnaby Rich's "Remembrances of the State of Ireland, 1612,'" *Proceedings of the Royal Irish Academy* 26 (1906/7): 125–42 (140).

96. For an occasion when women mourners attacked the Protestant minister who interrupted a funeral in Drogheda and threw him into the grave, see Patrick Moran, *Spicilegium Ossoriense: Being a Collection of Original Letters and Papers Illustrative of the History of the Irish Church*, 3 vols. (Dublin: Browne and Nolan, 1874–1878), 147–48.

97. Corish, *The Irish Catholic Experience*, 97.

98. Sir John Barnewall had been lord chancellor, and his nephew Patrick had been serjeant-at-law and one of the most influential members of the Commons in the 1530s. Bradshaw, *The Irish Constitutional Revolution*, 98–89, 106.

99. *Historical Manuscripts Commission: Report on the Manuscripts of the Earl of Egmont*, vol. 1, part 1 (London: His Majesty's Stationers, 1905), 33.

100. *Calendar of the State Papers Relating to Ireland, 1603–6*, ed. C. W. Russell and J. P. Prendergast (London: Longman, 1872), 389. See also Jon G. Crawford, *A Star Chamber Court in Ireland: The Court of Castle Chamber, 1571–1641* (Dublin: Four Courts, 2005), 290–321 (294).

101. Both this and the Barnewall case are discussed in Tait, *Death, Burial and Commemoration*, 55–57.

102. ODNB entry for Christopher Plunket.

103. *State Papers Relating to Ireland* 63, vol. 240, p. 163, cited in Brady, "Funeral Customs," 331.

104. Ibid.

105. Muir, *Ritual in Early Modern Europe*, 139.

106. Fry, *Burial in Medieval Ireland*, 85–87.

107. Meigs, *The Reformations in Ireland*, 137.

108. Patrick Moran, *Memoirs of the Most Rev. O. Plunket, Archbishop of Armagh* (Dublin, 1861), 117, cited in Brady, "Funeral Customs," 336.

109. Laurence Renehan, *Collections on Irish Church History* (Dublin: Duffy & Sons, 1861–1874), 158, cited in O'Súilleabháin, *Irish Wake Amusements*, 138.

110. Michael Comerford, *Collections Relating to the Dioceses of Kildare and Leighlin* (Dublin: Duffy and Sons, [1883–1886]), 81–82, cited in Brady, "Funeral Customs," 337.

111. Lysaght ("*Caoineadh*," 68) notes that in the nineteenth century, priests denounced keening from their pulpits and clashed with lamenting women, while the 1918 Code of Canon Law stipulated that funeral liturgy and Mass must take place in church, and inveighed against wake games and keening. She cites (70) a commentator in 1824 who noted, "The Irish funeral now is notorious, and although this vociferous expression of grief is on the decline, there is still, in the less civilized parts of the country, a strong attachment to the custom, and many may yet be found who are keeners or mourners for the dead by profession."

112. Canny, *Making Ireland British*, 446.

113. J.G.A. Prim, "Ancient Civic Enactments for Restraining Gossiping and Feasting," *Journal of the Royal Society of Antiquaries in Ireland* 1 (1849–1851): 436–41 (438–39).

114. Ibid., 439.

115. *Calendar of State Papers Relating to Ireland, 1611–1614*, ed. C. W. Russell and J. P. Prendergast (London: Longman, 1877), 193.

116. John T. Gilbert, "Archives of the Town of Galway, Queen's College, Galway," Historical Manuscripts Commission, 10th Report, *The Manuscripts of the Marquis of Ormonde, the Earl of Fingall, the Corporations of Waterford, Galway, & c.* (London, 1885), 473; also discussed in Tait, *Death, Burial and Commemoration*, 36.

117. Canny, *Making Ireland British*, 446.

118. "An Act for the English Order, Habit, and Language," 28 Hen. VIII. c. 15, reprinted in Constantia Maxwell, ed., *Irish History from Contemporary Sources (1509–1610)* (London: G. Allen and Unwin, 1923), 112. It is notable that when the sons of Clanricard rebelled in 1572, they discarded their English clothing as a marker of their rebellion; so, too, did the Earl of Thomond in 1570 (Canny, *Elizabethan Conquest*, 143).

119. Leerssen, *Mere Irish and Fíor-Ghael*, 41.

120. Sir William Herbert, *Croftus Sive de Hibernia Liber*, ed. Arthur Keaveney and John A Madden (Dublin: Irish Manuscripts Commission, 1992), 107.

121. Ibid., 45.

122. Spenser, *View*, 135, 93.

123. For eleven years following that rebellion, in fact, an intense scorched-earth war killed an estimated one-third of the population, and from 1653 the English Parliament ordered the transplantation of disloyal Irish subjects to Connacht or the Caribbean. Sean O'Callaghan, *To Hell or Barbados: The Ethnic Cleansing of Ireland* (Dingle: Brandon, 2001), 45, 116–17.

124. Sir John Temple, *The Irish Rebellion* (London: R. White for Samuel Gellibrand, 1646), 5.

125. Richard Stanihurst, "A Treatise Contayning a Playne and Perfect Description of Irelande," in Raphael Holinshed, *Chronicles of England, Scotlande, and Irelande* (London: John Hunne, 1577), part 3, 3.

126. Cox, "An Apparatus," *Hibernia Anglicana*, [n.p.] sig. l2v.

127. Thomas Hobbes, *A Dialogue between a Philosopher and a Student of the Common Laws of England*, ed. Joseph Crospey (Chicago: University of Chicago Press, 1971), 59.

128. Rich, *A New Description*, 12.

129. Edmund Spenser, *Colin Clouts Come Home Again* (London: William Ponsonbie, 1595), n.p., sig. B4r.

130. On Spenser's attitude toward Ireland and the Irish language and people, see *inter alia* Claire Carroll, *Circe's Cup* (Cork: Cork University Press, 2001); Eiléan Ní Chuilleanáin, "Forged and Fabulous Chronicles: Reading Spenser as an Irish Writer," *Irish University Review* 26, no. 2 (1996); Patricia Coughlan, ed., *Spenser and Ireland: An Interdisciplinary Perspective* (Cork: Cork University Press, 1990); Hadfield, *Edmund Spenser's Irish Experience*; Thomas Herron, *Spenser's Irish Work: Poetry, Plantation and Colonial Reformation* (Aldershot: Ashgate, 2007); Christopher Highley, *Shakespeare, Spenser, and the Crisis in Ireland* (Cambridge: Cambridge University Press, 1997); Willy Maley, *Salvaging Spenser: Colonialism, Culture and Identity* (Basingstoke: Macmillan, 1997); and Richard McCabe, *Spenser's Monstrous Regiment: Elizabethan Ireland and the Poetics of Difference* (Oxford: Oxford University Press, 2005).

131. Edmund Spenser, *The Faerie Queene* (London: [Richard Field] for William Ponsonbie, 1596), V.xii.38, 352.

132. Andy Wood, *The 1549 Rebellions and the Making of Early Modern England* (Cambridge: Cambridge University Press, 2007), 115.

133. Catherine A. Lutz, *Unnatural Emotions: Everyday Sentiments on a Micronesian Atoll and Their Challenge to Western Theory* (Chicago: University of Chicago Press, 1988), 62, 64.

4
Listening within the "Grief of Distortions"

ANN PELLEGRINI

In her now-classic 1981 essay "The Uses of Anger," poet and essayist Audre Lorde calls out guilt (and she is writing specifically about white feminist guilt) as "a device to protect ignorance and the continuation of things the way they are, the ultimate protection for changelessness."[1] This is guilt as a deflection of the other's experience and one's implication in it. She goes on to dare women of color to upset the feminist fantasy of unity without difference or differences of opinion, urging women of color to name and speak their anger aloud and challenging white feminists to hear it without getting defensive: "The angers between women will not kill us if we can articulate them with precision, if we listen to the content of what is said with at least as much intensity as we defend ourselves against the manner of saying. When we turn from anger we turn from insight, saying we will accept only the designs already known, deadly and safely familiar."[2] Instead of turning from anger, we need "to stand still, to listen to its rhythms, to learn within it."[3] Meeting Lorde's charge—to tarry with anger—remains no less urgent and no less discomforting today than it was when she issued her call in 1981.

I type these words the day before the presidential election of 2016. (I am returning to them for the last time on Inauguration Day, January 20, 2017.) My assertion for the value of anger, and the need for still more of it, may seem counter-productive at a time when polarization—and the outright demonization of those with whom one disagrees—has become the defining feature and feeling tone of US politics. Commentators bemoan the erosion of "political civility," a trend brought to negative apogee (that is, the highest point of decline) by Republican Party standard-bearer and, just under three hours from this sentence's writing, President Donald Trump. In the run-up to the 2016 election, *New York Times* op-ed writer David Brooks devoted multiple columns to Trump's incivility and its impact on shared common life: Trump has "shredded the unspoken rules of political civility that make conversation possible" (March 18, 2016), "abandon[ing] the Judeo-Christian aspirations that have always represented America's highest moral ideals: toward love, charity, humility, goodness, faith, temperance and gentleness" (July 28, 2016). Brooks's concern about a loss of civility and his linkage of norms of US political life to "Judeo-Christian aspirations" did not start with the 2016 presidential race. In a representative column from January 14, 2011, Brooks ends with a quotation from the Protestant theologian Reinhold Niebuhr: "Civility is a tree with deep roots, and without the roots, it can't last. So what are those roots? They are failure, sin, weakness and ignorance." I return to the way a dominant religious identity shapes US national affect—and affective normativity—later in this essay. But, might lamentations over the shattering of shared norms of civility, and calls for its return, be a different version of "making America great again"?

Some of this shattering has been set down to the fragmenting effects—and *affects*—of new media, with their appeal to increasingly specialized and identity-confirming sources of information. This "cyber-Balkanization" makes it possible to stay within one's own comfort zone, supposedly immunized from different viewpoints and uncomfortable affects.[4] Within the echo chambers of social media silos, feelings can calcify into facts and harden political positions. Anger is held to be especially corrosive. It distorts facts and thereby stands in the way of the kind of objective, reasonable debate and civil disagreement necessary for democratic life. Nonetheless, alongside this declension narrative of a dysfunctional United States, split into red versus blue, us versus them, we hear another and ostensibly more hopeful story: most Americans are in fact fed up with the ideological wings of both left and right, hate partisan rhetoric, and desire consensus and, above all, "civil" discourse.[5] One of the many interesting things about this claim is that it is often made as a rhetorical maneuver in order to silence those with whom the speaker disagrees—and, if that does not succeed, at least to morally aggrandize one's own position as the very measure of reason and reasonable compromise as against one's intractable "opponents." For the purposes of this essay, I am far less interested in these canny and self-conscious deployments of calls for civility than I am in their psychic underbelly. What can the disavowed or tranquilized viscera of negative feelings tell us about democracy and its discontents? What if we stay with anger and bad feelings?

In listening to the viscera, I mean to keep faith with Lorde's call to "learn within" anger. But we must proceed cautiously. There are uses of anger, and there are uses of anger. They are not all equivalent. Lorde is helpful on this point. She does not think that all forms of anger are equally usable or equally possible. In her essay, she is explicitly discussing anger "between peers." Peers have "common goals," Lorde says, but may be blocked from realizing them and even from recognizing each other across the gulf of self and other on account of "distortions" of history.[6] Importantly, too, the kind of peer-to-peer contact across differences that Lorde describes is precisely not a case of individuals or groups comfortably sticking with their own, so as to zero out exposure to other opinions and experiences.

In contrast, where there are deeply entrenched and activated asymmetries of power, all too often the furious hatred of the dominant can be enacted—sometimes with deadly force—against those with less power.[7] In drawing these distinctions, Lorde points to the material contexts and power-full histories that render anger usable or not, and contact survivable or deadly. Here is may be worth noting that the word "contact" comes from *con* (together with) + *tangere* (to touch).

Anger, on Lorde's analysis, does not *cause* distortion. It is in some sense activated by the distortions of structural oppression, by violences enacted, remembered, threatened, and/or anticipated. Anger haunts, is haunted. It may arise in "this" particular moment, between "you" and "me," but it invokes a larger history that precedes and exceeds this time and this particular "us." This is a very different diagnosis of the relation between facts and feelings from the one put forward by those who wring their hands at the unruly entry of emotions into US politics. The latter view holds out hope for the return to balance, to a Goldilocks of perfect moderation—not too much feeling, not too little—as it is embodied in an American political center. This Goldilocks is also Aristotle's golden mean: where there is anger, such anger should be "Righteous Indignation," directed at the correct "bad" objects and expressed in the right way.[8] But, whose bad objects?[9] Whose right of way? African Americans and other minoritized groups have long been denied the right to be justifiably angry. Instead their anger is seen as "scary," "excessive," un-American. As Tav Nyong'o underlines, in an essay provocatively entitled "Civility Disobedience," "the good star of 'civility' is offered, always provisionally to the charmed few."[10]

Those who occupy the center of American life are far more likely to have their feelings—including their negative feelings (of anger, disappointment, frustration, grief)—ratified as facts, literally legitimated through laws and policies, and supported in extra-legal realms that justify and strive to repair the hurt feelings of some individuals and groups more than others. The call for civility and consensus can thus mystify power relations and perpetuate social inequalities. Not only that, the romance of civility cleans up what it actually feels like to share space with others one knows and likes—let alone what it feels like to encounter those whom ones does not yet know, may fear, and may or may not even like after getting to know them. Calls for civility are frequently yoked to the notion that in political life and in other spheres of human relating, too, no one's feelings should ever be hurt. This is certainly a fantasy where the schoolyard and family dinner table are concerned. As a fantasy about the conduct of political life and, especially, as a fantasy about how we disagree with each other over morally charged issues—and what such disagreement *feels* like—the dream of consensus above all may actually block possibilities for vibrant and truly inclusive democratic life. As I have argued elsewhere, this does not mean democracy is going to feel "good."[11] In fact, it quite often means it will not.

Feelings do not occur in a vacuum. They have a political and social history as well as a psychic life. Feelings are raced; they also racialize. The dilemma is not solved, however, by bringing more subjects into the sphere of dispassionate secular reason. This is because reasonableness itself is raced. As José Muñoz argues, the "paradigms of communicative reason" that structure the majoritarian public sphere correlate affective and racial normativities.[12] It is not simply that the feelings *of* the dominant come to matter more; the deeper issue here is that some feelings predominate as the measure of proper democratic belonging and participation in shared public life.

This is a longstanding issue in American life. We can hear its strains in the majority opinion in *Plessy v. Ferguson*, the infamous 1896 Supreme Court case that held that separate was equal. Toward the end of his majority opinion, Justice Henry Brown offered an answer to the question of how to tell the difference between a law that promotes the "public good" (which would be constitutionally permissible) and one that was enacted for the "annoyance or oppression of a particular class" (which would not be). The short answer was "reasonableness." "In determining the question of reasonableness," Justice Brown wrote for the Court's 8–1 majority, the state "is at liberty to act with reference to the established usages, customs, and traditions of the people, and with a view to the promotion of their comfort and the preservation of the public peace and good order."

As legal and performance studies scholar Karen Shimakawa explains,[13] Justice Brown's appeal to the established "traditions of the people" and the majority's ongoing "comfort" serves to explain and justify the difference between reasonable laws and unreasonable discrimination, a distinction that produces, in her resonant words, "'reasonableness' as hegemonic 'comfort.'" This equation misrecognizes what substantive equality in the context of pluralism demands, and it effectively—and *affectively*—divides "us" from "them." In the context of *Plessy*, this meant a cut between a dominant white majority—whose comfort became the ultimate object of the majority's concern—and minoritized, racialized others. In sharp contrast to this result, Shimakawa calls for "a proliferation of 'comforts,'" a call in keeping with my own interest in cultivating the capacity, individually and collectively, to bear the discomforting pressure of difference.

The legal logic, if not the social practice, of separate but equal would at last be overturned in *Brown v. Board of Education*, in 1954. But, the demand—and a demand that has the force of a shared cultural logic—that the feelings of the majority and the preservation of their established traditions must be protected and "comforted" persists, in ways that are deeply disabling for democracy and social justice for all. Even *Brown*'s laudable concerns with African American children's "feeling of inferiority as to their status in the community that may affect their hearts and minds in a way unlikely ever to be undone" risks confusing feelings with substantive equality before the law.[14] Contemporary calls for civility—as well as the public feeling culture that converts such calls into a universal moral imperative—are haunted by a violent US history of racism and settler colonialism. Civility is an asymmetrical imperative, as we have seen in the condemnation of Black Lives Matter for its alleged anti-white racism and the quick conversion of quarterback Colin Kaepernick's carefully choreographed silent protest of US racism into an unpatriotic "assault" on American values. Implicit and explicit calls to move on, get over, and leave behind not just negative feelings of anger or outrage, but also forms of grief that disturb dominant conventions of mourning are ghosted by this violent history, too. Some bodies are always already seen as protesting too much, even when they are on bended knee.

In a suggestive passage in "The Uses of Anger," Lorde connects anger and mourning: "Anger is a *grief* of distortions between peers, and its object is change."[15] How might controversies over who can or cannot properly protest be linked to who can grieve and who and what are grievable?[16] Can we expand Lorde's claims for the politically transformative uses of anger, the possibilities of staying with and learning within it, beyond peer-to-peer encounters? I turn next to offer two case studies in and from bad feelings. Mindful of Lauren Berlant's important cautions about the elevation of "feeling *bad*" into "evidence for a structural condition of injustice,"[17] I offer these case studies not as lessons but as counter-pedagogies, perhaps even counter-rhythms.

In May 2010, a Manhattan community zoning board voted 29 to 1, with 10 abstentions, to grant approval for a fifteen-story, multi-use Islamic Community Center on the site of the former Burlington Coat Factory, just two blocks from where the World Trade Center buildings once stood. The store had been shuttered since September 11, 2001, when debris from one of the hijacked planes used in the attacks on the World Trade Center crashed through the top two floors of the store, which had not yet opened to customers for the day. None of the store's employees was injured; they were in the basement eating breakfast at the time.[18] The address of the Burlington Coat Factory was 45 Park Place; the proposed center would extend from 45 to 51 Park Place, lending its name to the project's official title: Park51. The project's developers—Imam Feisal Abdul Rauf, his wife Daisy Khan, and real estate developer Sharif El-Gamal—framed the center as an attempt to "bridge and heal a divide."[19] It "sends the opposite statement to what happened on 9/11."[20]

Opposition to the project was fierce, with opponents—fired up by the right-wing, anti-Islamic activist and blogger Pamela Geller—denouncing it as an example of "Islamic domination and expansionism."[21] Park51 was also decried for territorializing American grief. As C. Lee Hanson, whose son died in the attacks on 9/11, said to a *New York Times* reporter, "The pain never goes away.... When I look over there and I see a mosque, it's going to hurt. Build it someplace else."[22] In a *New York Times* op-ed published at the height of controversy, Imam Abul Rauf sought to portray the center as a site "for unification and healing" and offered a pluralist counter-history of the project: "Our name, Cordoba, was inspired by the city in Spain where Muslims, Christians and Jews co-existed in the Middle Ages during a period of great cultural enrichment created by Muslims. Our initiative is intended to cultivate understanding among all religions and cultures."[23] Imam Rauf's invocation of the peaceable coexistence in the past of Muslims, Christians, and Jews seemed pitched toward the present as a way to rebut incendiary associations—made by Geller and others—equating Islam and antisemitism.[24] Together, the two sentences attempt a kind of progressive expansion of the American religious imaginary: from the Judeo-Christian to the Abrahamic trio (Judaism, Christianity, Islam) and, from there, to "cultivat[ing] understanding among *all* religions and cultures" (emphasis added). This vision of religious pluralism sacralizes America's self-image of itself as endlessly extendible field of tolerance.

Dana Luciano argues that 9/11 was quickly transformed into a "transcendent trauma," the "gold standard of contemporary affective eventfulness." Anyone could mourn it, and everyone should. To respond with anything other than "the mingled awe and reverent sorrow that emerged as the appropriate affective response to the event," she suggests, lay one "open to the charge of inhumanity."[25] As became clear in the controversy over Park51, however, this charge awaited Muslim Americans no matter what they felt or how they displayed it. Imam Rauf's appeals to "a seemingly tolerant domestic multiculturalism," as David Eng puts it, were no match for the noisy normativity of mourning in the name of nation.[26] As recently as 2015, Geller was still fulminating about Park51, which she termed "a middle finger to the American people," and repeating her earlier claims about an "Islamic pattern" of territorial domination and triumphalism: "There has never been a mosque of reconciliation and healing built on the site of a jihadi attack. Ever."[27] She wrote these words in a piece for the right-wing media site Breitbart.com in which she also crowed, "Ground Zero Mosque Defeated!" Talk about sore winners. Her triumphalism is in keeping with what Donovan O. Schaefer—drawing on Sharon Patricia Holland's work on the "erotic life of racism"—has called Geller's "hedonicity of hate."[28] But, Geller's claims notwithstanding, Park51's ultimate demise was due more to changing economic circumstances and real estate values than to public opposition; financing for the center never came through. Imam Abdul and El-Gamal parted ways, and in 2015, El-Gamal announced plans to build a 70-story high condominium project at 45 Park Place instead.[29] Geller's real victory here was not that she stopped the center—she did no such thing—but that she was able to reframe the stakes. In a coup of misnaming, Geller and others had stamped this negative association between the Islamic center and "Islamic terrorism" in the public mind by reducing the multi-use community center to one function, a mosque, and calling it the "Ground Zero mosque." This shift in frame helped to set the ugly terms for the bait-and-switches to follow.

Congressman Peter T. King, a New York Republican, was a leading opponent of the project; he also led congressional hearings on the dangers of home-grown "Muslim terrorists." In August 2010, King publicly called for Muslims to cancel their plans to build on a space so filled with suffering and grief for all Americans—except, he implied, for Muslim Americans, who became a conceptual impossibility. They are, instead, "the Muslim community," and cast as apart from, not a part of, the suffering (w)hole. Drawing on a language of pain and suffering, he said: "It is insensitive and uncaring for the Muslim community to build a mosque in the shadow of Ground Zero. While the Muslim community has the right to build the mosque they are abusing that right by needlessly offending so many people who have suffered so much." King's remarks are illustrative, not exceptional (and foreshadow Trump's angry campaign promises to ban Muslims from the United States). They are one example of what happens when a call to repair hurt feelings is made without reference to existing social hierarchies or divisions of power. In such an instance, the feelings of some people must be protected, even if that means running roughshod over the *rights* of some others. If some Muslim Americans come away from this debate with hurt feelings or even limited free exercise rights, that is just the price they must pay for—eventual?—acceptance.[30]

Injured feelings are an unavoidable part of our lives with others. This does not make hurt feelings the great equalizer. The subjective experience of hurt or injured feelings does not cancel out the need for historical, political, and psychic mappings of the way hurt feelings are linked to, and rearticulate, differences in social power. How do we cultivate the capacity, individually and collectively, to bear disagreement and irresolvable differences? This is even our very starting place with others, not to mention our originary launching point if we are to be a self distinguishable from an other.

Liberalism gives lip service to being different; but, in a secular version of "love the sinner, hate the sin," too often difference is admitted into public life on the condition that it appear as more of the same. As in "I'm okay, you're okay, but could you keep your way to yourself?" Another term for this structure of feeling is *tolerance*; it may even be the US national affect. Tolerance is embedded in a long and specifically Protestant history of religious toleration at the same time that it also structures social relations—and affect is a social relation—in and for the secular state. As Janet R. Jakobsen and I argue in *Love the Sin: Sexual Regulation and the Limits of Religious Tolerance*, tolerance allows people to espouse punitive judgments and promote discriminatory policies against their neighbors and fellow citizens, all the while feeling themselves as "kind," "fair," and morally good. Tolerance demands likeness and then prides itself on its openness to difference.

Tolerance is in many respects a secular version of religious toleration in which an established church allows dissenters the right to worship without fear of persecution, but withholds from them equivalent public or civic rights and privileges. Although the United States is formally secular—the First Amendment promises disestablishment and free exercise of religion—Christianity (Reformed Protestantism) has long functioned as the backdrop against which claims to be a moral person or to have values achieve cultural legibility. To put this another way: the Christian assumptions underlying tolerance may also help to make sense of why the anti-Muslim feelings animating public debates over Cordoba House/Park51 are not seen or experienced as prejudice, at least not from the standpoint of the tolerant center. Indeed, the opponents of the proposed Islamic Center see themselves as defending a wounded post-9/11 America, and conserving the sacred grounds of "our dead." This is not, and has not been, the same thing as mourning them. As psychoanalyst Thomas H. Ogden argues, the "experience of mourning" requires symbolizing loss and a willingness to endure the painfulness—feelings of "terrible disappointment, aloneness and impotent rage"—of living on and into a new reality.[31] The "sacralization" of Ground Zero and cordoning off of its meaning entombs grief, collecting its unspent energies for potentially dangerous future uses.

In the case of September 11, 2001, the future was a mere nine days away. On September 20, President George W. Bush addressed Congress and the nation. After praising "the decency of a loving and giving people who have made the grief of strangers their own," he invoked anger and a call to action against "our enemies." He named this call and this action "justice": "My fellow citizens, for the last nine days, the entire world has seen for itself the state of our union, and it is strong. Tonight we are a country awakened to danger and called to defend freedom. Our grief has turned to anger and anger to resolution. Whether we bring our enemies to justice or bring justice to our enemies, justice will be done."[32] In the anger-charged chiastic crossing of "enemies" and "justice," no space remains for the ongoing work of mourning. In *Precarious Life: The Powers of Mourning and Violence*, Judith Butler cogently discusses this premature closing and the wall Bush sets up between a time for grief and a time for action. She also asks what it even means or feels like to complete the work of mourning—and how would we know? Who are the "we" who know? I want to reopen these questions, linking them to some others: what can we ever know about an other, and how much must we know in order to act on their behalf and alongside them? These questions take us far beyond either "sympathy" or, even, "empathy."

"Sympathy" was explicitly invoked by President Bush in another public address shortly after 9/11. Speaking to the United Nations General Assembly on November 10, 2001, President Bush simultaneously accepted and brushed off the expressions of sympathy that had flooded in from around the globe, countering with a martial reenvisioning of the stages of grief: "In this war of terror, each of us must answer for what we have done or what we have left undone. After tragedy, there is a time for sympathy and condolence. And my country has been very grateful for both. The memorials and vigils around the world will not be forgotten. But the time for sympathy has now passed; the time for action has now arrived."[33] This is an arresting passage, where "arresting passage" suggests not movement/passage, but detour or blockage. Read in continuation with the earlier speech to Congress and the nation, what emerges is a series of links and oppositions that pair the grief of the insider to the expressions of sympathy from outsiders. Both grief and sympathy are consigned to the past—what "will not be forgotten," but will and must be passed through and left behind in order to move forward and act in time. However, this containing wall between past and present becomes a barrier to remembering and to the active relationships memory requires to history as unfinished, in process. President Bush insists on capping the overflowing meanings of 9/11, freezing it into a known and knowable event with a set beginning and end, and putting it "all" behind us as a completed past. We will, we must, move on and take action. Grief will be arrested so as to put the past to rest. This does not end mourning, let alone commence questions of responsibility and reparation; if anything, the call to action refuses to submit to or stay in the space of mourning at all. Even less does it respond to the force of trauma and its temporal disruptions.

President Bush's November 2001 speech to the United Nations is preserved on an official archives page of the web site WhiteHouse.gov. Hauntingly, when you click on this page, the following notice appears at the very top: "This is historical material, 'frozen in time.' The web site is no longer updated and links to external web sites and some internal pages will not work." *Frozen in time:* is this a dead link or a link to the dead?

Freud's framework of mourning and melancholia is helpful here. In this famous essay, written in early 1915 during the early months of World War I, Freud traces an analogy between mourning (which he considers a normal psychological response to loss) and melancholia (which he describes as a pathological response).[34] He is seeking to show what mourning and melancholia have in common and, especially, where they differ. The array of objects that may be lost in grief includes not just loved persons, but also abstractions like patriotism, liberty, and other cherished ideals. For Freud melancholia—as opposed to mourning—involves an object-loss that has been withdrawn from consciousness and absorbed into the ego. Both mourning and melancholia are a relationship to loss, and in both cases the ego suffers profound withdrawal of interest in the outside world, inhibition of all activity, loss of capacity to love, and painful dejection. However, the melancholic suffers a blow to her or his inner world that seems to exceed the loss itself. "In mourning," Freud tells us, "it is the world which has become poor and empty; in melancholia it is the ego itself."[35] This diminution of self is marked by lacerating reproaches to self-regard,[36] a self-abasement not present in mourning; the mourner might lash out at a world suddenly bereft of his or her lost object, but does not, Freud says, turn the fire on himself. In contrast, Freud was deeply puzzled by the loquacious wretch so willing to pronounce judgment on him- or herself. This led Freud to speculate that the vocal self-judgments were actually bespeaking an unconscious identification with—and ambivalence about—the lost object.

All unknowing, Freud observes, "the shadow of the object fell upon the ego."[37] It is a dark shadow, underwritten by attachment's oscillating dance between love and hate, fort and da. Freud's focus is on individual "pathology." But his analysis of mourning and melancholia, and especially his allowance for ambivalence (the way attachments to others are run through with love and hate, hope and hostility, need and negativity), affords ways to consider the larger social and political contexts in which loss is lived and negotiated, not just individually and privately, but collectively and publicly. Where the *psychic* life of tolerance is concerned, we can, with Kathleen Skerrett, reconceptualize tolerance as a kind of melancholic reaction, or defense, that protects the agents of tolerance from knowing just how far short they have fallen from their own professed commitments to being fair and doing good.[38] Such a reconceptualization also shows how closely linked tolerance and violent anger are. This is not about the "hypocrisy," "bad faith," "false consciousness," or "social pathology" of some individuals or groups. Being and feeling "tolerant" are more than an individual's defense against feeling "bad" about him- or herself. These individual acts of "forgetting" connect to a larger national imaginary in which the often violent exclusions at the heart of American democracy are recast and misremembered as inclusiveness.[39] Tolerance is a form of racialized and "religionized" affective normativity. It is part of the production of whiteness and those beneficent subjects who bestow "goods" on deserving others.

Perhaps the feeling of tolerance is a wedge against recognizing and grappling with loss and the anger loss ignites. As long as "we" conduct our anti-democratic politics under the banners of civility and tolerance, "we" need not grieve, nor fight to restore, the lost objects of democracy, freedom, and justice. The moralizing strains of tolerance are here conceivable as self-reproach turned *outward*—a projection of unbearable aspects of oneself—onto those others whose ongoing inequality (and the irksome noisiness with which "they" proclaim it) threatens to bring lost ideals back into view. The constitutional promises of religious freedom were supposed to redress the inequalities built into tolerance, but these promises have never quite shaken themselves free from the dilemma of Christian dominance. In its flag-waving, finger-pointing moralism, perhaps tolerance betrays the trace of this specifically religious lineage.

This often high-decibel moralism connects to another crucial moment in Freud's analysis of mourning and melancholia, namely, the manic phase of melancholia. Mania, Freud suggests, is the voluble side of foreclosed mourning; it is how melancholia speaks and acts out—unthinkingly, often violently—when it stops berating itself and turns its force instead on the world outside.[40] The often vituperative verbal attacks on the Cordoba House project echo many features of President Bush's attempts to split grief from anger, passivity from action, and past from present. All may function as manic defenses—shields—against the pain of loss and its eruption of mixed feelings. This shield becomes a kind of reverse mirror, allowing pain and loss to be dumped onto irredeemable bad objects: look, now, what you will lose. This inability to stop and stay with the hard work of mourning and the reality of loss—the death that has already happened to one *you* love or the death that will happen to you—can easily become the "false witness" (Robert Jay Lifton's term) that outsources death anxiety to designated others.[41] In defeating and killing those others, there is the fantasy of overcoming difference—which is to say, death—itself.

What might democratic engagement with difference look like and feel like in practice? And how might it require giving up—mourning—the twin fantasy of a world without conflict and of grief freed of all anger? To return to an earlier point, democracy on these *agonistic* terms probably would not feel so good—and most certainly not for the culturally dominant. However, social relations, on scales large and small, are not only about beautiful feelings and everything going your way. This is among the reasons we need courts to protect the rights of unpopular minorities from the sentiments of majority rules. Moreover, what if, as Lorde suggests, risking discomfort and, yes, discomforting anger were actually a value for democratic life and possibilities of social justice, not to mention a necessity for the art of being mortal in a world shared with other beings, human and non-?

"People are different from each other." This is the deceptively simple first axiom of Eve Kosofsky Sedgwick's still revelatory, still necessary *Epistemology of the Closet*. Sedgwick continues: "It is astonishing how few respectable conceptual tools we have for dealing with this self-evident fact. A tiny number of inconceivably coarse axes of categorization have been painstakingly inscribed in current critical and political thought: gender, race, class, nationality, sexual orientation are pretty much the available distinctions." Were we to add additional categories—religion, for example, or bodily capacity—we would still make little headway toward resolving the problem or exhausting the *resources* Sedgwick here lays out for us. To wit: "Our families, loves, and enmities alike, not to mention the strange relations of our work, play, and activism, prove that even people who share all or most of our own positionings along these crude axes [of identity] may still be different enough from us, and from each other, to seem like all but different species."[42] In place of the settled claims of category, then, Sedgwick points us to the work of "nonce taxonomy" that is already underway—the ways that individuals and groups generate rich, unsystematized, often improvised hunches (maps on the go) for negotiating a social landscape far wider and wilder than the officially available terms.

For those on the margins of the named or namable, the space between *feeling* and *being* may be no space at all. But what do the margins feel like? Do they feel differently? And which margins, exactly? What do we do, for example, with the claims made by many US evangelicals and some Catholics that "religious liberty" is under attack and that they are being marginalized by a dominant secular culture? Instead of dismissing such claims out of hand as so much political rhetoric or "bad faith," what if we take them at face value? This does not mean evaluating them in a vacuum; instead, we must listen for the histories and the larger social contexts within which feelings are constituted and constitute people. It is thus helpful to make yet another distinction, this one between being minoritized, that is ascribed *as* "a minority" by dominant cultures, and identifying oneself and one's group as *in* the minority. Different degrees of accuracy obtain.[43] This feeling of marginalization remains active and galvanizing despite the undeniable impact conservative Christianity has had on electoral politics and policy making in the United States over the past three decades and counting. Christian conservatives develop their cultural power both by drawing on their connection to the religious aspect of a hegemonic Christian secularism *and* by asserting they are marginalized and even oppressed by this same secularism.[44]

The "same" feeling structure can work, and be put to work, in different ways. Think again of my earlier point about the multiple uses of anger. In the end, what or how we feel as individuals matters less than how feelings get taken up and plugged into social relations. Assuredly, what an individual or a particular group feels matters deeply to them and should not be discounted. But this does not require making these feelings law's or social policy's leading edge.

The case of *Snyder v. Phelps* illustrates some of these dilemmas. In 2006, family and friends gathered to mourn the death of Marine Lance Corporal Matthew Snyder, a US soldier killed in Iraq. At the same time, another extended family—all members of the Westboro Baptist Church (WBC)—staged a different kind of gathering: to celebrate Snyder's death. This small band of protesters, led by WBC's founder Reverend Fred Phelps and totaling seven in all, had traveled from their home base in Topeka, Kansas, to Westminster, Maryland, where a funeral mass was held for Matthew Snyder at St. John's Catholic Church, on March 10, 2006, a week after his death in the line of duty.

WBC was founded in 1955, and its membership is modest. At the district court trial, it was estimated to be between sixty and seventy members, with the large majority—approximately fifty—related to Phelps by blood or marriage. WBC is an Independent Baptist Church, unaligned with any larger Baptist organization. Their web site—notoriously entitled GodHatesFags.com—identifies the church as "an Old School (or, Primitive) Baptist Church," which adheres to a strict interpretation of the Bible, especially on matters concerning sexuality. To the extent that WBC can be said to have a recognizable theological orientation, it is Calvinist to the extreme, preaching total depravity of man due to original sin, redemption through God's grace alone, and unconditional election.

Phelps and his followers first came to national attention in 1998, when they picketed the funeral of another Matthew—murdered gay college student Matthew Shepard—holding up signs proclaiming "God Hates Fags" and depicting "Matt in Hell." This funeral protest was part of a much longer record of picketing funerals, gay pride parades, and other public events, dating back to 1991, to protest the wickedness of homosexuality, which WBC believes presents "a clear and present danger to the survival of America, exposing our nation to the wrath of God."[45] On their web site, WBC claims to have carried out 58,344 such protests, including conducting pickets at over 400 military funerals. These protests are not attempts to save or redeem sinners; only God's grace can do that. Instead, in keeping with their particular understanding of Calvinism, they are trumpeting—and with apparent glee—the bad news of humanity's utter fallenness. They well understand how to court and keep the media's attention, and they are in no way interested in cultivating public sympathy. They want to piss people off and shock sensibilities and seem enlivened by the frisson of their own fury—and the fury they incite in others.[46] A column on their homepage tallies various figures, including the number of pickets WBC has conducted and the number of soldiers that "God has killed in Iraq and Afghanistan." The list concludes with this final thumb of the nose: "0—nanoseconds of sleep that WBC members lose over your opinions and feeeeellllliiiiiings." WBC's triumphalism at the deaths of others is chilling testament to the human capacity to split off good subjects from bad, and recalls Freud's description of a manic "joy, exultation or triumph."[47]

The WBC's rhetoric is so extreme that other Christian groups—both "mainstream" and "conservative"—routinely distance themselves from WBC's language and protest activities. This is so, despite the fact that many of these same groups also decry homosexuality, equal rights for LGBTQ people, and same-sex marriage as threats to "the family." WBC openly connects homosexuality's threats to "the family" to threats to "the nation." As Michael Cobb points out, however, such a linking is hardly historically new or limited to WBC. What may be distinctive about WBC is that the group detests homosexuality so much that their anger spreads out in a negative embrace of "nearly the entire world."[48] WBC understands and celebrates the death of US soldiers as divine punishment for, in Cobb's words, the "permissiveness and sinfulness of a nation that does not hate fags enough."[49] Even the nationally consecrated events of 9/11 are not safe from their gleeful protest. "Thank God for 9/11," they cheer.[50]

On the day of Matthew Snyder's funeral, Phelps, two of his daughters, and four of his grandchildren stood approximately 1,000 feet from St. John's Church and held up signs they had made in Topeka, with such sayings as "Thank God for IEDs," "Thank God for Dead Soldiers," "God Hates the USA," "America is Doomed," "Semper Fi Fags," and "Pope in Hell." These sayings would all be familiar to anyone who has followed WBC pickets over the years. It was, by all accounts, a peaceful protest. The protesters remained in the public area designated by the police and made no attempt to contact the Snyder family or any of the mourners. They did, however, contact the media in advance of their arrival, and local news teams obliged.

Among those watching the TV news that night was Matthew Snyder's father, Albert. He had not known details of the protest nor the content of the signs until that moment. In June 2007, three months after the funeral, he filed a tort action lawsuit against Phelps and WBC in the US District Court for the District of Maryland, later adding the two Phelps daughters who had attended the protest (Shirley L. Phelps-Roper and Rebekah A. Phelps-Davis) to the list of defendants. Snyder père made five complaints: defamation, intrusion upon seclusion, publicity given to private life, intentional infliction of emotional distress, and civil conspiracy. In summary judgment at court, the district court dismissed two of the charges: defamation and publicity given to private life. The case went to trial on the remaining three charges. A jury found the defendants liable on all of them and assessed $2.9 million in compensatory damages and $8 million in punitive damages.[51] The district court judge reduced the punitive damages to $2.1 million.

The Phelpses appealed on First Amendment grounds, asserting their freedom of speech and, secondarily, the free exercise of religion. The Fourth District ruled in their favor, using a free speech analysis. Snyder, in turn, appealed to the Supreme Court, which accepted the case. Oral arguments took place in October 2006. In March 2011, in an 8–1 decision authored by Chief Justice Roberts, the Supreme Court upheld the Fourth Circuit and found that the First Amendment protected protests at a funeral and that the conduct of the protests had not crossed the line from protected speech into actionable conduct. The Court agreed that the distress caused to Snyder was severe: "The record makes clear that the applicable legal term—'emotional distress'—fails to capture fully the anguish Westboro's choice added to Mr. Snyder's already incalculable grief."[52] But it also held that, because the protests had not interfered with a private event (the funeral) and the speech in question concerned matters of public issue (the morality of homosexuality, the war in Iraq, the sex abuse crisis in the Catholic Church), First Amendment protections trumped any personal injury to Snyder. "Speech is powerful," the Court concluded. "It can stir people to action, move them to tears of both joy and sorrow, and—as it did here—inflict great pain. On the facts before us, we cannot react to that pain by punishing the speaker."[53]

Although the 8–1 majority decision probably got it right as a matter of law, it may have done so by missing or reading past the vital issues at *Snyder*'s core: not the interruption of "private" mourning, but grief and its necessary and potentially generative disruptions for both private and public life. What if this segregation is the kind of distortion of grief that can lead to grievance? Chief Justice Roberts's decision sought to distinguish between matters of public concern and those that are properly private (funeral rites and the pain of mourning). Although the case reached the Supreme Court during the Obama administration, it is important to remember that it began with a soldier's death and military action during the Bush administration. It was Pentagon policy during the Bush years to ban photographs of the returning coffins of American service members killed in Iraq and Afghanistan. The official reason for this ban was respect for the "privacy" of the surviving family members, who, we were told, needed to mourn in their own way. However, the ban on just seeing the coffins of American war dead actually effected a ban on public mourning. This segregation, this privatization, of loss was necessary to the construction of a nation willing to send someone else's sons and daughters off to fight for "our" freedom. We must not know what we will not see. With Freud we can say that this is not mourning but mania.[54]

Amid this division into public and private, a grateful nation and a grieving father, how could we begin to hear, let alone enumerate, Snyder's "incalculable grief"? Albert Snyder tried, using the language available to him and to court experts. At the district court trial, he spoke, tearfully, of the extreme distress he had suffered as a result of the plaintiffs' actions. This was crucial to establishing the injury of intentional infliction of emotional distress, or IIED, as it was called, following convention, in the court opinions and legal articles on the case. Expert witnesses testified that the Phelpses' protests and Snyder's own unrelenting memories of them had exacerbated his depression at his son's death and interfered with his ability to go through "the normal grieving process."[55] Underlying health conditions, such as diabetes, had also worsened due to the added stress.

Whenever Snyder tried to fix his mind on happy memories of his son, he was overcome: "There are nights that I just, you know, I try to think of my son at times and every time I think of my son or pass his picture hanging on the wall or see the medals hanging on the wall that he received from the [M]arine [C]orps, I see those signs."[56] The signs had driven out and tainted all that was good: "I see that sign when I lay in bed at nights. I [had] one chance to bury my son and they took the dignity away from it. I cannot re-bury my son. And for the rest of my life, I will remember what they did to me and it has tarnished the memory of my son's last hour on earth."[57]

The time-space of Snyder's mourning bears consideration. The injury from the protest arrived late: he learned of it after the funeral, while watching—re-viewing—coverage of the day's events. There is so much of trauma in the belated arrival of the signals of protest and the experience of injury. The TV news coverage brought him to see something he had missed at the time, something that had taken place just beyond the edge of his sound and sight. But now he cannot escape what he missed—which was what? The protest or his son's death? The two events overwrite each other in Snyder's imaginings. Snyder in fact has no memories of his son's last living hours on earth; he was not with him when he died, nor anywhere close. What he has are empathetic projections through which he seeks to close the epistemic gap and, more centrally, breach the reality principle: my son is dead, my son is not dead, my son is no-where. The intrusiveness of memories of the protest, which came to him through the mediation of TV, is interfering with these projections, with his ability to close the gap. Is this, then, the injury, the explosive IIED for which he demands repair, an interruption in his ability to project himself across time and space and consciousness?

For the Catholic Snyder, however, his son's last hours on earth outlast breath to include being with the body in death. Corpse is too sterile a word for this charged remnant, not-quite-here and not-yet-gone either. None of us can close this gap between the living and the dead. Death comes and when it comes, it comes for us alone. Our lives and bodies are entwined with others from the start, but at death we do and must part. The charged coffins of the dead show and hide this at once. Even a "normal grieving process" cannot return our dead to life. Perhaps the Phelpses become carriers of Snyder's grief and his fury and his confusion at this irretrievable loss.

While reading the court cases and the legal commentaries on *Snyder*, each time I saw the letters IIED, I stumbled and tripped. I kept seeing the letters IED (improvised explosive device) and hearing in this confusion of IIED and IED the horrifying gap of not-knowing when "it" might be coming—loss, death, grief—and what will finally trigger it. Seeking to preserve life at all costs by cutting off mourning—whether by declaring mourning over and done or through the cutting off that is consigning it to the private—all but guarantees carrying our grief to others in the form of violently dealing death to "our enemies." Phelps and his followers see death as something "more," too, but a very different more: it's a call to repent, a sign of our fallenness, and a cause for joyous celebration and reaffirmation that *they* are among the elect. In their manic exultation they do not want for repair.

The Phelpses won their case but lost in the court of public opinion. Their gloating performances of not-grieving solicited anger and repugnance from pretty much everybody: the jurors, the media (who nonetheless could not stop pointing their cameras at them), and even the justices. All invoked the need to grieve in private, undisturbed, as a moral imperative and a right-as-rite (or is that vice versa?). Things got ugly, and law offered no comfort to Albert Snyder. But comfort is not the law's role or place. It is easy enough to sympathize with Snyder, the grief-stricken father, maybe too easy, especially as its corollary is revulsion at the actions of WBC. But what if we hold back from this splitting of good objects and bad, hold back, too, on our disgust and the moral elevation that comes with it? As in: That's awful; *I* or *we* would never do or even feel *that*. The case of *Snyder v. Phelps* hardly seems to fit Audre Lorde's model of peers wrestling with the "distortions of grief" in service of personal and social change. (The Phelpses are trying to convert—radically change—their "audience," but they are not engaging in reciprocal exchange.) Nevertheless, I am interested in staying with the bad feelings sparked by the Phelpses and resisting, as long as I am able, the moral elevation and catharsis that comes with pity for Snyder and righteous anger, horror, disgust at the Phelpses.[58] This is an extreme case, to be sure, but what might this exercise in staying with offer to the work of sharing social space with others, loved and despised, known and unknowable?

NOTES

I am grateful to Austin Sarat and Martha Umphrey for inviting me to put law and mourning together and for assembling such a rich group of interlocutors during my visit to Amherst in spring 2013. The thinking, writing, and reimagining of this essay would not have been possible without the brilliant friendship and conversations over many years with Janet Jakobsen, Linda Schlossberg, Karen Shimakawa, and Kathleen Skerrett.

1. Audre Lorde, "The Uses of Anger: Women Responding to Racism," in *Sister Outsider: Essays and Speeches* (Berkeley, CA: Ten Speed Press, 1984), 130.
2. Ibid., 131.
3. Ibid., 129.
4. Toni M. Massaro and Robin Stryker, "Freedom of Speech, Liberal Democracy, and Emerging Evidence on Civility and Effective Democratic Engagement," *Arizona L. Rev.* 54 (2012): 415. In fact, as Massaro and Stryker report, there are conflicting studies on the question as to whether new media contribute to "balkanization" and lessen exposure to perspectives that conflict with one's own.
5. For a representative study, "Beyond Red vs. Blue: The Political Typology," Pew Research Center, see http://www.people-press.org/2014/06/26/the-political-typology-beyond-red-vs-blue/, accessed November 6, 2016.
6. Lorde, "The Uses of Anger," 129.
7. Ibid.
8. Aristotle, *Nicomachaen Ethics*, trans. H. Rackham (Cambridge, MA: Harvard University Press, 1982), 105. My argument here is indebted to Sianne Ngai's discussion of Aristotle and the long history of philosophic debates over the justifiability of anger. In the course of her discussion, Ngai also tantalizingly mentions Lorde's "Uses of Anger." See *Ugly Feelings* (Cambridge, MA: Harvard University Press, 2005), 182.
9. For an important recent postcolonial critique of the Kleinian conception of good objects, bad objects, and the liberal subject's reparation of harm done to good objects, see David Eng, "Colonial Object Relations," *Social Text* 34, no. 1 (March 2016): 1–19.
10. Tav Nyong'o, "Civility Disobedience," *Bully Bloggers*, https://bullybloggers.wordpress.com/2014/08/18/civility-disobedience/, accessed October 15, 2016.
11. Ann Pellegrini, "'A Storm on the Horizon': Discomforting Democracy and the Feeling of Fairness," *Secular Discomforts: Religion and Cultural Studies*, ed. Holly Randell-Moon and Sophie Sunderland, special issue of *Cultural Studies Review* 18, no. 2 (September 2012): 16–30.
12. José Esetaban Muñoz, "Feeling Brown: Ethnicity and Affect in Ricardo Bracho's *The Sweetest Hangover (and Other STDs)*," *Theatre Journal* 52 (2000): 68.
13. Karen Shimakawa, guest lecture on *Plessy v. Ferguson* and *Loving v. Virginia* for the course "Religion, Sexuality and U.S. Public Life," New York University, February 14, 2012.
14. *Brown et al. v. Board of Education of Topeka et al.* 347 U.S. 483 (1954). I am here grateful to Shimakawa for this connection.
15. Lorde, "The Uses of Anger," 128.
16. For questions about "grievable life," see Judith Butler, *Precarious Life: The Powers of Mourning and Violence* (London: Verso, 2004).
17. Lauren Berlant, "The Subject of True Feeling: Pain, Privacy, and Politics," in *Traumatizing Theory: The Cultural Politics of Affect in and beyond Psychoanalysis*, ed. Karyn Ball (New York: Other Press, 2007), 315.
18. Ralph Blumenthal and Sharaf Mowhood, "Muslim Prayers and Renewal near Ground Zero," *New York Times*, December, 8, 2009, http://www.nytimes.com/2009/12/09/nyregion/09mosque.html, accessed January 17, 2017.
19. Feisal Abdul Rauf, qtd. in Javier C. Hernández, "Vote Endorses Muslim Center near Ground Zero," *New York Times*, May 26, 2010, http://www.nytimes.com/2010/05/26/nyregion/26muslim.html, accessed January 17, 2017.

20. Feisal Abdul Rauf, qtd. in Blumenthal and Mowhood, "Muslim Prayers and Renewal." For an excellent account of the ultimately failed plans to build Park51, see Brendan O'Connor, "The Sad, True Story of the Ground Zero Mosque," *The Awl*, October 1, 2015, https://theawl.com/the-sad-true-story-of-the-ground-zero-mosque-dc222bd2c02 f#.vfbt98uqe, accessed January 17, 2017.

21. Qtd. in Donovan O. Schaefer, *Religious Affects: Animality, Evolution, and Power* (Durham, NC: Duke University Press, 2015), 136.

22. Qtd. in Hernández, "Vote Endorses Muslim Center."

23. Feisal Abdul Rauf, "Building on Faith," *New York Times*, September 7, 2010, http://www.nytimes.com/2010/09/08/opinion/08mosque.html, accessed January 17, 2017.

24. Schaefer is helpful here. See his *Religious Affects*, 135–37.

25. Dana Luciano, *Arranging Grief: Sacred Time and the Body in Nineteenth-Century America* (New York: New York University Press, 2007), 261–62.

26. David L. Eng, "The Value of Silence," *Theatre Journal* 54, no. 1 (2002): 89.

27. Pamela Geller, "It's Official: Ground Zero Mosque Defeated!," *Breitbart Newsletter*, September 26, 2015, http://www.breitbart.com/big-government/2015/09/26/its-official-ground-zero-mosque-defeated/, accessed January 17, 2017. Compare Geller's language in the 2015 essay to her claims in the 2010 interview with Alan Feurr, "Pamela Geller: In Her Own Words," *New York Times*, October 8, 2010, http://www.nytimes.com/2010/10/10/nyregion/10gellerb.html?pagewanted=all&_r=0, accessed January 18, 2017.

28. Sharon Patricia Holland, *The Erotic Life of Racism* (Durham, NC: Duke University Press, 2012); and Schaefer, *Religious Affects*, 125.

29. For details of this change in plans for 45 Park Place, see O'Connor, "The Sad, True Story of the Ground Zero Mosque"; Geller, "It's Official"; and Oshrat Carmiel, "Luxe Condos at 'Ground Zero Mosque' Site Aim High on Pricing," *Bloomberg News*, September 25, 2015, https://www.bloomberg.com/news/articles/2015-09-25/45-park-place-pricing-ground-zero-mosque-condos-aim-above-market-rate, accessed January 17, 2017. Note Carmiel's (or the editor's) use of "Ground Zero Mosque" in title of the article. In combination with the language of "Luxe Condos" and "high . . . pricing," this tag manages to insinuate something as American as apple pie—turning a huge profit on real estate—into a form of terrorism.

30. I discuss this controversy more extensively elsewhere, setting it alongside the anti-Shariah law movement in the United States. See "'A Storm on the Horizon.'"

31. Thomas H. Ogden, *This Art of Psychoanalysis: Dreaming Undreamt Dreams and Interrupted Cries* (New York: Routledge, 2005), 40.

32. "A Nation Challenged; President Bush's Address on Terrorism before a Joint Meeting of Congress," *New York Times*, September 21, 2001, B4. See Butler's discussion of this speech in *Precarious Life*, 29.

33. George W. Bush, "President Bush Speaks to United Nations: Remarks by the President to United Nations General Assembly," UN Headquarters, New York, November 10, 2001, http://georgewbush-whitehouse.archives.gove/news/release/2001/11/20011110-3.html, accessed November 6, 2016.

34. Sigmund Freud, "Mourning and Melancholia," in *The Standard Edition of the Complete Psychological Works of Sigmund Freud*, vol. 14, ed. James Strachey (London: Hogarth Press, 1957), 243–58.

35. Ibid., 246.

36. Ibid., 244.

37. Ibid., 249.

38. K. Roberts Skerrett, "Homosexuals, Heretics, and the Practice of Freedom; Commentary on *Love the Sin: Sexual Regulation and the Limits of Religious Tolerance*," *Studies in Gender and Sexuality* 6, no. 4 (2005): 387–98. See also Pellegrini and Jakobsen,

"Melancholy Hope and Other Psychic Remainders: Afterthoughts on *Love the Sin*," *Studies in Gender and Sexuality* 6, no. 4 (2005): 423–40.

39. David L. Eng and Shinhee Han, "A Dialogue on Racial Melancholia," in *Loss: The Politics of Mourning*, ed. David L. Eng and David Kazanjian (Berkeley: University of California Press, 2003), 347.

40. Freud, "Mourning and Melancholia," 253–58. Eng's essay on "The Value of Silence," cited above, has been very helpful for my own thinking about melancholia's manic turn. In it, Eng underscores the "value of silence" as a counter to the violent mania of US nationalism post-9/11. He proposes silence not as the opposite of speech, but rather as a precondition for the transformation of loss into meaning. I have also benefitted from the important prompts offered in Douglas Crimp's *Melancholia and Moralism: Essays on AIDS and Queer Politics* (Cambridge, MA: MIT Press, 2002).

41. Cathy Caruth, "Interview with Robert Jay Lifton," *Trauma: Explorations in Memory*, ed. Cathy Caruth (Baltimore: Johns Hopkins University Press, 1995), 139.

42. Eve Kosofsky Sedgwick, *Epistemology of the Closet*, 2nd ed. (Berkeley: University of California Press, 2008), 22. Sedwick's resort to the language of "species" at the end of this sentence is fascinating in light of recent and still-emerging work in queer theory and beyond that pressures the human/nonhuman divide—and the biopolitics of "species." Important examples from this literature include *Queering the Non-Human*, ed. Noreen Giffey and Myra J. Hird (London: Ashgate, 2003); "Queer Inhumanisms," ed. Dana Luciano and Mel Chen, special issue of *GLQ* 21, no. 2–3 (2015); "Tranimalities," ed. Eva Hayward Jami Weinstein, special issue of *TSQ: Transgender Studies Quarterly* 2, no. 2 (May 2015); Donna Haraway, *Staying with the Trouble: Making Kin in the Chthulucene* (Durham, NC: Duke University Press, 2016). For a critical examination of the biopolitics of species, see Nicole Shukin, *Animal Capital: Rendering Life in Biopolitical Times* (Minneapolis: University of Minnesota Press, 2009).

43. On this point, see Janet R. Jakobsen and Ann Pellegrini, *Love the Sin: Sexual Regulation and the Limits of Religious Tolerance* (New York: New York University Press, 2003), 118–19.

44. Janet R. Jakobsen with Ann Pellegrini, "Introduction," *World Secularisms at the Millennium*, ed. Jakobsen and Pellegrini, special issue of *Social Text* 64 (Fall 2000): 15. Elizabeth A. Castelli has recently tracked the emergence of a modern Christian persecution complex, which combines a long history of Christian martyrological discourses with the galvanizing rhetorics of contemporary identity politics. See Castelli, "Persecution Complexes: Identity Politics and the 'War on Christians,'" *differences* 18, no. 3 (Fall 2007): 152–80.

45. Accessed November 6, 2016, http://www.godhatesfags.com/wbinfo/aboutwbc.html.

46. Schaefer's discussion of Pamela Geller's delight in her hatefulness is helpful here. See *Religious Affects*, 127, 136–37.

47. Freud, "Mourning and Melancholia," 254.

48. Michael Cobb, *God Hates Fags: The Rhetorics of Religious Violence* (New York: New York University Press, 2006), 3.

49. Ibid.

50. Ibid.

51. All this is summarized by Judge King for the Fourth District Court. *Snyder v. Phelps*, 580 F.3d 206 (4th Cir. 2009). I am also drawing on additional details supplied by Benjamin C. Zipursky, in "*Snyder v. Phelps*, Outrageousness, and the Open Texture of Tort Law," 60 *DePaul L. Rev.* (2010–2011): 473–520.

52. *Snyder v. Phelps*, 562 U. S. 10 (2011).

53. Ibid.

54. See Eng, "Value of Silence," and Ann Pellegrini, "Habeas Corpus: Behold the Body," *TDR: The Drama Review* 52, no. 1 (Spring 2008): 179–82.
55. *Snyder v. Phelps*, 580 F.3d 206, 9 (4th Cir. 2009).
56. Qtd in. *Snyder v. Phelps*, 580 F.3d 206, 8 (4th Cir. 2009).
57. Ibid.
58. Ngai, *Ugly Feelings*, 6.

5
Psychoanalysis, Mourning, and the Law
Schreber's Paranoia as Crisis of Judging

MARK SANDERS

When humanists think mourning, they turn to psychoanalysis.[1] In its classic texts, the account of mourning given by psychoanalysis opens it toward law. In "Mourning and Melancholia," the motif signaling this opening is the self-reproaches that can come to the fore in mourning. "Where there is a disposition to obsessional neurosis," Freud writes, "the conflict due to ambivalence gives a pathological cast to mourning and forces it to express itself in the form of self-reproaches to the effect that the mourner himself is to blame for the loss of the loved object, i.e. that he has willed it."[2] A judgment takes place. The mourner finds himself guilty. Loss turns into murder.

A similar structure comes to light in the psychoanalytic fable for the origins of law in *Totem and Taboo*. Having placed before us the killing and eating of the primal father, Freud asks us to bear witness to what happens in its aftermath:

> After they had got rid of him, had satisfied their hatred and had put into effect their wish to identify themselves with him, the affection which had all this time been pushed under was bound to make itself felt. It did so in the form of remorse [*Reue*]. A sense of guilt [*Schuldbewußtsein*] made its appearance, which in this instance coincided with the remorse felt by the whole group. . . . The earliest moral precepts and restrictions in primitive society have been explained by us as reactions to a deed which gave those who performed it the concept of "crime."[3]

Law—in the form of moral precepts and restrictions—has its conditions of possibility in a being-conscious of guilt that coincides with the father-killers' remorse. The remorse (*Reue*) that they feel is, in the first place, not for the deed that they have done, but for the loss of the father: the affection that makes its presence felt after their hatred has been satisfied no longer has an object. This *Reue*, in other words, is mournful—as one might expect if one is used to hearing its Afrikaans cognate, *rou* (mourning).[4] A being-conscious of guilt ensues when the loss that is mourned is judged to have resulted from the deed. It is this being-conscious of guilt that gives the killers the concept of crime. And it is from this concept of crime that law springs.

Apart from its explicit account of the origin of law, the principal difference between the fable told in *Totem and Taboo* and the description of mourning given in "Mourning and Melancholia" is that, in the fable, those who mourn have *actually* murdered. As Freud reminds us, however, the fable is based on the psychoanalytic observation of neurotics; the compulsions of the obsessional neurotic, which often assume a ceremonial character, are like taboos. Whereas Freud thinks that the murder and eating of the primal father must have been actual deeds of "primitive men," he is emphatic in denying this to be so with neurotics: "We find no deeds, but only impulses and emotions, set upon evil ends but held back from their achievement. What lie behind the sense of guilt [*Schuldbewußtsein*] of neurotics are always *psychical* realities and never *factual* ones."[5] In other words, it is quite possible to think the origin of law as involving conditions of possibility *within* psychical reality: "The mere existence of a wishful *phantasy* of killing and devouring [the primal father], would have been enough to produce the moral reaction that created totemism and taboo."[6] The primacy of phantasy is emphasized over and over by Freud.[7] Law thus has its origin in mourning, to the extent that loss turns into a being-conscious of guilt that turns the mourner into the murderer. As in "Mourning and Melancholia," he or she has been found guilty. Law emerges in this act of judging.

This psychical nexus of mourning and finding oneself guilty of murder remains virtually unchanged, except for the introduction of the second topography, when, in his famous late essay, "Dostoevsky and Parricide," Freud establishes a clear distinction between criminal culpability and guilt. When the defense speaks in the trial of Dmitri Karamazov, Freud notes, there is a mockery of psychology, which is described as a "knife that cuts both ways" since it has been used to prove that he murdered his father, when it could as easily prove the opposite. But, Freud writes, "It is not psychology that deserves the mockery, but the procedure of judicial inquiry. It is a matter of indifference who actually committed the crime; psychology is only concerned to know who desired it emotionally and who welcomed it when it was done. And for that reason all of the brothers, except the contrasted figure of Alyosha, are equally guilty [*schuldig*]."[8] As Freud makes clear in his expert opinion in the case of Philipp Halsmann, a student from Innsbruck convicted in 1929 of murdering his father, this means that psychoanalysis makes no claims to decide criminal culpability. "Precisely because it is always present," Freud writes, "the Oedipus complex is not suited to provide a decision on the question of culpability [*Täterschaft*]."[9] The distinction between guilt and culpability, in a juridical sense, is crucial in what follows.

When Freud refers to the Oedipus complex, it might be thought to implicate the accused. But if the Oedipus complex is indeed omnipresent, would it not be operative as much for the judge as for the accused? And what would the effect be, in juridical terms, for judges, of being implicated in a psychical process in which they, in phantasy, were always already finding themselves guilty? Is there not the possibility that, if a certain mental mechanism were to bring about a substitution of accused for judge, the guilt of the judge might go to prove the culpability of the accused? If we acknowledge that law as judging—finding guilty or not guilty—itself has its conditions of possibility in psychical reality, then, in actual judgments, will there not always be the shadowing or doubling of decisions on *culpability* by a decision on *guilt*? A complicating factor is that, ostensibly, in the latter, taking place in the judge's psychical reality, the judge judges him- or herself, whereas in the former the judge judges the accused. Added to the doubling of culpability by guilt, this represents another doubling.

What would happen if the two lines of judging could no longer be held apart—and just as the accused's guilt may be used to prove his culpability, as in the trial of Dmitri Karamazov, so might that of the judge? In that case there would be a crossing of "I am guilty" and "He is culpable," or even a syllogism: "I am guilty therefore he is culpable." Might inklings such as this lie behind Freud's idea that the judicial proceedings in *The Brothers Karamazov* are deserving of mockery? He never says so explicitly, either in "Dostoevsky and Parricide" or in his opinion in the Halsmann case.

The closest that Freud comes to posing—and perhaps even suggesting answers to—questions of this order is in his history of a case of paranoia, published in 1911, which he based on an autobiographical account by Daniel Paul Schreber, who, as everyone knows, was a judge in Prussia, and quite a senior one. In that case history, as has perhaps not sufficiently been registered by humanists, the nexus for the genesis of law in mourning set out in *Totem and Taboo* the following year makes a prior appearance. It is, however, only when we return to Schreber's own writings that we discern clearly how the judge's paranoia (delusion of persecution, projection, and so forth) will have constituted what I call a *crisis of judging*. It is quite possible to imagine that, for judges, the cognitive lines of judging oneself, and judging the accused, never cross, but it is equally imaginable that the one line, powerfully charged, may, from time to time, switch the judge onto the other in a kind of short circuit. Read as a turn in the process of mourning, the theory of paranoia, developed by Freud and those who came after him, tells us *how* this might happen.

Freud's Case

When he published his *Memoirs of My Nervous Illness* in 1903, Daniel Paul Schreber had recently been discharged at his own request from Sonnenstein asylum, the third in a series of asylums in which he had lived for a decade.[10] In his book, Schreber takes the aural and visual hallucinations that characterized the second and more serious of his two illnesses to be revelations concerning the nature of God. The challenge presented to established religious doctrine by some of them is, he says, his reason for publishing the book. Appended to *Memoirs of My Nervous Illness* are several brief essays elaborating upon its religious ideas, as well as an addendum of legal documents pertaining to Schreber's application that the tutelage imposed on him be lifted, and that he no longer be confined in an institution against his will. In his book Schreber describes how his illness came about: God, who is made up of nerves, established "nerve contact" with human beings. This takes place through nerves known as divine "rays." Because this contact was against the "order of the world," it led to the destruction of the world, leaving Schreber as the "last man." Other people he encounters are, by his account, not real people but miraculously created "fleeting-improvised-men." Through a miracle brought about through nerve contact, Schreber becomes "unmanned": "This process of unmanning consisted in the (external) male genitals (scrotum and penis) being retracted into the body and the internal sexual organs being at the same time transformed into the corresponding female sexual organs."[11] He came to believe, from what the voices told him, that this was so that he could be abused sexually by a human being. Playing a role in this plot, just as he will have instigated nerve contact against the order of the world, was a certain Flechsig. "I do not dare maintain," Schreber writes, "that Professor Flechsig took part in it in his capacity as a human being."[12] For this was also the name of Schreber's doctor: Professor Paul Emil Flechsig, director of the psychiatric clinic of the University of Leipzig, who treated him during his first illness and at the beginning of his second. Flechsig is also accused of "soul murder." Because Schreber's "unmanning" only increases the attraction of divine rays and human nerves,[13] God tries to undo nerve contact by destroying Schreber's reason.[14] This is the cause, for Schreber, of the incessant voices, the "compulsive thinking," the "writing-down system" and the accompanying "tying to heavenly bodies"[15]—all of which make intellectual activity difficult for him, and are the formidable obstacles that he needed to overcome in order to put his book down on paper. An important change occurs for Schreber when he learns that his unmanning has a different purpose—not sexual abuse, but repopulation of the world through his impregnation by God. When the meaning of unmanning changes, persecution turns into triumph verging on megalomania. *Memoirs of My Nervous Illness* is preceded by a preface, and an open letter to Professor Flechsig, in which Schreber makes insinuations against his doctor that suggest that he continues to regard him as his persecutor: "I beg you ... my dear Sir—I might almost say: I *implore* you—to state without reservation. ... Whether during my stay in your Asylum you maintained a hypnotic contact with me in such a way that even when separated in space, you exerted an influence on my nervous system."[16]

Early in *Psycho-Analytic Notes on an Autobiographical Account of a Case of Paranoia (Dementia Paranoides)* (1911), Freud gives a basic outline of his interpretation. Based on the theory of paranoia being developed by him, Karl Abraham, and others, this outline is elaborated in subsequent pages:

> The relation between the patient and his persecutor can be reduced to a simple formula. It appears that the person to whom the delusion ascribes so much power and influence, in whose hands all the threads of the conspiracy converge, is, if he is definitely named, either identical with some one who played an equally important part in the patient's emotional life before his illness, or is easily recognizable as a substitute for him. The intensity of the emotion is projected in the shape of external power, while its quality is changed into the opposite. The person who is now hated and feared for being a persecutor was at one time loved and honoured. The main purpose of the persecution asserted by the patient's delusion is to justify the change in his emotional attitude.[17]

Freud makes three key assumptions. First, when affect *changes into* its *opposite*—or more precisely when love turns into hate, since a reversal in the other direction seems to require no such justification—this change has to be justified psychically. Although Freud does not use the word "guilt" here, it is clear, by definition, that a justification is a way of warding off guilt, or at least of heading off accusation. Second, this justification takes the form of *projection:* the feelings in their reversed form are attributed to the one who was formerly loved. Third, this projection may occur in transference, in relation to a "substitute." In the practice of psychoanalysis, the last in the line of substitutes would be the analyst.[18] Freud identifies Flechsig, Schreber's psychiatrist, as the "substitute." The transference is, to begin with, positive: Flechsig cures Schreber's first illness. The judge's phantasy, at the onset of his second illness, that "it must be nice to be a woman submitting to the act of copulation," which occurred at the same time as he dreamed that his illness had returned, Freud speculates, might have been associated with the longing that "I wish I could see Flechsig again!"[19] "The exciting cause of his illness, then," Freud sums up, "was an outburst of homosexual libido; the object of this libido was probably from the very first his doctor, Flechsig; and his struggles against the libidinal impulse produced the conflict which gave rise to the symptoms."[20]

Freud has referred to a "masculine protest"—Adler's term—against the "feminine" phantasy, in which affectionate dependence on the doctor has somehow become erotic desire. Given Freud's outline of the theory of paranoia, however, what is ruled out is not a homosexual libidinal impulse per se, but the hostile feelings that contradict this impulse. Both sets of feelings are unconscious. But it is the hostile feelings that require justification—hence the phantasy of being prepared for sexual abuse by Flechsig, which is an unconscious projection of those feelings. So what is actually being repudiated is not love for the doctor—as substitute figure—but hatred for the figure for whom the doctor substitutes. This turns out to be Schreber's father, an eminent physician famous for his system of medical gymnastics that some commentators imply must have been at the root of the son's problems. But the actual father, who he was, and what he was like is less relevant for Freud than he makes it appear, since it is the father's symbolic position that makes hatred of him unacceptable, because what he is owed is love. When Freud elaborates the "mechanism of paranoia," it is clear that the struggle and conflict described are not against the homosexual libidinal impulse—say, because it is socially unacceptable—but because the love in question brings into relief the *hatred* that it *contradicts*. This is consistent with what ensues in *Totem and Taboo* when the murderers of the primal father mourn him. Hatred turning into love requires no justification, but the hatred presupposed does. Thus when Freud writes that "what lies at the core of the conflict in cases of paranoia among males is a homosexual wishful phantasy of *loving a man*,"[21] and he is taken to be saying what popular prejudice says about repressed homosexuals, the closet, and paranoia (let J. Edgar Hoover be a synecdoche),[22] it is time to read more carefully. We have precedents in our literature for a more lucid understanding; George Orwell, who was probably alluding to the gay closet in *Nineteen Eighty-four* when he described the furtive exchanges between Winston Smith and O'Brien, makes it clear that what the Party actually demanded of Winston, all of whose experiences may be interpreted as an elaborate realization of paranoid phantasy or delusion, was that he love Big Brother.[23]

The operation of such an imperative becomes palpable when, in setting out what John Forrester has called the "propositional structure of neurosis,"[24] Freud writes:

> The familiar principal forms of paranoia can all be represented as contradictions of the single proposition: '*I* (a man) *love him* (a man),' and indeed that they exhaust all the possible ways in which such contradictions could be formulated.
>
> The proposition 'I (a man) love him' is contradicted by:
> (a) Delusions of *persecution;* for they loudly assert:
> 'I do not *love* him—I *hate* him.'
>
> This contradiction, which must have run thus in the unconscious, cannot, however, become conscious to a paranoic in this form. The mechanism of symptom-formation in paranoia requires that internal perceptions—feelings—shall be replaced by external perceptions. Consequently the proposition 'I hate him' becomes transformed by *projection* into another one: '*He hates* (persecutes) *me,* which will justify me in hating him.' And thus the impelling unconscious feeling makes its appearance as though it were the consequence of an external perception:
> 'I do not *love* him—I *hate* him, because HE PERSECUTES ME.'
>
> Observation leaves room for no doubt that the persecutor is some one who was once loved.[25]

In this passage, Freud restates his initial interpretative outline in a different way. The immediately preceding pages have set out his theory of how homosexuality is linked to the etiology of psychosis (regression, fixation at phase of auto-erotism or narcissism, hence cathexis of ego instead of objects). The theory is crude, in that it identifies the *auto-* with the *homo-*. But it accounts for how, when entering into a discussion of paranoid psychosis, Freud thinks that he can without further ado assume a homology: "I love him" is, in effect, "I love myself."[26] The ego takes the place of the object. Neurosis becomes psychosis. But the structure of Freud's explanation is also continuous with that for neurosis. As in *Totem and Taboo*, guilt coincides with a being-conscious; the propositions "I love him" and "I hate him" exist together in the unconscious, and the contradiction makes itself felt in the negation of the one. The negation itself is, as I read it, not unconscious, and neither, therefore, is the contradiction. Although the letter of the passage leads us to think that the contradiction itself sounds (*lauten*) in the unconscious, the passage does not really make sense unless we assume, as Freud does in "Negation" (1925), that negation, and thus also contradiction, is a function of the ego (or of consciousness, in the first topography). *Totem and Taboo* tells us this too when it registers a being-conscious of guilt (*Schuldbewußtsein*). The long dash separating "I do not love him" and "I hate him" might then indicate that, for the unconscious, the "Widerspruch" is just another "-spruch." In the German,[27] the syntax of "Ich l i e b e ihn nicht—Ich hasse ihn ja" shows how the negation (*nicht*), because it parallels the redundant intensifying affirmative particle (*ja*), might be read as an equally redundant afterthought; the first proposition in the formulation "Ich l i e b e ihn ja nicht—ich h a s s e ihn ja—weil *er mich verfolgt*" places side by side "ja" and "nicht," suggesting that negation can take place through a word ostensibly meaning "yes," but which works here as a particle that intensifies the negation. It is not the word but the negating function—or judgment—that matters. The emphasized verbs "love" and "hate" are Freud's names for what are, strictly speaking, cathexes of psychical energy that continue to abide side by side without contradiction in the unconscious. For the paranoiac, however, the simple contradiction cannot become conscious, and the negation that is symptomatized differently for the neurotic, who, for example, obsessively fears harm coming to his Lady Love,[28] occurs in the form of projection. The continuities between this passage and the initial outline given by Freud are clear. Without mentioning guilt, Freud tells us that guilt is at the heart of the mechanism—or what the mechanism automatically produces as a conscious feeling for the subject. What brings about the conflict, and what makes the hateful utterance *wider-*, is that love is what *will have been owed* to the phantasied persecutor. The future perfect is important, since guilt comes *after*. It is because of this debt that, if I hate him, my hatred has to be justified: "*He hates* (persecutes) *me, which will justify me in hating him*' . . . . 'I hate him, because HE PERSECUTES ME.'"

If we introduce the German *Schuld,* we can say that the paranoiac is in debt to/ guilty before the other. Another way of saying this is that he or she is, in effect, before the law. But the paranoiac does not *know* this, since the contradiction cannot come to consciousness in the requisite form; "guilt" is structural, but, for the paranoiac, not subjectively felt.

There is another way of interpreting this passage. Because of the guilt-producing consequences of its contradiction outlined by Freud, I began by treating the sentence "I love him" as the sign of an imperative to love (with George Orwell providing added documentation). Guilt is evident in the endeavor to justify a contradiction of the imperative. An imperative, however, is a verb. And the contradiction of the verb, in this case, is one of a series of contradictions of the sentence "I love him." In the other types of contradiction, the subject or the object of the sentence changes, and the verb remains the same. You will have noticed an "(a)" in the quotation above, but not a "(b)" or a "(c)." In fact, Freud goes on to detail propositions and their contradictions through "(c)," and adds a fourth, as follows:

> (b) Another element is chosen for contradiction in *erotomania* . . . "I do not love *him*—I love *her*". . . . And in obedience to the same need for projection [as in (a)], the proposition is transformed into: "I observe that *she* loves me". . . . (c) The third way in which the original proposition can be contradicted would be by delusions of *jealousy* . . . . "It is not *I* who love the man—*she* loves him" . . . Delusions of jealousy in women are exactly analogous. "It is not *I* who love the women—*he* loves them" . . . . But in fact a fourth kind of contradiction is possible—namely, one which rejects the proposition as a whole: "*I do not love at all*—*I do not love any one.*"²⁹

Although he does not cite the fourth contradiction when he comments on this passage in his seminar on *The Psychoses* (1955–56), Jacques Lacan changes the order in order to show how "(a)" represents a complication of "(b)" and "(c)." Lacan observes that "projection has to intervene as a supplementary mechanism whenever there is no effacement of the *I.*"³⁰ Forrester sums up Lacan's exegesis by writing that "*admissible transformations of the primal sentence ['I love him'] must not include the subject as first person of the statement.*"³¹ This rule is easily satisfied in "(b)" and "(c)," in which object and subject change. But when the *verb* is contradicted, yielding "I hate him," then "I" remains the subject of the sentence, and "he" remains the object. It is because the rule has still to be satisfied that "he" takes the place of "I," and what results is psychosis. What I am calling guilt, and what Freud formulates in terms of psychical justification, may thus be viewed as a function of this contradiction—which Lacan is explaining, with appeal to his theory of the imaginary, in terms of the alienation of the subject, whose desire is the desire of the other: not mine, but his. "In the third case [i.e., Freud's "(a)"]," says Lacan, "we are dealing with something much closer to negation. It's a converted alienation, in that love has become hatred. The profound deterioration of the entire system of the other, its reduction ratio, the extensive nature of interpretations about the world, shows you here the properly imaginary disturbance at its maximum extension."[32] Hence what we have here is not only, *one*, the potential for a judge to pass judgment on the basis of his own guilt (projection), but, *two*, a possible explanation for how a judgment—say, "soul murderer"—will always fall on "him" because the verb (and its contradiction) can never take "I" as its subject. This is not to say that all judgments will fall out in this way, but to identify a mechanism whereby a judgment could systematically never be one of non-guilt. I shall return to the second eventuality later. For now, however, let us concentrate on how—even if we decide that the propositional model should be viewed as having logical priority—Freud continues to elaborate his theory of paranoia according to a topography of conscious/unconscious and an economy of libidinal investment and displacement.

Freud's elaboration of his theory of paranoia links guilt to *mourning*—as one would expect, having read *Totem and Taboo*. This is first apparent when Freud makes a point of ascertaining whether Schreber's eminent father, and Schreber's elder brother, are still alive.[33] His reasoning appears to be that, if they are dead, then it is more likely that Flechsig could have become a substitute for one of them, and a focus of the projection that will have existed in relation to them.[34] Freud thus observes that the reproaches against Flechsig as a physician could easily have been reproaches against Schreber's father, "from whom he had been so early separated by death,"[35] a focus of the usual boyish mix of reverence and rebellion. He also observes that they take the form of "the *tu quoque* mechanism used by children, which, when they receive a reproof, flings it back unchanged upon the person who originated it. Similarly the voices [heard by Schreber] give us grounds for suspecting that the accusation of soul-murder brought against Flechsig was in the first instance a self-accusation."[36]

We noted that in "Mourning and Melancholia," published only a few years later, Freud explains how, for neurotics, mourning can bring about self-reproach. As in that text, in the Schreber case, mourning in the narrow sense—that is, for the dead—is a clue to a more general sense of mourning as what happens when the libido is detached from any previously loved object. This is clear from Freud's definition of repression:

> We may say, then, that the process of repression proper consists in a detachment of the libido from people—and things—that were previously loved. It happens silently; we receive no intelligence of it, but can only infer it from subsequent events. What forces itself so noisily upon our attention is the process of recovery, which undoes the work of repression and brings back the libido again on to the people it had abandoned. In paranoia this process is carried out by the method of projection. It was incorrect to say that the perception which was suppressed internally is projected outwards; the truth is rather, as we now see, that what was abolished internally returns from without.[37]

As Freud observes, withdrawal of libido occurs in "normal mental life (and not only in periods of mourning) [and] we are constantly detaching our libido in this way from people or other objects without falling ill."[38] The key, of course, is that, for neurotics (*Totem and Taboo*, "Mourning and Melancholia"), withdrawal of libido is felt not simply as loss of the object, but also as a failure to devote to the object what is due to it. The subject thus feels guilty and engages in self-reproach. The symptom is, however, formed in a more complicated way for paranoiacs. Projection—and here Freud combines topography, economics, and dynamics—would thus allow the reproach to be directed outward toward another. This would not be in the form "I hate him," which is ruled out because the "I" would be the subject of the sentence, and would for Freud be answerable to the imperative to love, but rather in the form "He hates me." Transference allows the identity of the accused to change: when Flechsig is accused of "soul murder," and projection and transference are taken into account, what has happened is that Schreber has turned his withdrawal of libido from his father, which means a loss of that loved object, whether the father is dead or not, into a crime in which he, as he will tell us in his *Memoirs*, stands "represented" in phantasy as the murderer of that object. Mourning, thus generalized, becomes through this turn a condition of possibility for paranoid judgment.

Klein's Elaboration

When Melanie Klein elaborates and transforms Freud's theory and practice through her analytic work with children, radically shifting the focal point of psychoanalysis from father to mother—who herself is thought of as derivative of the breast, which for the young infant is split into "good" and "bad"—she places what I am framing as the turn from loss to murder at the center of her theory of the "paranoid-schizoid position." In "A Contribution to the Psychogenesis of Manic-Depressive States" (1935),

Klein tells us that prior to the age of six months, the infant encodes any satisfaction and frustration that it experiences as arising from two distinct agencies. Explaining how projection and introjection operate in complementary fashion, Klein refers to these agencies, which derive from the breast, as "good" and "bad" objects. Good objects satisfy, and bad objects, which frustrate, are experienced as persecutory:

> It is because the baby projects its own aggression on to these objects that it feels them to be "bad" and not only in that they frustrate its desires: the child conceives of them as actually dangerous—persecutors who it fears will devour it, scoop out the inside of its body, cut it to pieces, poison it—in short, compassing its destruction by all the means which sadism can devise. These imagos, which are a phantastically distorted picture of the real objects upon which they are based, become installed not only in the outside world but, by the process of incorporation, also within the ego. Hence, quite little children pass through anxiety-situations (and react to them with defence-mechanisms), the content of which is comparable to that of the psychoses of adults.[39]

A pivotal role is played in these processes by what Klein terms "scotomization, the *denial of psychical reality*," which is "one of the earliest methods of defense against the dread of persecutors."[40] Instead of acknowledging the role of its own cognitive processes in splitting the object into "good" and "bad," the infant holds that, just as there are ones that bring it satisfaction, there are malign agencies at work persecuting it.[41] By about the age of four or five months, however, "the ego is faced . . . with the necessity to acknowledge psychic reality as well as the external reality to a certain degree. It is thus made to realize that the loved object is at the same time the hated one."[42] It thus becomes possible for the child to recognize that "good" and "bad" are attributes that it ascribes to the mother, and not her inherent qualities; these are also, we could say, the conditions of possibility for it to be able to view projection *as* projection.

Here is where Klein describes what transpires in terms of mourning. It is at this stage, "when the child comes to know its mother as a whole person and becomes identified with her as a whole, real, and loved person . . . that the depressive position . . . come[s] to the fore. This position is stimulated and reinforced by the 'loss of the loved object' which the baby experiences over and over again when the mother's breast is taken away from it."[43] As Klein adds in "Notes on Some Schizoid Mechanisms" (1946), "The loved and hated aspects of the mother are no longer felt to be so widely separated, and the result is an increased fear of loss, states akin to mourning, and a strong feeling of guilt, because the aggressive impulses are felt to be directed against the loved object."[44] But as a result of feeling guilt for having in phantasy attacked the "bad" breast, which turns out to be part of a (whole) object that is (also) good, there may occur a regression involving the denial of psychical reality, as well as external reality: "If persecutory fear, and correspondingly schizoid mechanisms, are too strong, the ego is not capable of working through the depressive position. This forces the ego to regress to the paranoid-schizoid position and reinforces the earlier persecutory fears and schizoid phenomena."[45] The "good" part objects, like the bad, in addition to being *projected*, have also been *introjected* to become parts of the infant's ego. Because the infant identifies with the good object, its own existence is at stake: "Preservation of the good object is regarded as synonymous with the survival of the ego."[46] The good objects are thus split off from the "bad" ones in order to protect the former from the phantasied attacks of the latter—hence a position that is *both* paranoid and schizoid.

Klein thus builds on Freud's account of *regression* and *fixation*, in which parts of the ego are cathected instead of external objects. In psychosis there is a complete withdrawal of libido from external objects—hence the inaccessibility of transference for the psychotic, and the limited efficacy of psychoanalysis for psychotics, except when there is the type of "recovery," noted by both Freud and Klein, in the course of which external objects are newly cathected. "Denial of psychical reality," however, means that the subject cannot recognize that this withdrawal has taken place.

It is because of those shared infantile conditions of possibility for schizophrenia and paranoia that, whatever the most accurate clinical diagnosis of Schreber might have been,[47] we may draw from Klein a general picture of the phantasy involved in fostering those conditions: whether my object returns from without (paranoia) or cannot be cathected at all (psychosis), the loss of that (good, loved) object is due, in the final analysis, to my attacks on it; if I am being persecuted it is because I am guilty; if I *mourn* it is not simply because I have *lost* that object, but because I have *murdered* it. This account is, of course, not available to the delusional subject, whether paranoid or psychotic—unless, of course, that subject recovers sufficiently to perform the *Umkehrung* of projection that allows Freud and those who come after him to translate the delusion into the common tongue.[48]

How might this generalization of mourning as loss cast as murder apply to what I am calling Schreber's crisis of judging? Neither Freud nor

Klein, nor yet any other of the principal psychoanalytic commentators on Schreber—surprisingly, this goes for Lacan too—refers in any operative way to Schreber's profession as a judge.[49] In what follows I would like to propose how, for humanist scholars of law and mourning, it would be illuminating to do so.

The Scales

In the fourth chapter of *Memoirs of My Nervous Illness*, Schreber briefly describes the onset and course of his two illnesses. Schreber never recovered from the second one, to which the bulk of his book is devoted. From the first illness, however, he did recover—thanks, he says, to his treatment by Professor Flechsig. He nevertheless sees fit to point out certain "mistakes" made by his doctor. There are, first, the "white lies" (*Nothlügen*) told to him by Flechsig, in order, Schreber appears to presume, to keep him hoping for a cure, but which "were hardly ever appropriate in my case, for he must soon have realized that in me he was dealing with a human being of high intellect, of uncommon keenness of understanding and acute powers of observation."[50] One of those white lies was "to put down my illness solely to poisoning with potassium bromide, for which Dr. R. in S., in whose care I had been before, was to be blamed (*zur Last zu legen sei*)."[51] Commonly prescribed as a sedative in Schreber's time, when it was used in psychiatric treatment, potassium bromide can have a range of side effects, including delirium, memory loss, disturbance of speech, and depression. Indeed, as is specified in Schreber's medical records, brought to light in the 1950s by Baumeyer, on admission to the University Clinic in December 1884 "he showed retardation of speech and emotional lability."[52] Since his second illness is the main subject of his *Memoirs*, Schreber only makes passing mention of his first illness and its symptoms. It is here that he makes his second criticism:

> I believe I could have been more rapidly cured of certain hypochondriacal ideas with which I was preoccupied at the time, particularly concern over loss of weight, if I had been allowed to operate the scales which served to weigh patients a few times myself; the scales used in the University Clinic at the time were of a peculiar construction unfamiliar to me. All the same [this and the white lies] are only minor points on which I place little importance; perhaps it is unreasonable to expect the Director of a big Asylum with hundreds of patients to concern himself in such detail with the mental state of a single patient.[53]

Of the "mistakes" that he mentions from his six-month stay in Flechsig's asylum, Schreber chooses to mention this. It and the white lies, he says, are "minor points on which I place little importance" (*Nebendinge, auf die ich kein großes Gewicht lege*). Freud, however, teaches us that when something is declared to be a side issue, it could be a sign that it is in fact what is most important. Commenting specifically on Schreber, Freud observes:

> He himself not infrequently presses the key into our hands, by adding a gloss, a quotation or an example to some delusional proposition in an apparently incidental manner, or even by expressly denying some parallel to it that has arisen in his own mind. For when this happens, we have only to follow our usual psycho-analytic technique—to strip his sentence of its negative form, to take his example as being the actual thing, or his quotation or gloss as being the original source—and we find ourselves in possession of what we are looking for, namely a translation of the paranoic mode of expression into the normal one.[54]

Let us therefore strip Schreber's sentence of its negative form: "auf die ich kein großes Gewicht lege" (on which I lay no great weight) becomes "on which I lay great weight." Why should Schreber lay any great weight on what is, as his book is organized, the second of Flechsig's mistakes—and which, in any case, relates to his first illness, from which he recovered? I think we can guess why, if we allow that the scales that he chooses to mention are, in addition to being an instrument for monitoring the weight of patients, also a symbol of justice, a reminder—even if he was not conscious of it—of Schreber's métier as judge; he was, in 1884, at the onset of his illness, chairman of the Country Court at Leipzig. Several significant elements are condensed into the scales. Schreber's illness prevents him from performing his job; the immediate cause is "mental overstrain" (*geistige Ueberanstrengung*) occasioned by his candidacy for the Reichstag, but, as with his second illness, which he ascribes to the "extraordinary burden of work" (*ungewöhnliche Arbeitslast*) associated with his promotion to Senatspräsident of the Court of Appeal in Dresden, we can assume an incapacity to work.[55]

Eric Santner has insightfully discussed the professional pressures that somebody in Schreber's position might have experienced. Relying on Bourdieu, and drawing a broad parallel between how psychoanalysts and judges gain their authority institutionally, Santner ascribes Schreber's two breakdowns to a "*crisis in symbolic investiture.*"[56] When Santner writes that "whether one is performing the role of psychoanalyst or judge, one's performance must be authorized,"[57] the parallel he draws is too sweeping.[58] I am putting forward a more specific explanation, proposing that we have before us a crisis of judging (which, if I were prepared to argue from etymology, would be *krisis* in its original sense, inviting me to insert a colon to produce a syntax close to but not quite that of a definition: crisis: of judging). I am with Duncan Kennedy when he observes that the legitimacy of a judge depends on the manner in which he or she decides cases.[59] Schreber can no longer judge well. He sees himself has having become emaciated—*Abmagerung* is starker than "loss of weight," closer to emaciation—because, he tells us, he does not understand how the scales work, and is not given leave to operate them himself. The scales may work perfectly, but his faculty of judgment does not. He thus believes himself to weigh less than he actually does, for, as he acknowledges in retrospect, his weight loss is one of his "hypochondriacal ideas." Indeed, as Schreber's medical records attest: "*1 June* [1885]. Departure for Ilmenau [in Thuringia, presumably where he went to convalesce]. He imagines that he has lost thirty to forty pounds in weight. Has in fact gained two kilogrammes. Complains that he is being purposely deceived about his weight."[60] Schreber's hypochondria shades into paranoia: they are trying to starve him to death. If we allow the scales their full judicial symbolism, however, Schreber has, in his mind, been weighed and found wanting. The scales have tilted against him. He has been found *guilty*. It may have been possible to blame Dr. R. for the bromide, but Schreber, being of uncommon keenness of understanding, knows that accusation to have been a lie, however expedient. And even Professor Flechsig, who will become the main focus of all the paranoid ideas of his second illness, eludes the symbolic economy of the scales: "Perhaps it is unreasonable to expect the Director . . . to concern himself in such detail with the mental state of a single patient."[61] When Schreber writes that these are only side issues on which he places little weight (*kein großes Gewicht*), we suspect that, with his capacity impaired accurately to weigh—and to weigh himself—the weight he unwittingly places on the episode is greater than he says. "The main point was that I was eventually cured." Yet even after he returns to give Flechsig "in my opinion an adequate honorarium" (*ein nach meinem Dafürhalten angemessenen Honorar*), his wife, who kept Flechsig's likeness on her desk for many years, "felt even more sincere gratitude and worshipped Professor Flechsig as the man who had restored her husband to her." Once again, Schreber is found wanting; he considers his honorarium to be "adequate" (or "commensurate"), but the scales are tipped against him. He cannot relieve himself of the guilt of not feeling a gratitude more inward. And here this guilt is bound up with rivalry, for he believes that Flechsig has his wife's heart. The couple is childless, and it is easy to see how, at one level, Schreber might have feared displacement as husband. At another level, it is possible to suspect what Freud called a paranoia of jealousy.

Schreber's account of the onset of his second illness again betrays a crisis of judgment, an absence of due measure. Keeping to the metaphorics of weight, he mentions the "heavy burden of work" (*Die Arbeitslast . . . war . . . ungemein groß*), but adds that "I was driven, maybe by personal ambition, but certainly also in the interests of the office, to achieve first of all the necessary respect among my colleagues and others concerned with the Court (barristers, etc.) by unquestionable efficiency."[62] In other words, by preempting an imagined accusation—a questioning of his efficiency—he has already found himself guilty of not working hard enough. His labors are thus in excess of any reasonable measure, or at least in excess of what his job actually demands; to work in order to gain "respect," a symbolic object, can be to embark on a potentially endless series of labors. "The task was all the heavier (*schwerer*)," he observes, because of the seniority and experience of the judges over whom he was to preside. Schreber fails in his office not because he cannot work hard, but because he has lost the ability to judge what is adequate to his task. The onus of work at the Court is unusually (*ungewöhnlich*) and uncommonly (*ungemein*) heavy, not because it has been determined to be thus by some reliable measure or instrument, applied by him or anybody else, but because Schreber finds himself guilty in advance of not being able to bear it.

Crime and Culprit

Shortly after the onset of his second illness in 1893, and his readmission to the Leipzig University Clinic, what Schreber describes as supernatural occurrences begin to take place. These assume the form of voices, visions, and transformations of his body, and above all what Schreber describes as "nerve-contact" with Flechsig and with God.[63] Aided by the vocabulary used by the voices that speak to him,[64] Schreber develops, during his years in the two asylums to which he was transferred after his brief second stay at Flechsig's clinic, an elaborate explanation of his "nervous illness."

That some *crime* has been committed is central to Schreber's delusion. Although suspects are named, Flechsig first among them, the way in which Schreber's ideas acquire their phrasing allows the identity of the culprit to change. To his basic explanation of nerve contact as contrary to the order of the world, he adds a historical and genealogical dimension. "I presume," Schreber writes, "that at one time a bearer of the name Flechsig—a human being carrying that name—succeeded in *abusing* nerve-contact granted him for the purpose of divine inspiration or some other reasons, in order *to retain his hold on the divine rays.*"⁶⁵ Schreber builds an ever-more complex narrative out of simple grammatical elements, combining proper names with a concept, and allowing that concept to imply a verb: "the leading roles . . . were played on the one hand by the names of Flechsig and Schreber (probably not specifying any individual member of these families), and on the other by the concept of *soul murder*"—which in one passage Schreber defines as "tak[ing] possession of another person's soul in order to prolong one's life at another soul's expense, or to secure some other advantages which outlast death,"⁶⁶ but in another place what he wrote on soul murder is, as a note explaining a truncated chapter indicates, not deemed fit to print.⁶⁷

The syntactic openness that results when the impulse to explain latches onto a proper name, yokes onto it the name of a crime, and connects the two with a verb, an openness that parallels the elliptical manner in which the "souls" speak,⁶⁸ allows Schreber himself to be positioned as the accused—and, of course, for him to be accused, albeit under the sign of negation, of "soul murder." Thus when he relates that "the crisis that broke upon the realms of God was caused by somebody having *committed soul murder,*" he adds that "at first Flechsig was named as the instigator of soul murder but of recent times in an attempt to reverse the facts [*Umkehr des Verhältnisses*] I myself have been 'represented' as the one who had committed soul murder."⁶⁹ In soul language, "representing" is "giving to a thing or a person a semblance different from its real nature (expressed in human terms 'of falsifying')."⁷⁰ When Schreber writes, employing the impersonal "one" (*man*), that "one did not want to admit that what had happened was not my fault [*ohne meine Schuld geschehen war*], but one always tended to reverse the blame by way of 'representing' [*das Schuldverhältnis im Wege des 'Darstellens' umzukehren*],"⁷¹ we can follow Freud and remove the "not" or "without" (*ohne*), and apply the rule that whenever it is a question of an *Umkehr* or *Umkehren,* another turn may be added in order to place in relief the thought, negated by Schreber, that he is the guilty one.⁷² That the other instances of *Darstellen* occur in the sphere of masturbation and "voluptuous excesses" will lead Freud to suspect a connection between "soul murder" and forbidden infantile sexual activity.⁷³

In an important elaboration of Schreber's narrative, his "unmanning," which, exchanging a causal for a teleological explanation, he believes to have been "for purposes *contrary to the Order of the World* (that is to say for the sexual satisfaction of a human being)"—namely, Flechsig[74]—is said to lead to a restoration, through repopulation, of the world that has been destroyed.[75] Having at the start of his second illness had the idea that it would be most pleasant to be a woman succumbing to sexual intercourse, an idea he would then have rejected had he been fully conscious[76]—an event that Freud and subsequent commentators debate a great deal—Schreber begins to see himself as having a woman's breasts, at which time his doctor finds that he is gaining weight (*zunehmende Leibesfülle*).[77] In broad outline, the emphasis of Schreber's narrative shifts from his having been a victim of crime—the destruction of his body is described in vivid detail—to a triumphal return with the "palm of victory" earned by his religious insights as well as his new role and gender.[78] "The scales of victory [*Wagschale des Sieges*] are coming down on my side more and more," Schreber writes, "the struggle against me continues to lose its previous hostile character, the growing soul-voluptuousness makes my physical condition and my other outward circumstances more bearable [*erträglicher*]."[79] Although the megalomania is typical of the paranoiac, the figure of the scales returns in the final pages in order to emphasize a judgment in his favor, or at least a tendency toward an alleviation of feelings of persecution that, ultimately, stem from his feelings of guilt. If dynamics of mourning operate, they do so in the background, at a different level. The feelings of voluptuousness—which, he says, are in no way masturbation[80]—have a higher purpose. Freud sees Schreber's delusional transformation as a sign of recovery—since it begins to bring him out of the psychosis. But the main delusion of persecution, which persists in his open letter to Flechsig that prefaces *Memoirs of My Nervous Illness*, remains.

The key theoretical claim made by Schreber throughout his *Memoirs* is that in his "nervous illness" the influences he describes come *from outside*, that his "nerves have been set in motion *from without*."[81] If what he sees comes from outside then it is, by definition, a vision and not a hallucination. This leads him into a polemic with the psychiatry of the day; Emil Kraepelin is named several times.[82] And in his open letter to Flechsig that prefaces the *Memoirs* he asks his doctor to entertain the possibility of there having been hypnotic or other suggestion. Although not supernatural, suggestion would also have been *from outside*. The explanation remains paranoid. (Not all of the commentary on Schreber, when it vilifies the father or the doctor, reproducing old engravings of the former's contraptions and quoting the latter's precepts, is free of the paranoia that besets the judge.) When Schreber makes a legal case for his discharge from the asylum, he emphasizes that he suffers not from a "mental illness" but from a "nervous illness."[83] His elaborate explanations and distinctions are thus also motivated by the existing legal code's reference to "mental illness." If he has a "nervous illness"—the supernatural one he describes—the state has no legal authority to detain him. He must be released—and is, but not because of his hair-splitting; although he falls ill again, never to recover, and perishes in an asylum in 1911.

Crisis of Judging

> The case of the delusional system of a paranoiac is similar: unless specially touched upon it will easily remain hidden from other people, and hardly be noticeable in his ordinary conduct, whereas in reality it forms the substrate of his mental life. It is therefore neither rare nor remarkable that paranoiacs although perhaps for a long time considered oddities, carry on their business sufficiently well and their professional duties in an orderly manner, can even work scientifically with success, although their mental life is seriously disturbed and they are in the throes of a delusional system which is frequently quite absurd. Such cases are known in large numbers to every psychiatrist of some experience, indeed they illustrate nicely the special features of paranoia. In this always chronic illness the patient may be disturbed by some event in the *modus vivendi* he has maintained towards the outer world, his pathological ideas collide in some way with his environment, he exceeds the limits of what is tolerable in his actions, and thus he is recognized as ill and treated as such. This is common experience; but it can hardly be denied that some cases of paranoia never reach the orbit of medical experience, but remain outside it, recognized perhaps only by their closest associates, and lead the ordinary life of a citizen without any marked disturbance. —Dr. Weber's Expert Report of 5th April 1902.[84]

Senatspräsident Schreber's crisis of judging first made itself manifest as an inability to gauge proportion, to give due weight to the matter at hand, and even to judge his own body weight. It evolved into an inability to define the culprit, notwithstanding a conviction that a crime had been committed and somebody was culpable. Psychoanalysis can be used to explain this in terms of a general theory of mourning, which, as I have shown, is also an account of the genesis of law. Law in its most basic form of "thou shalt" and "thou shalt not" makes its presence felt when the loss of an object—generalizable as the subject's withdrawal of libido from it—is experienced as murder of that object. The identity of the murderer can change. If mourning is the name we give to our response to loss, then to the extent that loss is experienced in this way, mourning may be regarded as the source of law as prescription and proscription. Schreber's crisis of judging is implicated in these dynamics.

We might infer—though this is, for understandable reasons, not alluded to in his *Memoirs*—that the judge's crisis extended to cases before him. From a psychoanalytic perspective, the symptom of this crisis was that, in spite of the enormous energy Schreber spends preparing an indictment of Professor Flechsig, and even God, for "soul murder," the only other identifiable culprit ends up being the judge himself. Schreber's self-accusation—veiled as it is—is what prevents him from carrying out his office as judge. In other words, it is *as if* he were to have asked himself: How can I mete out punishment if I myself am the one who must be punished? The "as if" needs to be underlined, since, for the paranoiac, it is not "I" who is to be punished. Any accusation of the self is an *Umkehrung* of the facts, and any "representation" to that effect is false. It is always only "he" who is culpable—of soul murder, or of any other crime. In other words, instead of being incapable of passing sentence, the paranoid judge will do so *only too well*. That contemporary US culture's hyperbolic investments in criminal prosecution follow such a pattern has recently been persuasively underlined by Vanessa Place in *The Guilt Project*.[85]

If law makes itself felt as a prohibition or prescription when loss is encoded as murder, then can there be, in all rigor, any act of judging that is not shadowed by the sort of crisis that besets Schreber and makes him unable to carry out his office? When matters come full circle, and Schreber submits his case for rescission of the tutelage imposed upon him by the Dresden District Court in March 1900, his psychiatrist, Dr. Weber, may have thought not. What is remarkable is that his judges appear to have differed. When Schreber's suit was decided on appeal at the Dresden Country Court in July 1902, the judges, apparently led by a former colleague of his,[86] observed that "even the District Court in the order placing him under tutelage held that he is still capable of presiding over a panel of Judges, of deciding the most intricate cases and delivering the most difficult counsel's opinions with striking juristical reasoning."[87] Both Schreber and his psychiatrist deny that he would be so capable, for the voices—or "interferences"—make it impossible for him to engage in sustained intellectual work.[88] The court is nevertheless so impressed by the part played by Schreber in the proceedings that it adduces it as a positive ground for deciding whether he would be incapable of managing his own affairs as a consequence of his mental illness—the criterion for tutelage under the Civil Code: "All this affords indisputable proof that in *this* field plaintiff has no need of protection by a guardian."[89] The legal documents pertaining to his appeal to rescind his tutelage, which he made the addenda to his *Memoirs,* evaluate, for the most part, Schreber's capacity to judge (*beurtheilen*) in spheres other than the juridical. His psychiatrist nevertheless appears to have grounds for suspecting that a more pervasive crisis of judging could spring from Schreber's paranoia. Dr. Weber writes, for instance, that "what objectively are delusions and hallucinations are to him unassailable truth and adequate motive for action. It follows from this that the patient's decisions at a given moment are quite unpredictable; he may follow and turn into action what his relatively intact mental powers dictate or he may act under the compulsion of his pathological mental processes."[90] Weber feebly cites the publication of the *Memoirs* as an example, and Schreber rightly challenges his statement as an unsubstantiated generalization.[91] Because the import of Weber's observations, stated in different ways in all three of his reports,[92] is that, since mental life forms a unity, delusional ideas from one sphere of thinking can encroach on other spheres, even if this is not readily apparent, attention is given to it by the judges too.[93] The court demands facts about what has happened, not theoretical speculation about what might.[94] What neither Schreber's psychiatrist nor his judges draw our attention to, however, is that Schreber's relentless indictment of Flechsig is a prime example of how an unpredictability could impinge upon the juridical sphere. In his well-crafted appeal of July 1901, Schreber himself writes that "it is correct that I have reported certain events which I must believe were true from the information of the voices that talked to me and which, if they were true and did refer to the *human being* Doctor Flechsig, could be calculated to lower him in public esteem, and if they were untrue would be libellous."[95] The court takes him to be referring to Flechsig's being "accused of soul-murder and worse," but decides that "even here plaintiff is not in any way talking for himself or acting on his own behalf, but only reporting what the voices of miraculous spirits told him."[96] Even though there is nothing that will shift Schreber's conviction that Flechsig is the culprit, the court can ignore this because it is not directly relevant to the matter at hand—namely whether Schreber foresees that Flechsig might have grounds for suing him should he publish his book. To claim to be "reporting" what the voices say might defend one against an accusation of libel (although it would be a long shot), but to base an indictment or judgment on their assumed truth is a different matter. The courts may, however, ignore Schreber's accusations and their pathological quality because, Schreber having been permanently retired in 1895 after being declared legally incompetent,[97] they are not ruling on his capacity to carry out the office of judge—even if, magnanimously, in *obiter dicta,* the District Court affirms it, and then in its *ratio decidendi,* the Country Court acknowledges his expertise in pleading his case in the course of ruling on his capacity to judge in his own affairs. There is indeed no evidence to show that any actual case before Schreber was influenced by his crisis of judging. The terms of the decision of the court to release him from tutelage nevertheless could suggest that his fellow legal minds, if only by their express affirmation of the contrary when the matter of his judgeship is moot,[98] knew very well what the effect of Schreber's madness might be: a mania of indictment. Where there is only guilt (for "me"), there can be no nonguilt (for "him"). The scales will tilt only one way.

I began this essay by showing a continuity, in the unfolding of Freud's thought, between the case of Schreber and *Totem and Taboo*. It is possible, however, to object that the "moral precepts and restrictions" referred to in *Totem and Taboo* do not constitute *law* in the sense in which a lawmaker or jurist would understand it, thereby challenging the idea that Freud's text gives a fable for the origins of law. Although Freud does not assimilate these precepts and prohibitions with law, since they are neither systematic nor grounded in reason—something that they, like the compulsions of the neurotic, share with Kant's categorical imperative—he never departs from the assumption of his contemporaries that they evolve into positive law.[99] And, indeed, in psychoanalytic tradition, there is little doubt that Freud "wanted to demonstrate the origin of universal Law in the primal crime in *Totem and Taboo* in 1912."[100] More striking, however, is the fact that the explanation given by Freud for these precepts and prohibitions does indeed lend them a systematic and reasoned character. A set of conditions must be satisfied before the "concept of 'crime'" can emerge.[101] Although the story of the murder of the primal father and its consequences are chronological, these conditions are logical: if remorse, then guilt; if guilt, then "crime"; if crime, then "precepts and prohibitions." This is usefully viewed as a structure of co-implication. Yet when we think of law in the narrow sense, the order of logical priority appears to be the reverse: if law, then crime; if crime, then guilt—or rather, culpability. In a naïve way, we may see this as being the shape of judgment. But also in a not-so-naïve way: the theory of judging as subsumption under rule is an elaboration upon this structure.[102] Freud leads us to suspect that with the system of logical co-implication that is set to work in judgment, there is always the possibility of a reversal of logical priority because the condition of possibility for law itself must be thought of as giving primacy to guilt.

Although Freud does not appear to have addressed directly the implications of psychoanalysis for judges at law, he does investigate the cognitive activity of judgment in a number of texts, dating back to the "Project for a Scientific Psychology" (1895).[103] Perhaps the most far-reaching of these works is "Negation" (1925), a short and dense essay in which Freud enters into its "psychological origin."[104] There Freud writes that "the function of judgement is concerned in the main with two sorts of decisions. It affirms or disaffirms the possession by a thing of a particular attribute; and it asserts or disputes that a presentation has an existence in reality."[105] As Jean Hyppolite observed in explicating "Negation" for Lacan's seminar of 1953–54, this is a working distinction "in accordance with what everyone learns about the elements of philosophy."[106] Freud tells us that, in the genesis of the human subject, the conditions of possibility for a judgment of attribute come before those for a judgment of existence. By this time, Freud has formulated two principles of mental functioning—namely, the pleasure principle and the reality principle—and is working with the second topography (id, ego, superego).[107] In terms that anticipate Klein, Freud explains that a judgment of attribute originates with the pleasure ego: an object that I take in is "good," whereas an object that I expel is "bad." A judgment of existence is a function of the reality ego, which, according to Freud's account, depends on the pleasure ego:

> Experience has shown the subject that it is not only important whether a thing (an object of satisfaction for him) possesses the "good" attribute and so deserves to be taken into his ego, but also whether it is there in the external world, so that he can get hold of it whenever he needs it. . . . The first and immediate aim, therefore, of reality-testing is, not to *find* an object in real perception which corresponds to the one presented, but to *refind* such an object, to convince oneself that it is still there. . . . The reproduction of a perception as a presentation is not always a faithful one; it may be modified by omissions, or changed by the merging of various elements. . . . But it is evident that a precondition for the setting up of reality-testing is that objects shall have been lost which once brought real satisfaction.[108]

When Freud writes of the subject's refinding of an object in reality, it is presupposed that an object that brought satisfaction in reality will have been *lost*. Structurally, then, here too the origins of judgment lie in mourning, since the former shares its basic conditions of possibility with the latter. It looks to be axiomatic for Freud that it is only objects that satisfy that are lost, and are refound in reality.[109] But the object can be distorted in its presentation. We see this assumption working in Freud's interpretation of Schreber: once loved, the object now persecutes. Thus, if a judgment of existence depends on a judgment of attribute,[110] "He exists" presupposes that "He is good" ("I love him"), but in paranoia this is distorted as "He hates me." For the paranoid, then, the object that is refound only exists in this distorted form. Thus, for the paranoid judge, "He is guilty" is the only possible verdict, since if "he" exists, then he is also guilty. The question then becomes whether the accused or defendant in a given case could occupy the position of that "he." "Negation" thus adds another dimension to explaining how, because of an aberration in the refinding of the object on which "reality testing" depends, a given judgment can shift tracks.[111] In Freud's case history of Schreber, when the proposition "He hates me" is produced through the contradiction of the primal sentence "I love him," love turns to hate, but, because "I" cannot be the subject of the transformed sentence, or because hatred must be justified psychically—propositional and economic models of the psyche meet without necessarily coinciding—"I" must turn into "he." Once this has taken place, the "he" in the proposition "He hates me" must be refound in reality. And, in paranoia, "he" *is* refound. This is what Freud emphasizes when he talks about the repressed returning from without; as Lacan, who decisively linked the Schreber case with Freud's essay on "Negation," keeps reminding us, it *does*, for the psychotic.[112] In Schreber, "he" takes on a name: Flechsig. For a paranoid judge, it could just happen that a defendant or respondent in a given case assumes the relevant position. Under certain circumstances a judge might find herself shifting from one sequence to the other, so that her guilt becomes his culpability: "I am guilty" therefore "He is culpable." My guilt becomes his culpability. This would be a crisis of judging. Is there any evidence that this has ever happened, or might ever have happened; and what would count as evidence? If only the distortion is available to the paranoid, and not its underlying mechanism, since paranoia rules out "I am guilty" as a conscious proposition, if such a thing happened it is unlikely that anybody would ever know for certain that it had.

Jury Duty

In the United States of America, the labor of judging is a citizen's duty. This brings me to an anecdote. In June 2012 I served as a juror in a civil case in New York City. As a juror I was empowered to judge, something that I am often uncomfortable doing. Toward the end of the trial, after experiencing a stinging sensation, I looked in the mirror to find on my left shoulder blade the characteristic bull's-eye left by the bite of a tick carrying Lyme disease (the deer tick, or *ixodes scapularis*). I also had a serious headache, a sore neck, and aching knees, all elements in the classic syndrome. My doctor immediately prescribed a four-week course of antibiotics. But two antibody tests came back negative. Although false negatives are common with the test, I am tempted now to wonder in retrospect whether I was not going through my own crisis of judging. The target on my back reminded me of the letter "M" chalked behind the left shoulder of the child murderer played by Peter Lorre in Fritz Lang's 1931 film *M*. There was surely some overdetermination in that *ixodes scapularis* had, literalizing its Greek name, chosen to stick itself to my shoulder blade. And to be a juror places a heavy burden of responsibility on a citizen's shoulders. I was well enough, following deliberations, to add my vote to what was a unanimous verdict in favor of the respondent, but perhaps my resistance to judging had made its penumbra of paranoia felt through hysterical conversion, which Freud teaches us will find the physical path of least resistance.

NOTES

1. In addition to the works by Freud cited below, one thinks of Melanie Klein, "Mourning and Its Relation to Manic-Depressive States" (1940), in *Love, Guilt and Reparation, and Other Works 1921–1945* (London: Vintage, 1998), 344–69; Alexander Mitscherlich and Ruth Mitscherlich, *The Inability to Mourn: Principles of Collective Behavior*, trans. Beverley R. Placzek (New York: Grove, 1975); Nicolas Abraham and Maria Torok, *The Shell and the Kernel: Renewals of Psychoanalysis*, trans. Nicholas Rand (Chicago: University of Chicago Press, 1994); Jacques Derrida, *The Work of Mourning*, trans. Michael Naas and Pascale-Anne Brault (Chicago: University of Chicago Press, 2001); and numerous other works that take their bearings from these. For their rigorous and insightful responses to an earlier version of my essay, I thank Austin Sarat, Lawrence Douglas, Adam Sitze, and Peter Goodrich.

2. Sigmund Freud, "Mourning and Melancholia" (1917), *The Standard Edition of the Complete Psychological Works of Sigmund Freud* (London: Hogarth, 1953–), vol. 14, 251.

3. Sigmund Freud, *Totem and Taboo: Some Points of Agreement between the Mental Lives of Savages and Neurotics* (1913), *Standard Edition*, vol. 13, 143, 159. It is important to

note that, in other passages in *Totem and Taboo*, the affection toward/ from the father functions as the counter-force to hatred; it is as if what we call the law—the prescription to love—is simply the influence of this force. To have presupposed a prohibition on hatred would have been to beg the question of the origins of law. In technical terms, whereas we also find a topographical explanation—"pushed under"—in these later passages, in earlier ones dynamic and economic models come to the fore without appeal being made to psychic topography. "The prohibition [against touching] is accepted, since it finds support from powerful internal forces [i.e., from the child's loving relation to the authors of the prohibition], and proves stronger than the instinct which is seeking to express itself in the touching." Freud, *Totem and Taboo*, 29 and 29n.2; see also 49.

4. The word for *remorse* in Afrikaans is *berou*, which is cognate with *rou*.
5. Freud, *Totem and Taboo*, 159.
6. Ibid., 160.
7. For instance, in "Formulations on the Two Principles of Mental Functioning" (1911), *Standard Edition*, vol. 12, 225–26; "Dostoevsky and Parricide" (1928), *Standard Edition*, vol. 21, 183–85.
8. Freud, "Dostoevsky and Parricide," 189.
9. Sigmund Freud, "The Expert Opinion in the Halsmann Case" (1931), *Standard Edition* vol. 21, 252; translation modified.
10. The relevant chronology is from F. Baumeyer, "The Schreber Case," *International Journal of Psycho-Analysis* 37 (1956): 65.
11. Daniel Paul Schreber, *Memoirs of My Nervous Illness*, trans. Ida MacAlpine and Richard Hunter (1955; Cambridge, MA: Harvard University Press, 1988), 51, 53. When making reference to this book, I use the page numbers from the original German edition, provided by MacAlpine and Hunter in the margins of their translation.
12. Ibid., 56.
13. Ibid., 94, 127.
14. Ibid., 61–62.
15. Ibid., 125–26.
16. Ibid., xi.
17. Freud, *Psycho-Analytic Notes on an Autobiographical Account of a Case of Paranoia (Dementia Paranoides)* (1911), *Standard Edition*, vol. 12, 41.
18. Freud, "The Dynamics of Transference" (1912), *Standard Edition*, vol. 12, 100.
19. Freud, *Psycho-Analytic Notes*, 42.
20. Ibid., 43.
21. Ibid., 62.
22. *J. Edgar* (dir. Clint Eastwood, 2011), the latest mass-entertainment version of the tale, of course does nothing to dislodge the prejudice.
23. George Orwell, *Nineteen Eighty-four* (1949; New York: Plume, 1983), 18–19, 245. On Orwell's engagement with psychoanalysis, see Alex Zwerdling, "Orwell's Psychopolitics," in *The Future of Nineteen Eighty-four*, ed. Ejner J. Jensen (Ann Arbor: University of Michigan Press, 1984), 87–110. For an insightful Kleinian psychoanalytic reading of *Nineteen Eighty-four*, see Martha C. Nussbaum, "The Death of Pity: Orwell and American Political Life," in *On Nineteen Eighty-four: Orwell and Our Future*, ed. Abbot Gleason, Jack Goldsmith, and Martha C. Nussbaum (Princeton, NJ: Princeton University Press, 2005), 279–99.
24. John Forrester, *Language and the Origins of Psychoanalysis* (New York: Columbia University Press, 1980), 141–65, esp. 154–58.
25. Freud, *Psycho-Analytic Notes*, 63.

26. See also Karl Abraham, "The Psycho-Sexual Differences between Hysteria and Dementia Praecox" (1908), in *Selected Papers of Karl Abraham*, trans. Douglas Bryan and Alix Strachey (New York: Basic Books, 1953), 74–75.

27. Sigmund Freud, "Psychoanalytische Bemerkungen über einen autobiographisch beschriebenen Fall von Paranoia (Dementia paranoides)," *Gesammelte Werke*, vol. 8, 299.

28. I allude to the Rat Man. See Freud, "Notes upon a Case of Obsessional Neurosis" (1909), *Standard Edition*, vol. 10, esp. 189–92.

29. Freud, *Psycho-Analytic Notes*, 63–65.

30. Jacques Lacan, *The Seminar of Jacques Lacan; Book III: The Psychoses 1955–1956*, trans. Russell Grigg (New York: Norton, 1993), 53. Page numbers for *The Psychoses*, which are given in the margin of Grigg's translation, refer to the original French edition.

31. Forrester, *Language and the Origins of Psychoanalysis*, 155. In his careful account of Freud's "propositional analysis," Forrester writes that "Freud's propositional model was intended to contribute to a general theory of the paranoiac psychoses. All of these, he thought, arise from the repression of a primary 'idea,' a 'primal sentence,' expressive of homosexual love. The idea that suffers repression and subsequent transformation can best be expressed in the form of a simple sentence: 'I love him.'" Forrester continues, arguing that "the mechanism of projection is not a necessary condition for this group of transformations. Rather, one might wish to couch the principle as follows: admissible transformations of the primal sentence must not include the subject as first person of the statement." In other words, as Forrester convincingly shows, a topology of projection and introjection comes into conflict with a grammatical model. His account of the repression of the primal sentence does not, however, explain what Freud calls the "impelling unconscious feeling" in paranoia being not love but hate, a difficulty that Forrester partially, and somewhat confusingly, acknowledges in a footnote: "One notes that this proposition, 'I hate him,' seems to disobey the principle of the exclusion of the first person subject," upon which he cites Laplanche and Pontalis as pointing out that "the hatred felt for the other [is] the primary symptom [sic] of paranoia," when the *symptom* is the other's hatred of me. Forrester, *Language and the Origins of Psychoanalysis*, 154–55, 240 nn. 23, 25.

32. Lacan, *The Psychoses*, 54.

33. Freud, *Psycho-Analytic Notes*, 47.

34. Another line of reasoning, apparent in Freud's "Dostoevsky and Parricide," is that the actual death of a father, by realizing the son's parricidal phantasy, would intensify the repression of parricidal wishes and hence also the burden of guilt. Freud, "Dostoevsky and Parricide," 186.

35. Freud, *Psycho-Analytic Notes*, 51.

36. Ibid., 52–53.

37. Ibid., 71.

38. Ibid., 72.

39. Klein, "Contribution to the Psychogenesis of Manic-Depressive States" (1935), in *Love, Guilt and Reparation*, 262.

40. Ibid., 262.

41. Klein, "Notes on Some Schizoid Mechanisms" (1946), *Envy and Gratitude, and Other Works, 1946–1963* (1975; London: Virago, 1988), 15.

42. Klein, "Contribution to the Psychogenesis of Manic-Depressive States," 285–86.

43. Ibid., 286.

44. Melanie Klein, "Notes on Some Schizoid Mechanisms," 14.

45. Ibid., 15.

46. Klein, "Contribution to the Psychogenesis of Manic-Depressive States," 264.

47. The consequences of a diagnosis of schizophrenia for interpreting Schreber's case are explored most fully by Ida MacAlpine and Richard A. Hunter, "Translators' Analysis of the Case" (1955), in Daniel Paul Schreber, *Memoirs of My Nervous Illness*, trans. MacAlpine and Hunter (Cambridge, MA: Harvard University Press, 1988), 369–416.

48. Although locating their shared conditions of possibility, Klein marks a clear divergence between depression and paranoia; Klein, "Psychogenesis of Manic-Depressive States," 269.

49. Correspondingly, as Peter Goodrich notes in an important series of articles addressing the lacuna, lawyers have in fact not addressed the case of Schreber; Peter Goodrich, "The Judge's Two Bodies: The Case of Daniel Paul Schreber," *Law and Critique* 26, no. 2 (2015): 117–33; "Miscarriages of Transmission: Body, Text, and Method," *International Journal of Law and Psychiatry* 48 (2016): 77–84.

50. Schreber, *Memoirs*, 35.

51. Ibid., 35.

52. Baumeyer, "Schreber Case," 61.

53. Schreber, *Memoirs*, 35.

54. Sigmund Freud, *Psycho-Analytic Notes*, 35.

55. In a different interpretation alert to dynamics of law and working with psychoanalysis, Peter Goodrich decisively reads Schreber's candidacy for the Reichstag as a bid to escape law for politics, which Goodrich views as opposed to law by being a "world of . . . of greater creativity and the embodiment of passions." Because Schreber's attempted escape into politics was unsuccessful, according to Goodrich, Schreber cultivates femininity, which he himself views as definitively precluding a career in law. The idea of politics as an escape from law, or as opposed to law, however, is not a construction made by Schreber, who, as Goodrich notes, does not reveal in his *Memoirs* that his candidacy was unsuccessful. Building on these assumptions, Goodrich makes an interesting case for the critical significance of Schreber's position, historically: "an extreme but recognizable revision of juridical theology or, to paraphrase Kantorowicz, 'the judge, Law's son, becomes Law's father.' . . . Schreber's revival and rewriting of juridical theology offers a radical critique of the legal philosophy of the late 19th century and specifically of the resurgent neo-Kantian science of law that coincided with the promulgation of the German Civil Code of 1900." Goodrich, "Judge's Two Bodies," 120–22.

56. Eric Santner, *My Own Private Germany: Daniel Paul Schreber's Secret History of Modernity* (Princeton, NJ: Princeton University Press, 1996), 26.

57. Ibid., 26.

58. Pointing to the fact that Schreber arranged the publication of a new edition of his father's book, Peter Goodrich argues, contra Santner, that "it is not authority that is the primary issue," but rather the "nihilism of legal reason," its lack of "human passion." On Goodrich's subtle reading of the *Memoirs*, what Schreber's father could not give him was desire. Goodrich, "Judge's Two Bodies," 131.

59. According to Kennedy, "No one will be able to say much about 'what kind of judge he is' from my decision to go along with the collective initial impression [of how the law applies to a given case]. Going along would be costless in terms of legitimacy. My legitimating power is depleted or augmented only when I try to do something out of the ordinary. . . . I can build up my legitimating power through instances of persuading people through legal argument. If they have had the experience of my 'being right' before, experiences of my changing their view of the law, then they will be susceptible in the future to believe what I tell them the law is, quite independently of the argument I can muster." Duncan Kennedy, "Freedom and Constraint in Adjudication: A Critical Phenomenology," in *Legal Reasoning: Collected Essays* (Aurora, CO: Davies Group, 2008), 29–30.

60. Baumeyer, "Schreber Case," 61.
61. The same qualification is made by Schreber in his appeal for rescission of his tutelage, with reference to his psychiatrist, Dr. Weber. Schreber, *Memoirs*, 424.
62. Ibid., 37.
63. Ibid., 44.
64. Ibid., 12n.6.
65. Ibid., 25.
66. Ibid., 22–23.
67. Ibid., 33.
68. Ibid., 48n.26.
69. Ibid., 23.
70. Ibid., 128n.62.
71. Ibid., 160.
72. Freud, *Psycho-Analytic Notes*, 52–53.
73. Ibid., 56.
74. Schreber, *Memoirs*, 61, 56.
75. Ibid., 51–52, 114–15, 124, 177, 289, 293.
76. Ibid., 36.
77. Ibid., 384. I thank Louisa Barta for bringing to my attention the connection, in this passage, between Schreber's increasing bodyweight and his feminization.
78. Ibid., 293.
79. Ibid.
80. Ibid., 282.
81. Ibid., 47.
82. Ibid., 78, and 78n.42.
83. Ibid., 268.
84. Ibid., 458.
85. Vanessa Place, *The Guilt Project: Rape, Morality, and Law* (New York: Other Press, 2010), esp. 211–29.
86. The judge in Schreber's case was Hardraht; no first name given. In an annual directory of German courts published in 1895, the name Hardraht appears among the *Räthen* of the *Oberlandsgericht* in Dresden, whereas Schreber's still appears among the *Senatspräsidenten*, indicating that his retirement was not yet in effect although he had been ill since November 1893. Carl Pfafferoth, *Jahrbuch der deutschen Gerichtsverfassung* (Berlin: Karl Heymann, 1895), 122.
87. Schreber, *Memoirs*, 476.
88. Ibid., 399. Schreber, however, maintains that he would be able to do so in *writing*; *Memoirs*, 426.
89. Ibid., 494, 502; cf. 479–80.
90. Ibid., 401–2.
91. Ibid., 427–28.
92. See also ibid., 385, 470–71.
93. Ibid., 498.
94. Ibid., 500.
95. Ibid., 444.
96. Ibid., 514.
97. Zvi Lothane, *In Defense of Schreber: Soul Murder and Psychiatry* (Hillsdale, NJ: Analytic Press, 1992), 93.
98. Evidently Schreber, after his release in 1902, "occasionally did some private work which was always faultless."Baumeyer, "Schreber Case," 65.
99. Freud, *Totem and Taboo*, xiv, 18, 24, 39, 123.

100. Jacques Lacan, "A Theoretical Introduction to the Functions of Psychoanalysis in Criminology," in *Écrits: The First Complete Edition in English*, trans. Bruce Fink (New York: Norton, 2006), 130. I cite the page numbers corresponding to the 1966 French edition of *Écrits*, which appear in the margin of Fink's translation.

101. Freud, *Totem and Taboo*, 159.

102. See, for example, Kennedy, "Freedom and Constraint in Adjudication." It is clear from the addenda to the *Memoirs* that Schreber's judges reasoned in precisely this fashion.

103. Freud, "Project for a Scientific Psychology" (1895), *Standard Edition*, vol. 1, 328ff.

104. Freud, "Negation" (1925), *Standard Edition*, vol. 19, 236.

105. Ibid., 236.

106. "Appendix I: A Spoken Commentary on Freud's 'Verneinung' by Jean Hyppolite," in Jacques Lacan, *Écrits: The First Complete Edition in English*, trans. Bruce Fink (New York: Norton, 2006), 883.

107. Freud, "Formulations on the Two Principles of Mental Functioning" (1911), *Standard Edition*, vol. 12, 213–26.

108. Freud, "Negation," 237–38.

109. See Lacan, *Psychoses*, 97–98.

110. Lacan notes this "unusual priority," adding that "there is in Freud's dialectic an initial division into the good and the bad that can only be understood if we interpret it as the rejection of a primordial signifier." *Psychoses*, 171.

111. Freud also notes that "negation" is the "successor" to primitive expulsion of what is "bad." He notes that judgment as an intellectual function depends on the "symbol" for negation, which gives the subject a "first measure of freedom from the consequences of repression and the compulsion of the pleasure principle." Freud, "Negation," 239. In other words, if repression (withdrawal of libido; distortion: good represented as bad) and the pleasure principle (refinding of good object) can combine to produce paranoid delusion, then it is only through negation as symbolic—that is, repeatable apart from context of specific expulsions?—that judgments of existence are no longer subject to the conditions of possibility for judgments of attribute that, for Freud, are their precursor. This appears to be what is at stake when Lacan makes a key part of his explanation of paranoia, and psychosis more generally, "the rejection of a primordial signifier." Lacan, *Psychoses*, 171. See also Lacan, "Response to Jean Hyppolite's Commentary on Freud's 'Verneinung,'" and "On a Question Prior to Any Possible Treatment of Psychosis," *Écrits*, 381–99, 531–83.

112. Lacan, *Psychoses*, 20–21.

6
Does Mourning Become the Law?
Commodity Fetishism and Political Contestation

CATHERINE KELLOGG

The title of this book—*Law and Mourning*—immediately brings to mind two of Gillian Rose's last books. *Mourning Becomes the Law* is a meditation on post-Hegelian philosophy, and *Love's Work* is an autobiographical reflection on her life, her love, and her work.[1] Both books were written as she battled ovarian cancer, and the shadow of her imminent death is a constant theme. I loved these books and read them with a strong sense of wanting very much to speak with her about their themes, but I heard of them only after she died. My contribution to this volume is thus motivated by that wanting-to-speak with Gillian Rose, a feeling I have not lost, even after twenty years. But I find I run into trouble in my first breath because in responding to these two books I immediately come up against two contrary directives. Let me explain.

In the autobiographical text, *Love's Work*, Rose describes metaphysics most aptly as the perplexity of finding the path from the law of the concept to the purely particular; as she puts it, it is the task of finding the way between the *idea* of the nose to *this* stubbornly snub one.[2] In the philosophical text, *Mourning Becomes the Law*, Rose rails against what she perceives as deconstruction's *attack* on metaphysics, which is to say, deconstruction's attack on the task of finding that path. Most damningly, she argues that because of what she calls "postmodern" thinkers, justice, freedom and the good have not *lost* their metaphysical guarantee, but were never metaphysically guaranteed to begin with, the lost object that postmodernism mourns is not gone, but was *always missing*. This has left postmodern thinkers in a state of interminable grief, a state in which mourning can never be completed. The interminability of this grief means that mourning itself, rather than justice or the good, "becomes the law."

Interestingly, despite railing against deconstruction, Rose writes in its style, with both hands, as it were; the philosophical text cut across and through with the autobiography. And whereas the philosophical text is concerned with the law, justice, and the good, it is beautifully illuminated by the autobiographical one, which is concerned, characteristically, with her loves, her illness, and her work. In this sense, in her writing, she has in fact *described* a path from her singular, unrepeatable life to the universality of philosophy. Now, there is something most interesting going on here. For while the philosophical text ends with the bleak thought that she may die before her time, the autobiography ends with the announcement that reason has always been radically ungrounded. Strikingly, these irreconcilable endings—the personal cry ending the "philosophical," and the triumphant philosophical pronouncement ending the "autobiographical"—form a *chiasmus* that itself describes the rhythm of deconstructive reading: what Derrida might call a double bind.

Indeed, the bind I found myself in—the contrary directives—is most aptly described by the claim Derrida ascribes to Walter Benjamin: "Translate me, but, whatever you do, don't translate me."[3] What this injunction attempts to capture is that while the desire to be translated is the desire to be understood, that is, to make an idiomatic expression or experience understandable—"translate me"—there is also a second desire at work: the desire to remain intact, the desire not to be betrayed: "whatever you do, don't translate me." Rhetorically I notice she has made Benjamin's very entreaty: translate me, but whatever you do, don't translate me.

Do I take her at her word, then, that deconstruction is the monster ravaging contemporary philosophy? Or do I take a scholarly tone and point out that for all her claims to the contrary, she has nonetheless written in a deconstructive style? Neither of these suit, for the truth of the matter is that reading her voluptuous philosophy was an intimate experience, and one from which I emerged feeling something like love. On this basis, I feel bound by the injunction to respect her; to leave her thought be and to speak for itself. But at the same time, I am drawn by my respect for her work to want to argue with her, to tell her that she missed some of the most important dimensions of deconstructive thought. For instance, despite her claim that without completing the task of mourning we lose the possibility of political discrimination, I would argue that mourning can no more be completed than can the task of enumerating all of the possible variations on human noses. For mourning is thought's *own* gesture, and its aim is to tidy up the remainder between structures of repetition—like language or law or philosophy itself—on the one hand, and those countless possibilities on the other. On the reading I provide here, then, "mourning" is another name for the *aporia* of metaphysics; the endless and unavoidable negotiation between the irreplaceability of the singular and the law of the concept.

If it is just the interminability of mourning that Rose would contest, we can perhaps understand it. For knowing that she was dying as she wrote these books throws her palpable desire for an origin and, by implication, for a return into a stark relief. However, her beloved Hegel himself can be read as positing the impossibility of an origin. Indeed, I have argued elsewhere that Hegel's notion of 'mechanical memory' acts in fact as a kind of double forgetting.[4] It is meant to draw the mind away from the fact the singular thing itself is *not* the origin of the word or the sign; in a certain sense, then, to encourage mind to forget that there is *nothing to forget*. Mechanical memory is the process by which Hegel suggests that Mind can be led away from the unthinkable: away from the necessary *loss* at work in the path from the peculiarity of each instance to the law of the concept.

However, the implications of this loss are momentous. If representation cannot be made complete because it relies upon a negativity for which it cannot account, then the stability of meaning and knowledge is always more uncertain than it seems. At the same time, if knowledge cannot be made certain, neither can it be compensated for by *belief*. For even though the singular can never be represented as such, neither is it like God, radically exterior to thought. Rather, the singular is always a disruptive force *internal* to representation. In this sense, neither reason nor God can work to guarantee philosophy. Philosophy is always radically unguaranteed, an unguaranteeability which Derrida calls the "risk of absolute surprise" that is nothing less than the risk of politics.

Thus, while philosophy attempts to enclose thought, both philosophy and thought are always necessarily opened by what thought cannot think. Philosophy is always necessarily breached. That this breach or opening is intolerable to thought or to philosophy does not prevent it from happening. On Jacques Derrida's analysis, this opening has a name: it is deconstruction. It is for this reason that deconstruction is not a 'thing' at all; rather, as Derrida says, "Deconstruction takes place, it is an event that does not await the deliberation, consciousness or organization of a subject."[5]

This event of deconstruction has been most scandalously formulated by Derrida as "justice." However, this statement is less scandalous than it might seem, for even in its most commonplace meaning, "justice" refers to the coming together of the singular instance and a general law. Justice, in other words, is understood to be the matching of a singular occurrence to a rule or law so general, so universal, that it can accommodate even that unforeseeable eventuality. Now, despite the impossibility of just such an encounter, *justice happens anyway.* There are situations, in other words, in which we might argue that justice has been done. This impossibility is made possible by virtue of a strange occurrence in the law itself: as something like the phenomenon of case law indicates, the uniqueness of each case means that the law is transformed—it is remade—with each singular application of it. Importantly, however, because the law is remade in each of its applications, it cannot call on anything that predates it for its own legitimacy. In this regard, a judge's decision is always elementally ungrounded; this is the "mystical foundation" of the law to which Derrida refers, and it is equally the source of the law's "force." This impossible event, then—the meeting of the unrepeatable occurrence and the newly made law—is nothing other than law deconstructing. The deconstruction of the law through its encounter with the unrepeatable singular occurrence—the remaking of the law in order to accommodate the singular infraction for which, in order to be law, it must have always-already been designed—*is* justice.

To demonstrate this, it is helpful to remember Derrida's insistence that Marx's *own* unthematized notion of justice is predicated upon just such an insight. Thus, while Gillian Rose reserves a special kind of exasperation for Derrida's Marx—that there is no materialism in Derrida's Marx, that his call for a New International is most annoying in that it must be very secret indeed if it can include no bodies—I think she might be surprised to hear me agree with her, but with my own exasperation. For Derrida never claimed that his reading of Marx should or could replace Marx himself. Indeed, it seems clear to me that Derrida did not so much claim deconstruction for Marxism, but has rather indicated a certain deconstructive moment at work in Marx; indicated a genealogical debt or inheritance that he would not renounce. In this sense, Derrida's reading of Marx is not significantly different than his reading of many others: deconstruction's strength is that it does not present itself as a new way of thinking philosophically about *politics:* rather, it offers a way of rethinking the political itself, that realm of negotiation between the purely particular and the law of the concept.

The important differences between Rose and Derrida's readings of Hegel and Marx are made most clear when looking at how they respectively understand the fetishism of commodities; that famously difficult and important part of volume 1, chapter 1 of *Capital*. Marx began that analysis, we remember, by looking at the commodity from two points of view: as a "use-value," a *quality,* an object outside of us that satisfies our desires in some way, and as an "exchange-value," a relation that appears, at first sight, to be *quantitative*. Rose insists that use-values have a kind of ontological status insofar as it is possible to argue that, in a certain sense, there *was* an intact, self-identical *quality* prior to the object's *quantification* or commodification—before the "sensuous object" was thrown into the system of equivalences. It becomes most important to make that argument when talking about the commodity whose expenditure—like the proverbial goose that lays the golden egg—produces more value in being consumed than it takes to produce: namely, human labor power. Importantly for my purposes, because all commodities' quantification results from the flattening out, the abstraction (or killing) of the labor power congealed within them, there is, consequently, a "spirit" that emerges from that "death." On Derrida's reading of Marx, on the other hand, what is buried in the commodity must be understood to be *un*dead: it is not a disembodied soul but a *specter*. It makes no sense to speak of an original, authentic qualitative object—a singular object, or a singular "moment" of laboring time—that became "lost" through the processes of commodification. Indeed, on his reading of Marx, the social practices of capitalist production themselves are what *produce* the illusion of a qualitative, self-identical object. Thus mourning can never restore a "lost paradise" because it was never lost. More pointedly, Derrida's analysis suggests that mourning "abstraction" actually inscribes absolute loss *within the law itself,* whether that's within the law of appropriation governing capital or within positive law. Insofar as mourning is thought's own gesture, meant to tidy up the remains of capitalization, in fact, it *covers over* or depoliticizes commodification, and so is, in fact, *complicit* with the very processes Rose decries. In short, I argue that Rose's reading of Marx ultimately *spiritualizes* law, whereas Derrida's *politicizes* it.

In what follows, I demonstrate that following Derrida's reading of Marx, this understanding of "use-value" wherein there is a referent for a simple, homely, self-identical object designed simply for human use, is itself a kind of fable. Indeed, it is a fable that works as compensatory reinstatement of an imaginary lost unity. From this point of view, Gillian Rose's desire to mourn the spirit of dead labor time congealed within it is a nostalgic strategy that works to depoliticize the very process of fetishization Marx's analysis tried to politicize in the first place.

Mourning, Law, and Commodity Fetishism

The point of contention between Rose and Derrida emerges when Derrida suggests that the sensuous thing, the object that Marx analyzes as both use and exchange-value, was *never identical to itself* as a sensuous thing. Specifically, Derrida says that the thing's haunting does not *begin* when it becomes an exchange value, or when it enters into exchange. Rather, Derrida says that the haunting or spectralization of the thing "began before the said exchange-value, at the threshold of the value of value in general." This is because, as he says, "the use-value"—the simple table waiting to enter into exchange—"is in advance contaminated, that is, preoccupied, inhabited, haunted by its other."[6] Rose responds by saying that while Derrida is quite right to notice that the commodity *exchanged* is haunted by the laboring activity congealed within it, she goes on to say that "once *use-value* is also conceived as 'phantasmagoric,' then the world of capital circulates among the crowds of dim and doubtfully real persons who are equally insubstantial whether they stand for wage-labour or the personification of the commodity."[7] In other words, once *use*-value is understood as a retrospective creation, as Derrida proposes, one loses the entire point of Marx's analysis that goes to show that the commodification of human labor power is precisely the condition for all commodities *as commodities* in the first place.

What Derrida is pointing to—and what infuriates Rose—is a fundamental *undecidability* at work in Marx's analysis of the commodity. What is undecidable is whether the commodity emerges before or after the process of "capitalization." On Derrida's reading, Marx's writing suggests two contradictory things at once: both that the table stands quietly as a use-value until it enters into exchange, *and* that the commodity's valuation *precedes* even its vocation as a "use-value." Derrida says that while Marx does seem to imply that there was an original "use-value purified of everything that makes for exchange value," this itself suggests that there was a commodity *form before itself,* for without that commodity form there would be no way that the object could "be identified throughout its repetitions."⁸ Derrida's point is that if you read Marx carefully, the status of the commodity is equivocal: on one reading, the simple quality emerges as a commodity—which is to say, as a quantitative relation—*only* with its exchange. On another reading, the object is "commodified" in a strange sense *prior* to its commodification.

In order to understand Derrida's point, we have to see that there are two modes of commodification at work in Marx's analysis that are not equivalent. There are two modes of abstraction that produce the object as exchange *and* as use-value. The first is simply idealization or abstraction itself; indeed, this mode of commodification is what Marx calls the commodity-*form*. To imagine that the table once sat quietly, identical to itself, or that there was a unique "moment" congealed as "labour time" is to cover over the question of how those things or events—those "singularities," if you will—became representable, intelligible, or recognizable as "things" or "events" at all. It is to assume an "experience" of self-identity or of singularity. But Derrida points out that "the only experience the singular can have is [an] experience of loss." In its original "iteration" as a "table" or as "labouring activity," both the object and the subjective determinants of value were *already* lost. As Derrida says: "In its original iterability . . . a use-value is thrown onto the market of equivalences. This is not simply a bad thing, even if the use-value is always *at risk* of losing its soul in the commodity. The commodity is a 'born cynic' because it effaces differences, but although it is congenitally levelling, this original cynicism was already being prepared in use-value, in the wooden head of that dog standing, like a table, on its four paws."⁹ This is precisely why this experience of loss—the only experience possible for any singularity—is also "the possibility of capital." In the very second that a singular thing or event is thrown on the market of equivalences, in the moment it is identified as some*thing* which may or may not be valuable, it has already lost itself. This is because, as he points out, in order for any*thing* to be regarded or understood as useful, it is in effect understood as useful *for another person*, or for *another time;* this is precisely what its usefulness consists of. Indeed, in this regard Derrida quotes Marx who says, "Commodities must be realized as values before they can be realized as use-values."¹⁰ Because commodities must be realized as values before they can be use-values, Derrida argues, "just as there is no pure use there is no use-*value* which the possibility of exchange and commerce has not in advance inscribed as an *out of use*."¹¹ (I will return shortly to this out-of-useness.)

The second mode of commodification is the one with which we are more familiar. It is the process by which singular things and events are quantified, flattened, where the unequal is made equivalent. It is the process by which each use-value "loses its soul." But if we understand Derrida's point, Marx's argument is precisely against the illusion that a "soul" might be trapped in the commodity, that the object might have once been a simple use-value. Indeed, it is among the most vital dimensions of *Capital* that while political economy is the science whose question is "what is value?" it is working in tandem with the effect of the hall-of-mirrors-thrown capitalist social relations, to the extent that it imagines that "value" inheres in commodities themselves. Indeed, Marx famously anthropomorphizes commodities, suggesting that, were they able to speak, they would tell us themselves that "our use-value may interest men but it does not belong to us as objects" (*Capital*, 176). The use-value—the substance of value—does not *inhere* in the object, even though the usefulness of the object *is* "the physical body of the commodity itself . . . which is the use-value or useful thing" (*Capital*, 126). Indeed, in the opening pages of *Capital*, Marx is working hard to combat the impression that we are presented by a simple body—a use-value—and an *external* exchange-value. As he says, the "exchange value appears first of all . . . as the proportion in which use-values of one kind exchange for use-values of another kind." Because this proportion is constantly changing—the exchange value of any given object is never constant—"exchange value appears to be something accidental and purely relative" (*Capital*, 130).

What, then, is the value that is the *proper* property of commodities? This, of course, is the socially necessary labor time it requires to produce them. For under conditions of generalized commodity production, a product of labor is, for its *seller*, merely a value-equivalent for some portion of the remainder of the total social product that s/he may subsequently purchase. Under generalized commodity production, in other words, any table I may make is useful to me only insofar as it represents other commodities or goods I might need. It is useful to me as an *exchange value*, but not a use-value. On the other hand, in order for it to fulfil its function of value-equivalence for me, the product must prove itself to be endowed with the physical properties that make it a use-value at all—namely *for someone else*, or, as I just pointed out, *for another time*. Once the product of labor has acquired this second "social objectivity" of being a value, it is then the physical objects themselves that bear this social form that thereby acquire the attribute of exchangeability in regular proportions. It is this coincidence of social form and physical thing that is the basis for the "fetishism of commodities."

Combating the illusion created by the fetishism of commodities is the task of science. Specifically, Marx tells us "reflection on the forms of human life, hence also scientific analysis of those forms, takes a course directly opposite to their real development. Reflection begins *post festum*, and therefore with the results of development ready to hand" (*Capital*, 168). The mysterious animated appearance of the commodity results from the retrospective appearance of a "use-value" that is produced (as originary) only after the commodity is realized as a value in general (and therefore animate). The "use-value"—the inert, pre-animated body—is an original *that never was*.

In order to make sense of the retrospective nature of the "plain" and "homely" form of commodities—their appearance *post festum*, so to speak, as use-values—it is important to remember that Marx made it clear that the mysterious and enigmatic character of the commodity emerges only when observed as an exchange value (*Capital*, 138). The mysterious character of the commodity form, Marx says, "consists simply in the fact that the commodity reflects the social characteristics of men's own labour as objective characteristics of the products of labour themselves, as the socio-natural properties of these things" (*Capital*, 164–65). The commodity, as Derrida points out, is a kind of mirror that cannot reflect back "those who are looking for themselves in it." When we look at a commodity what we see instead is its value "branded on its forehead," misrecognizing the price as the marker of value as a quasi-natural property of those things themselves (*Capital*, 167).

Marx tells us that we must first notice that "all different kinds of private labour . . . are continually being reduced to the quantitative proportions in which society requires them" (*Capital*, 168). He seems to suggest, in other words, that one might be able to identify a relatively simple *difference* between labour's quality and its quantity simply by calculating what is left over once we subtract the qualitative laboring activity from the product. He seems to imply that one could, in fact, identify a simple *quantity* of laboring energy that remained as a residue in the wake of its utility. For instance, he says:

> Let us . . . look at the residue of the products of labour. There is nothing left in them in each case but the same phantom-like objectivity: they are merely congealed quantities of homogenous human labour, i.e. of human labour power expended without regard to the form of its expenditure. All

these things now tell us is that human labour power has been expended to produce them, human labour power is accumulated in them. As crystals of this social substance, which is common to them all, they are values—commodity values.[12]

Significantly, moreover, Marx almost always qualifies his references to the residue or remains of labor's product by suggesting that its objectivity—what is most often called its materiality—is not a thing but a "phantom." As he says, "If we leave aside the determinate *quality* of productive activity, and therefore the useful character of the labor, what remains is its quality of being an expenditure of human labor power. Tailoring and weaving, although they are qualitatively different productive activities, are both a productive expenditure of human brains, muscles, nerves, hands etc."[13] The "phantom-like" objectivity to which Marx refers is neither a substantive entity, nor a mere expenditure of physical energy, but rather what Derrida might call a trace or the remains; it is what is *retroactively* produced by the object's commodification. It is its "out-of-useness." Listen carefully to Marx's language: "*If we . . . disregard* the use-value of commodities, only one property remains, that of being products of labour. . . . *If we make abstraction* from its use-value, we also abstract from the material constituents and forms which make it a use-value. It is no longer a table, a house, a piece of yarn or any other useful thing. All its sensuous characteristics are extinguished" (*Capital,* 128). The conditional language—"if we abstract" or "if we disregard"—is precisely what alerts us to the fictional nature of the simple qualitative object or simple qualitative labouring power, which might be thought to be waiting to lose its soul in its exchange. Marx is quite clear that we can only speak of a table, house, piece of yarn, or any other useful thing as sensuous self-identical entities, as use-values, *if* we abstract from the process that produces them in the first place. Thus, Derrida points out that,

> Like every thing, from the moment it comes onto the stage of a market, the table resembles a *prosthesis* of itself. . . . Two genres, two generations of movement intersect with each other in it, and that is why it figures the apparition of a specter. It accumulates undecidably, in its uncanniness, their contradictory predicates: the inert thing appears suddenly *inspired*, it is all at once transfixed by a *pneuma* or a *psyche*. Become like a living being, the table resembles a prophetic dog that gets up on its four paws, ready to face up to its fellow dogs: an idol would like to make the law. But, inversely, the spirit, soul or life that animates it remains caught in the opaque and heavy thingness of the *hulé,* in the inert thickness of its ligneous body. . . . The Thing is neither dead nor alive, it is dead and alive at the same time. It survives.[14]

Each commodity only *resembles* a prosthesis of itself because the original self-identity is a retrospective fiction; it is a kind of fantasy that compensates for what was never truly lost. A prosthesis or a fetish acts to replace what was *never lost*. In short, the "use-value" is only how commodities must *appear*.

Because, for Rose, it is possible to speak of an object, a use-value that was once identical to itself, unmarked by the "dead" labor time" or abstraction melancholically interred within it, because the commodity only becomes commodified, if you will, when it goes to market, mourning can undo the damage of that abstraction; it can restore the object to its previous incarnation as a qualitative object, quietly identical to itself. On Derrida's analysis, in contrast, to mourn the "dead" labor time trapped in the commodity is to mourn its out of use-ness or its remains. Mourning the dead labor time trapped in the commodity is to tidy up the process of repetition known as capitalization. What is interred in the commodity is not "alive," nor is it fully dead. It is a specter—an undead or congealed abstraction. Mourning this "specter" does not "bring it back to life," but covers over its death *as abstraction*. The significance of this difference comes into view when we look more carefully at the phenomenon of mourning.

Mourning and Melancholia

On the psychoanalytic view, mourning is understood to be the incorporation and eventual displacement of the emotional investment in singular, irreplaceable lost objects. It emerges from a demand from the ego: get back what one has given away. Indeed, according to Freud, grief for a lost object is painful precisely because the work of mourning is utterly absorbing. Each memory, each way in which the ego is tied to the lost love object, must be gone through and *hypercathected* in order that all libido tied up with it be freed up. In this sense, the mechanism of mourning can be likened to a kind of intensive psychic sorting; the energy that was once "invested" in the lost person or object must be slowly displaced from "out there" and reinvested, or introjected back into the structure of the ego itself. This is accomplished through a process of identification with the lost object; in effect the subject temporarily "becomes" the object that it once loved, giving the lost object a certain period of continued life. The utter absorption of the ego in this meticulous and exacting work leads to the symptoms we generally associate with mourning: depression, decreased interest in the outside world, sleeplessness, loss of appetite, loss of the capacity to love, and a general inhibition of activity. As Freud tells it, mourning is the process whereby "reality-testing has shown that the loved object no longer exists, and it proceeds to demand that all libido shall be withdrawn from its attachments to that object."[15]

While this demand "arouses understandable opposition," because "people never willingly abandon a libidinal position," he goes on to say that "normally, respect for reality gains the day."[16] The difficult circumstance of mourning is one in which the reality principle temporarily overrides the pleasure principle in order that libidinal energy be freed up. For mourning is considered to have been "successful" when the process of identification is complete. In this case, the energy once given to the lost object has been introjected back into the ego, and the subject is free to displace those libidinal energies elsewhere. Thus, despite the tremendous pain involved in the work of mourning, when it is complete, the ego "becomes free and uninhibited again."[17] What was once *irreplaceable* in what was lost—attachments, memories, etc.—has now been replaced.

Analogously, on a non-psychoanalytic account mourning can be understood as the social process by which death is spiritualized; it is the process of honoring and dignifying the bodily remains of the dead so that they might be returned to the spiritual/abstract order of universality. On either view, therefore, it emerges that mourning's work is to abolish the irreplaceability, the singularity of the singular. On this view, the success of mourning means the *death* or the end of singularity. It is the gesture that lets go, or "moves on," from this singular being to another one.

This process can be compared to that attending the other mental deviation Freud described alongside mourning: melancholia. To highlight the difference between them in a way that is most useful for my purposes, it is necessary to heed the ambiguity at the heart of melancholia itself. That is to say, not only is melancholia the illness that attends the loss of an ambivalently loved object but, perhaps more importantly for my purposes, a radical ambiguity or ambivalence sits at the heart of Freud's description of the peculiar pain that is melancholic passion itself.

The first dimension of this ambiguity is found in the two symptoms that distinguish the melancholic from the mourner: the severity of self-reproach and the opacity of the object lost. On the first count, Freud made careful note of the grandiosity of the melancholics' self-hate, and so drew an important conceptual link between melancholia and primary narcissism. As he says: "The melancholic displays an extraordinary diminution in self-regard, an impoverishment of his ego on a grand scale. . . . The patient represents his ego to us as worthless, incapable of any achievement and morally despicable, he reproaches himself, vilifies himself and expects to be cast out and punished."[18] Freud speculates that this self-hate is a displacement: "The self reproaches are reproaches against a loved object which have been shifted away from it onto the patient's own ego." The melancholic refuses to work through the loss of the object by withdrawing all libidinal investments from the object lost into his/her ego itself, thus avoiding the painful work giving up or relinquishing attachments to the lost object, by providing a refuge for them in a strategy of narcissistic identification.

The trouble with this strategy is that while the love for the object is not lost or given up, neither is the hate. "If the love for the object—a love which cannot be given up though the object itself is given up—takes refuge in narcissistic identification, then the hate comes into operation on this substitutive object, abusing it, debasing it." The narcissistic identification with the lost object means that the "shadow" of all of the attachments to the object—both love and hate—"fall upon the ego." Thus, whereas the mourner and the melancholic are both burdened by "painful dejection, cessation of interest in the outside world, loss of the capacity to love," and so on, "in mourning it is the world which has become poor and empty; in melancholia it is the ego itself."[19]

Interestingly, because the ego has treated itself as an object, attacking itself from within so to speak, the melancholic does not exhibit the shame or remorse one might expect to find in someone crushed by self-reproach. Rather, the melancholic is "insistently communicative," finding no shame in his/her abjection, but rather "satisfaction in self-exposure." This curious self-aggrandizement proceeds from the fact that because the object lost is actually tucked away within the structure of the ego, the only thing the melancholic subject is fully aware of is "what he has lost in him." The progression of libidinal cathexes characteristic of melancholia—which move defensively away from the object lost and toward loss *as such*—is explained by the second distinguishing feature of melancholia: the peculiar opacity of the object lost.

Indeed, Freud comments on the "unknown" nature of the loss; "one cannot see clearly what it is that has been lost." On this view, as Giorgio Agamben points out, the melancholic subject's refusal to mourn might be better understood as a preemptive denial of loss, one that covers over the real inaccessibility of its object by determining its loss in advance. As Agamben says, "From this point of view, melancholy would be not so much the regressive reaction to the loss of the love object as the imaginative capacity to make an unobtainable object appear *as lost*."[20] He goes on to say, "If the libido behaves as if loss had occurred, although nothing has in fact been lost, this is because the libido stages a simulation where what cannot be lost because it has never been possessed appears as lost, and what could never be possessed because it had never perhaps existed may be appropriated insofar as it is lost."[21] The melancholic's insistence on "unknown loss" functions against the fact that the object "lost" was never hers for the having. In short, as Rebecca Comay puts it, "Melancholia would thus be a way of staging a dispossession of that which was never one's to lose in the first place."[22]

On this view, Gillian Rose is quite correct when she argues that mourning—the process of working through, letting go of the irreplaceability or singularity of the singular—becomes the law. She is quite correct, in other words, when she says that mourning enhances or opens the law. She is correct, too, when she argues that mourning is a process that enlarges reason, but it does not, as she also argues, make reason "big hearted." For mourning is thought's own gesture, whose aim is to tidy up the remainder between structures of repetition—like capitalism, language, law, or philosophy itself—on the one hand, and the infinite variability of the world on the other.

Mourning is the process by which the singular thing or event is rendered intelligible to the law, and thus entered into exchange. But it is also the process by which what is necessarily lost in the path from the universal to the purely particular is covered over or buried. Thus, while mourning may very well be necessary for the function of law, not only does it not guarantee justice, it covers over the very moment of political contestation. Mourning may indeed "become" the law, but this process does not guarantee justice. On the contrary, it is the process that makes law's reach to justice impossible.

In order to clarify this point, it is useful to remember Derrida's striking argument that justice must be thought as the necessary but impossible encounter between universalizing law, on the one hand, and the unique case, on the other. Justice must be thought this way because, as Derrida points out, the peculiar nature of a notion like justice is that it refers to the adequation between a thing and its ideal, the coming together of what is said, on the one hand, and what that saying promises, on the other. Thus, justice cannot be conceptualized as an ideal for law, but is, rather, in a strange sense, the condition of possibility for *all ideality* or idealization itself. On this view, insofar as law announces itself as a rule designed for all and any circumstances, to do justice to the *law,* the absolutely unique case, must come before a law designed exclusively for it.

An encounter so described, however, is logically impossible. For while the law "always aims at the singular" (as Derrida says, this is its "promise and its destination"), it also necessarily generalizes, and consequently it does a kind of violence to the singular.[23] It is in this regard that Derrida speaks of the "force of law," a force that is most powerfully demonstrated by the necessarily violent nature of judgement. Because each case is unique, each application of the law is, in effect, the *re*making of the law, a remaking that is neither authorized nor fully deauthorized by law. In other words, because judgment is both the conservation and the destruction of the law, in the *moment* of judgment, the law is both "regulated and *un*regulated."[24] At the moment when the law is remade to fit the case that comes before it—when the law strains to fulfil itself and thus to do justice—the law is, in fact, suspended. To the extent that it is unauthorized, then, the law is simply *force*. It follows from this paradox, Derrida says, "that there is never a moment that we can say *in the present* that a decision *is* just."[25] And it is precisely this force that Rose refuses to acknowledge in her understanding of ethics as the willed development of the impossible path from the purely particular to the universal, that is, in her advocacy of a certain metaphysics.

In a vernacular perhaps more familiar to legal scholars, no instance of infraction against the law is ever ideally suited to the law it encounters, nor is the law ever ideally suited to every possible case to which it might apply. Without deciding what the singular *is*—for instance, by interpreting this singular case in terms of previously decided cases that render it into a broader vernacular—the singular case or infraction would remain unintelligible. The interpretation of any singular event or thing, then, names into newly being what had previously been undecidable and thus unrecognizable.

In this process, the *singularity* of the singular is lost. Between the singular case and the universal law there is always an unassimilable remainder: a remains. This remainder is politically important because the decision of what a singular event or thing *is*, the moment of interpretation, is precisely the moment of force. For that reason, it is also the moment that can be politically contested. Exactly what that political contestation might be, however, is by definition infinitely open. For what those singular events might be—how they will be idealized and thus rendered intelligible—and thus what kind of violence we might say has been done to them cannot be determined in advance.

The singularity of the singular, like the value of the commodity prior to its commodification, like the quality of labor that is left over—its quality as an "expenditure of human labour power"—is precisely what has not yet been appropriated, taken up, or re-presented through processes of idealization like law, philosophy, or language. Our *experience* of the singular, then, is of a radical or absolute alterity. As it cannot have happened yet, we cannot know, anticipate, or foreclose it. Thus, the encounter between law and the singular case—justice—is always coming. What is explosive about Derrida's insight is that this coming is not in the future present—as a Kantian ideal, a messianic promise, or some other horizon—but is rather always-already: *here-now*. One does not wait with hope for the messiah, for that would be "calculation." For as Derrida points out, the "present" can only be collected, organized, gathered into being, and imagined retrospectively. It is only ever afterward, when the event has already happened, that we may say "it *is*." While the singular event or thing, to be possible, must be "to-come," it can only be known once it has happened. Thus, the promise of law, like the promise of the use-value that animates the commodity, is this: what cannot be known or experienced is coming, but its coming is not *not-yet*, but rather *already*.

The gap between the "not-yet" and the "already" is precisely "the moment of suspense" within which "juridico-political revolutions take place."[26] This suspension or opening of the law *is* justice. It bears pointing out that, paradoxically, justice is what "happens" (impossibly) when the law is most perilously balanced: over an abyss. This "moment of suspense"—the opening of the law—happens *impossibly* not because we have reconstructed a law "able to face both power and contingency," but, on the contrary, because it is not really a "moment" at all. Because all events—including the law's suspension—are always "not-yet" or "already," the opening of the law never "appears" in a moment we can identify as "now." Strictly speaking, then, justice can never be experienced. To reconstruct it through the work of mourning, as Rose advocates, is thus to deny rather than to affirm the *aporia* of law, precisely when its stakes are highest.

The *im*possibility of this experience is significant because it points toward the dual nature of law's opening. On the one hand, justice "happens" when the law is transformed to accommodate the singular: what it has never encountered before. On the other hand, the suspension of the law is also necessarily a moment of arbitrary judgment; it is the moment when what was "to-come" is rendered "always-already" through a *coup de force*. Thus, not only is the law transformed, so too is the *singularity* of the singular event or thing which is ushered into meaning. For in order to have an experience of the event or thing, what was "to-come"—or in Derrida's language, *undecided* and undecidable—must be determined to be a "being" that was "always-already." This is precisely how the singular is smuggled into the law, the singular that was undecidable, is determined or decided and thus introduced into a process of idealization. While "justice" is what "happens" when the law opens and transforms itself to admit a case that is unique, this opening also always entails a violence to the uniqueness of that case.

I want to end with the thought that Gillian Rose might have been horrified to know that her work was pivotal to an argument such as this. That is to say, she might have been horrified to learn of this translation and thus betrayal of her work. But this is always the risk of reading, which, like the risk of politics itself, cannot be contained or known in advance.

NOTES

1. Gillian Rose, *Mourning Becomes the Law* (Cambridge: Cambridge University Press, 1996); Gillian Rose, *Love's Work* (New York: New York Review of Books, 2011).
2. Rose, *Love's Work*.
3. Jacques Derrida, *Ear of the Other* (New York: Schocken Books, 1998).
4. Catherine Kellogg, "Making History: Representation and 'Forgetting to Forget,'" in *Law, Culture and the Humanities* 1 (February 2005): 103–18.
5. Jacques Derrida, *Letter to a Japanese Friend*, in *Derrida and Difference*, ed. David Wood and Robert Bernasconi (Warwick: Parousia Press, 1985), 1–5.
6. Jacques Derrida, *Specters of Marx: The State of the Debt, the Work of Mourning and the New International*, trans. Peggy Kamuf (New York: Routledge, 1994), 61.
7. Rose, *Mourning Becomes the Law*, 67.
8. Derrida, *Specters of Marx*, 160.
9. Ibid.
10. Ibid., citing *Capital*, 179.
11. Derrida, *Specters of Marx*, 160.
12. Ibid., 128.
13. Marx, *Capital*, vol. 1, introduction by Ernest Mandel, trans. Ben Fowkes (New York: Vintage Books, 1977), 134.
14. Derrida, *Specters of Marx*, 154.
15. Freud, "Mourning and Melancholia," in *On Metapsychology: The Theory of Psychoanalysis*, trans. James Stachey, compiled and ed. Angela Richards, Penguin Freud Library, vol. 11 (London: Penguin Books, 1984), 253.
16. Ibid., 260.
17. Ibid., 262.

18. Ibid.
19. Ibid.
20. Giorgio Agamben, *Stanzas: Word and Phantasm in Western Culture*, trans. Ronald Martinez (Minneapolis: University of Minnesota Press, 1993), 20.
21. Ibid.
22. Rebecca Comay, "Perverse Desire: Fetishism and Dialectic," in Walter Benjamin, *Research in Phenomenology* 29 (1999): 51–62, at 52.
23. Jacques Derrida, *Force of Law*, in *Acts of Religion* (New York: Routledge, 2002), 20.
24. Ibid., 23.
25. Ibid.
26. Ibid., 20.

About the Contributors

ANDREA BRADY is Professor of Poetry at Queen Mary College, University of London.

LAWRENCE DOUGLAS is James J. Grosfeld Professor of Law, Jurisprudence, and Social Thought at Amherst College.

CATHERINE KELLOGG is Associate Professor of Political Science at the University of Alberta.

SHAI J. LAVI is Professor of Law, director of the Edmond J. Safra Center for Ethics, and co-director of the Minerva Center for the Interdisciplinary Study of End of Life at Tel Aviv University.

RAY D. MADOFF is Professor at Boston College Law School.

ANN PELLEGRINI is Professor of Social and Cultural Analysis, Performance Studies; and director of the Center for the Study of Gender and Sexuality at New York University.

MARK SANDERS is Professor of Comparative Literature at New York University.

AUSTIN SARAT is Associate Dean of the Faculty, the William Nelson Cromwell Professor of Jurisprudence and Political Science, and Professor of Law, Jurisprudence, and Social Thought at Amherst College.

MARTHA MERRILL UMPHREY is director of the Center for Humanistic Inquiry and Bertrand H. Snell 1894 Professor in American Government in the Department of Law, Jurisprudence, and Social Thought and Class Dean at Amherst College.

Index

Abraham, Karl, 121
Absalom, 51
acceptance: of God's ways, 60; and law, 15
Acuña, Cristóbal, 64
Aeneid (Virgil), 62
Afghanistan, 108, 110
afterlife of the living, 15
Agambem, Giorgio, 160–61
alcohol, 64, 68, 76, 73
Alcor, 22
Alyosha, 119
ambivalence, 104, 117
American Law Institute, 34n36
American Society for Reproductive Medicine, 40
American Society of Clinical Oncology, 56n10
Antigone (Sophocles), 4–7
Appel, Jacob, 18
Aragno, Anna, 23
Archbishop of Canterbury, 78–79
ars moriendi, 71, 73
Atkins, Alison, 29
Atkins, Jaclyn, 29
Aubrey, John, 63
autobiography, 149. See also *Memoirs of My Nervous Illness* (Schreber)
autopsy, 20–21, 33n18
Ayash, Chen, 56n16

bagpipe, 68

Barnewall, James, 78
Barnewall, Sir John, 91n98
Barnewall, Sir Patrick, 91n98
Baumeyer, F., 130
bean caointe, 66
Beckelman, Martha, 41
Ben-Gershon, Zelina, 47
Benjamin, Walter, 149
Berlant, Lauren, 99
Bible, 50–55, 71
biological wills. *See* wills
Bishop of Kildare, 80
Black Lives Matter, 98
blood drinking, 73–75
Blood, Diane, 41
Blood, Stephen, 41
bodily hexis, 61
bone-type objects, 49–50
Book of Common Prayer, 76, 78
Borneo, 48–49
Bourdieu, Pierre, 61
Brady Handgun Violence Prevention Act, 35n44
Brady, Andrea, 8–9, 59–93
Brady, James, 35n44
brain death, 17–19, 56n16
Breitbart.com, 100
Brooks, David, 95
Brothers Karamazov (Dostoyevsky), 118–19
Brown v. Board of Education, 98
Brown, Henry, 97–98

Buddhism, 17
burial: in *Antigone*, 4–5; Malay practices of, 48–49; night, 91n92; premature, 16
Bush, George W., 102–3, 105
Butler, Judith, 6, 13n16, 13n22, 61, 102–3

Cacique, 64
Calvin, John, 71
Camden, William, 63
Campion, Edmund, 60
cancer: brain, 18; treatment of, 38–39, 42, 56n10
caoineadh, 66, 74, 84. *See also* keening
Capital (Marx). *See* Marx, Karl
Castelli, Elizabeth A., 115n44
catharsis, 45
Catholicism, 61–62, 69, 72, 76–80, 106–7, 110, 111; as superstition, 67. *See also* Counter-Reformation; religion
Century City Hospital (Los Angeles), 36
"Character of Ireland" (Dunton), 73–74
charitable foundations, 31–32
charitable gifts, 30–31
Charron, Pierre, 68
Cheng, Cho Fook, 17
Chichester, Sir Arthur, 78
children: development of, 127–29; welfare of, 44
Christianity, 67, 70–79
Christy, Daniel Thomas, 41
Chrysostom, John, 71
civil conspiracy, 109–12
civility, 59, 61, 69, 71, 94–97, 105; asymmetry of, 98
Clanricard, 92n111
classical literature: keening in, 62
closure, 18–19
Cobb, Michael, 108
Code of Canon Law (1918), 92n111
Cohen, Keivan, 45–48
Cohen, Rachel, 45–48

Colin Clout's Come Home Again (Spenser), 84–85
"The Collective Representation of Death" (Hertz), 48–49
colonialism, 9, 59–60; resistance to, 61. *See also* "To Weep Irish: Keening and the Law" (Brady)
Comay, Rebecca, 161
commodity fetishism: and use-value, 11, 152–58, 163; and exchange-value, 152–53, 155
common law, 61, 34, 81, 84
conclamatio, 73
Constitution, 105
contract law, 29
"A Contribution to the Psychogenesis of Manic-Depressive States" (Klein), 127–28
Conway, Sir Edward, 78–79
Cordoba House. *See* Park51
Corish, Patrick, 77–78
corpse, 111; community's right to, 78; disposition of, 3, 19–21, 33n16, 54–55
Counter-Reformation, 76, 80
Court of Castle Chamber, 77–79
Cox, Sir Richard, 68, 83
crisis of judging, 10–11, 120, 129–30, 136–42
crying, 69. *See also* keening
cryonics, 21–22, 34n21
cryopreservation of gametes, 38–39, 42, 56n10, 56n16
culpability: and guilt, 10, 118, 139, 141; and psychoanalysis, 119, 136–37
cy pres, 27
cycle of life and death, 8, 37, 38, 45, 48, 52, 55

Davys, Sir John, 83
Dayak tribes, 48–49
the dead: calls from, 5, 8, 45; duty to, 52; renegotiation with, 26–27
death: brain function as definition of, 17–19, 32–33n9; cardiopulmonary definition of, 15–17, 32–33n9;

moment of, standards of, 3, 7,
    14–19, 32–33
decision maker hierarchy, 20, 33n17
deconstruction, 11, 148–51
defamation, tort of, 29–30, 109
denial, 18–19, 129
depraved indifference, 13n12
Derrida, Jacques, 7, 11, 149–58, 161–64
Deuteronomy, 50–51
deviance from norm, 25
difference, 94–96, 98, 101–2; democratic engagement with, 105–7
dirges, 65–66
disinheritance, 24, 27
disposition of corpse. *See* corpse: disposition of
divorce, 34n30
"Does Mourning Become the Law? Commodity Fetishism and Political Contestation" (Kellogg), 11, 148–65
"Dostoevsky and Parricide" (Freud), 118–19, 144n31
Douglas, Lawrence, 1–13
dreams, 46
Dresden, courts of, 137–39
drinking. *See* alcohol
Druids, 63
Dublin, Ireland, 60, 77–78
Dunton, John, 73–76

egg donation, 23, 56n10
ego, 12, 46–47, 104, 124, 128–29, 140–41, 159–60
Egypt, 62
electronic memorial material, 7, 28–29
El-Gamal, Sharif, 99–100
emotional distress, intentional infliction of, 109–12
Eng, David, 7, 100, 115n40
England: law of, 41; and Reformation, 63, 72, 76–77; values of, defined against Irish, 9, 59–93
Epistemology of the Closet (Sedgwick), 106, 115n42

Er, 50
erotomania, 125
European Society for Human Reproduction and Embryology, 43
evangelicalism, persecution complex of, 106–7, 115n44
Evans, Missy, 23
Evans, Nikolas, 23
exchange-value. *See* commodity fetishism: exchange value

Facebook, 28–29
father, 145n58; primal, 10, 117–18, 123, 139, 143n3. *See also* Shapira, David; Snyder, Albert
feelings, 95–99, 106–7, 112; hurt, 97, 101–2
Feerick, Jean, 70
fees and fines, 77, 78
feminism, 94
Fiduciary Access to Digital Assets Act, 29
fileadha, 66
First Amendment, 102, 109–10
Flechsig, Paul Emil, 121–22, 126–27, 130–35, 138, 141
flesh-type objects, 49–50
Forrester, John, 123, 144n31
Fourth Circuit, 109
free speech. *See* First Amendment
freedom of testation. *See* testation, freedom of
French law, testation and, 24–25, 27
Freud, Sigmund, 1, 144n31; and exorcism, 34n37; and mania, 105, 110. *See also* melancholia; *individual works by*
Fry, Susan Leigh, 63, 79–80
funerals, 9–10, 30; and Book of Common Prayer, 76; and class, 90n76; night, 77. *See also* keening

Gaelic language, 60, 65, 66–68, 84–85
Galway, Ireland, 81

gametes. *See* cryopreservation of gametes
Gaza Strip, 36
Geller, Pamela, 99–100
gender, 9, 40, 106, 135, 145n55. *See also* keening: and gender
Genesis, 50–52
genitals, 120–21
Gerald of Wales, 65–66
German language, 124
God, contact with, 120–21
Goodrich, Peter, 145n55, 145n58
Gorer, Geoffrey, 2
Greece, 62
Ground Zero Mosque. *See* Park51
guilt, 10, 117–19, 122, 124–27, 129, 132–35, 139–41, 144n34

haliza, 53
Halsmann, Philipp, 119
Hanson, C. Lee, 99
Hardraht, 146n86
hatred, 96, 117–18, 122–26, 141, 143n3, 144n31, 160
Hegel, Georg Wilhelm Friedrich, 150
Henry IV, Part I (Shakespeare), 67
Herbert, Sir William, 82
Herodotus, 62, 87n13
Hertz, Robert, 48–49, 53
Heslin, Neil, 31
Hobbes, Thomas, 83
Holland, Sharon Patricia, 100
Holloway, Beth, 19
Holloway, Natalee, 19
Homer, 62
homosexuality, 108–10, 122–23, 144n31
Horst-Warhaft, Gail, 70
Human Fertilisation and Embryology Authority, 41
humans, social nature of, 14
humoral science, 69–70
Hyppolite, Jean, 140

identification, 158–60
IIED. *See* emotional distress, intentional infliction of

inheritance, 27, 34n34, 51
introjection, 11, 128–29, 144n31, 158–59
intrusion upon seclusion, 109–12
investigations, 33n18
Iraq, 107, 108, 110
Irish (people), 9; as barbaric, 63, 64, 67–68, 75, 81–84; and cultural reform, 76, 78, 81–83; law of, 59–60; and religious law (*see* Counter-Reformation; Reformation); stereotypes of, 59–60, 70–71; war cry of, 85
The Irish Hubbub, or, The English Hue and Crie (Rich), 70–71
Irish Privy Council, 81
Irish Rebellion (1641), 82, 93n123
Islamic Community Center, 99
Isle of Anglesey, 63
Israel, 36; law of, 40–41, 43
Italy, 30, 70

Jakobsen, Janet R., 101–2
jealousy, 125, 132–33
Jones, Sir Roger, 78
Judah, 50
Judaism, 26; and keening, 64; and mysticism, 51
judging, 119–20, 162, 145n59. *See also* crisis of judging
jury duty, 142
justice, 4–6, 11, 151, 161–62

Kaepernick, Colin, 98
Karamazov, Dmitri, 119
Kazanjian, David, 7
keening, 8–9, 59; aesthetics of, 65–68; across cultures, 62–65; doctrinal implications of, 70–74; and gender, 62, 68–70; and law, 79–83; as noise, 66–67, 74–75, 84; punishment for, 79–80and religion, 67, 70–74, 92n111; and resistance, 74–79; sincerity of, 59–60, 71, 74. *See also* Irish (people)
Kellogg, Catherine, 11, 148–65

Kelly, John Q., 19
Kennedy, Duncan, 132, 145n59
Kerrigan, John, 66
Khan, Daisy, 99
Kildare, Ireland, 73, 75
Kilkenny, Ireland, 81
Killeen, Lady (Susanna), 78
King, Peter T., 101
Klein, Melanie, 127–30
knowledge, 150
Koochin, Jesse, 18–19
Kraepelin, Emil, 135
Kruse, Amy, 41

labor power, 152–53, 155–58, 163
Lacan, Jacques, 125–26, 130, 140–41, 147n111
Lady of the Fountain, 63
Larson, Heather, 64
Lavi, Shai J., 3, 8, 36–58
law: Brehon, 60–61; and justice, 151, 161–62; origins of, in mourning, 10, 117–18, 136–37; positive, 4–6; private and public, 31–32; and singularity, 11, 149–51, 161–64; and understanding, 23–25
laws: named after people, 31; state, 32–33n9, 34–35n39. *See also* individual laws
Leach, Edmond, 52
legacy, 30–31
Leipzig University Clinic, 121, 130–33
levirate marriage, 8, 50–53; justifications for, 50
liberalism, 47, 101
libido, 12, 122, 126–27, 129, 136, 147n111, 158–61
life support, 16–18
Lifton, Robert Jay, 105
Lindbergh Law, 31
"Listening within the 'Grief of Distortions'" (Pellegrini), 9–10, 94–116
Lorde, Audre, 94, 98–99

Love the Sin: Sexual Regulation and the Limits of Religious Tolerance (Pellegrini and Jakobsen), 101–2
Love's Work (Rose), 148
Lucian, 62–63
Luciano, Dana, 100
Lutz, Catherine, 86
Lysaght, Patricia, 92n111

Mabinogion, 63
mac Con Brettan, Blathmac, 65
Madoff, Ray D., 3, 7–8, 14–35
Man, Paul de, 2
Marbhnai, 66
marriage, 15, 26. *See also* levirate marriage
Marx, Karl, 151–57
masculine protest, 122
Massachusetts, 33n17; disposition of corpse in, 19–20
materialism, 151
meaning in life, 30
media: fragmenting effects of, 95
medical decisions: autonomy in, 18
Megan's Law, 31
Meigs, Samantha, 80, 90n76
melancholia, 2, 4, 6–7, 46–48, 104–5, 117, 159–61
Memoirs of My Nervous Illness (Schreber), 120–23, 130–33, 137–38, 145n55–56, 145n58preface of, 121, 135–36
memorial material, 28–29, 46
memorial services, 30
memory, 6, 28–32; mechanical, 150
Meredythe, Thomas, 77–78
metaphysics, 148–50, 162
Middleton, Marmaduke, 76
ministers, assaulted, 77–79
minoritization, 106–7
missing persons, 19
Molyneux survey, 75
Monk, Thomas, 73, 75
Moore, Lord, 78

mother, 6–7, 19, 23–25, 30, 78; and child development, 127–28; and PMSR, 40, 42, 44–48, 54
"The Mourning After: Posthumous Sperm Retrieval and the New Laws of Mourning" (Lavi), 3, 8, 36–58
"Mourning and Melancholia" (Freud), 2, 10, 46, 104–5, 117–18, 126–27
"Mourning and the Law: An Introduction" (Umphrey, Sarat, and Douglas), 1–13
Mourning Becomes the Law (Rose), and metaphysics, 11, 148–51
"Mourning in America: What's Law Got to Do with It?" (Madoff), 3, 7–8, 14–35
mourning: of abstractions, 104; anthropology of, 2–3, 8, 48–50; and children, 128–29; and conflict, 20; definitions of, 1–2, 14, 46, 102, 158–59, 161; interrupted, 9–10, 102–3, 105, 112; and metaphysics, 148–50, 152–53; private, 10, 109–10, 112; and processing, 28; regulation of, 70; and remorse, 117–18; and reorientation, 14; and ritual, 5, 60–65 (*see also* keening); substituting, 4, 37, 126; war and, 9. *See also* law: origins of, in mourning; melancholia
Muir, Edward, 79
Muñoz, José, 97
Munster, Ireland, 82; murder, 32n2, 108, 119, 129, 137; and origins of law, 10, 117–18, 123, 139; soul, 121, 126–27, 134, 137–38; and ventilators, 16–17
Muslim Americans, 99; intolerance toward, 100–101

names, 133–34; perpetuation of, 50–54
narcissism, 123, 159–60
negation, 124, 126, 134, 147n111

"Negation" (Freud), 124, 140–41, 147n111
neurosis, 117–18, 124
New Family (NGO), 36
New International, 151
New Jersey, 32–33n9
New York City, 99–102
New York Times, 99
Newtown massacre, 31
Ní Dhomhnaill, Nualaith, 68
Niebuhr, Reinhold, 95
9/11, 99–103
Nineteen Eighty-Four (Orwell), 123
normativity, 95, 97, 100, 105
"Notes on Some Schizoid Mechanisms" (Klein), 128–29
Nyong'o, Tav, 96

Ó Dálaigh, Cúchonnacht, 72
O'Brien, Murrough, 75
obsession, 47–48, 117–18, 134
Oedipus complex, 119
Ogden, Thomas H., 102
Onan, 50–51
organ donation, 15, 19, 56n16
Orwell, George, 123
ova retrieval, 56n10, 56n16

Paganism, 67, 75, 84
Pale, Ireland, 69, 78, 81
Palmer, Patricia, 67–68
paranoia, 10, 132–33, 135–38, 141–42; Freud's theory of, 121–27; Klein's elaboration on, 127–30
Park51, 100, 102, 105
Parkes, Colin Murray, 23
Paulinus, Suetonius, 63
Pellegrini, Ann, 9–10, 94–116
persecution. *See* paranoia
Petrarch, 70
phantasy, 118, 123, 128–29
Phelps, Fred, 107–12
Phelps-Davis, Rebekah A., 109
Phelps-Roper, Shirley L., 109

philosophy: and thought, 151–52. *See also* deconstruction; *individual philosophers*
photographs, 30
Piers, Sir Henry, 75
Pigman, G. W., 72
Plessy v. Ferguson, 97–98
Plunket, Lucas, 78
PMSR. *See* postmortem sperm retrieval
politics, US, 9, 94–95
Posner, Richard, 26–27
posthumous birth, 38, 46
posthumous meddling, 25–28
posthumous sperm retrieval. *See* postmortem sperm retrieval
postmodernism, 11, 148–49
postmortem sperm retrieval (PMSR), 8, 22–23, 36, 38–39; children from, 44; ethics of, 3, 37–38; the individual and, 54; and intent of decedent, 40–43; and levirate marriage, 51–55; novelty of, 37, 52–53; and parents of deceased, 43–48; partnerless, 45–48; psychological soundness of, 47; regulation of, 37, 39–45; and waiting period, 43–44
potassium bromide, 130
Praeficae, 63, 65
Precarious Life: The Powers of Mourning and Violence (Butler), 102–3
pregnancy, 78
Prigerson, Holly, 23
privacy rights, 29
professional mourners, 59, 62, 64, 71, 74–76, 80, 92n111; prohibited, 80
"Project for a Scientific Psychology" (Freud), 140
projection, 121–23, 126–28, 144n31
property: and social media, 28–29; and testation, 24, 27
protest, 107–12
Protestantism, 61, 67, 76, 77–79, 82, 83, 91n96, 95, 101–2. *See also*
evangelicalism; Reformation; religion
"Psychoanalysis, Mourning, and the Law: Schreber's Paranoia as Crisis of Judging" (Sanders), 10–11, 117–47
Psycho-Analytic Notes on an Autobiographical Account of a Case of Paranoia (Dementia Paranoides) (Freud), 121
psychology: mockery of, 118–19
psychosis, 123–25, 129, 135, 141, 147n111
publicity given to private life, 109

race, 61, 96–102, 106; and discourse, 96–97; and feminism, 94
Rambam Hospital (Israel), 42
Rauf, Fiesel Abdul, 99–100
reanimation, 21
reason, 149
recovery from mental illness, 130–31
reflection and understanding, 23
Reformation, 63, 72, 76, 82–83, 86
regression, 129
Reichstag, 131, 145n55
religion, 106; clashes of, in Ireland, 61–62; and death standards, 3, 17–18, 32–33n9; and disposition of corpse, 20–21; and superstition, 67. *See also* keening: and religion; *individual religions and religious concepts*
remorse, 117–18, 139
repression, 126–27, 147n111
reproduction clinics, 36–37
Restatement (Third) of Trusts, 27–28
restatements, 34n36
Rich, Barnabe, 66–67, 77, 84

rigorism, 72
Roberts, John, 109–10
Rome, 69
Rose, Gillian, 6, 11, 148–53, 158, 161–64. *See also individual works by*

INDEX

Rothman, Cappy, 36–37
Russia, 64–65
Ryan White Care Act, 31

Sanders, Mark, 10–11, 117–47
Santner, Eric, 131
Sarat, Austin, 1–13
scales, 130–33
Schaefer, Donovan O., 100
Schiesari, Juliana, 70
schizoid mechanisms, 127–29
Schreber, Daniel Paul, 119–21; discharge of, 136, 146n98; Freud on, 121–23, 126–27, 131, 141; and judging, 130–33, 137–41. See also *Memoirs of My Nervous Illness* (Schreber)
Scythians: Irish compared to, 63
Sedgwick, Eve Kosofsky, 106, 115n42
Seeman, Don, 52–53
sexual abuse, 121
Shakespeare, William, 67
Shapira, Daniel, 26–27, 34n34
Shapira, David, 26–27
Shepard, Matthew, 108
Sherard, Abigail, 71
Shimakawa, Karen, 98
silence, 115n40
Simms, Katharine, 68
Skerrett, Kathleen, 104
Smith, Anna Nicole, 33n16
Snir, Idan, 42
Snyder v. Phelps, 10, 107, 109–12
Snyder, Albert, 109–12
Snyder, Matthew, 107, 109–12
social media, and echo chambers, 95. See also electronic memorial material
social workers, 44
soldiers: coffins of, 110
Solon, 62
soul, 8, 48–50, 54
Spain, 65–66
Sparta, 62, 87n13
Spenser, Edmund, 63, 75, 82, 84–85

sperm banks, 39
sperm. *See* cryopreservation of gametes; postmortem sperm retrieval
Stanihurst, Richard, 68, 83
Star Chamber, 77
stethoscope, 16
Stoicism, 70–71
Strathern, Marilyn, 54
Strocchia, Sharon, 70
suicide, 30–31
Supreme Court of the United States, 97–98, 109–10
surrogacy, 23
Swartz, Aaron, 31
Sydney, Sir Henry, 60
synods, 80

Tacitus, 63
Tait, Clodagh, 60
Tamar, 50
Tangiers, 64
taxonomy, 106
Taylor, Jeremy, 71
Temple, Sir John, 82–83
testation, freedom of, 7, 24–25
Thomond, Earl of , 92n111
time, 52
tolerance, 9, 100–101; as melancholia, 104–5
Totem and Taboo, 117–18, 123–24, 139
"To Weep Irish: Keening and the Law" (Brady), 8–9, 59–93
transference, 121–22, 127
translation, 67, 149
transplant, 17, 20
trauma, 111; transcendent, 100
Trump, Donald, 95

uielleann pipes, 68
Umphrey, Martha Merrill, 1–13
Uná, 72
understanding, and law, 15. *See also* reflection and understanding
undue influence, 25
Uniform Anatomical Gifts Act, 41

Uniform Determination of Death Act, 17
Uniform Law Commission, 29, 34–35n39
unmanning, 120–21, 135
"The Uses of Anger" (Lorde), 94, 98–99
use-value. *See* commodity fetishism: use-value

Venbroux, Eric, 49
ventilator, mechanical, 16–18
Vernoff, Gabby, 36
voices, hearing, 120–21, 126, 137, 138

wakes, 75–76, 79
Wales, 63

Weber, Dr. ___, 136–38
Weever, John, 64, 91n92
weight, 130–33
Westboro Baptist Church, 10, 107–12
Wetherfield, Alison, 31, 35n45
white lies, 130
widowhood: and PMSR, 43–44
Williams, Ted, 22
wills, 22, 24–25, 29, 42; biological, 36, 40–41
Winslow, Jean Jacques, 16
Winston, Lord, 51
Wood, Andy, 85

Yorkshire, England, 63